DATE DUE

Political Culture and Soviet Politics

Also by Stephen White

The USSR: Portrait of a Super-power

Britain and the Bolshevik Revolution: a Study in
the Politics of Diplomacy, 1920–1924

Political Culture and Soviet Politics

Stephen White

Lecturer in Politics, University of Glasgow
Scotland

St. Martin's Press   New York

ISBN 0-312-62249-X

Library of Congress Cataloging in Publication Data

White, Stephen, 1945–
   Political culture and Soviet politics.

   Includes bibliographical references and index.
   1.   Political participation—Russia. 2.   Russia—
Politics and government—1917–   I. Title.
JN6581.W45   1979   320.9'47'084   79–18077
ISBN 0-312-62249-X

Contents

List of Tables

Preface

This is a relatively short book about a large subject. It has, I believe, two principal justifications. The first stems from what I have felt for some time to be a serious shortcoming in much of the existing literature on Soviet government and politics, its lack of an historical perspective. Most of the general textbooks begin with an account of the ideology; they include a chapter or two about political developments since 1917; and then they go on to discuss institutions, groups and processes, the staple of the study of Soviet politics as of that of most other countries. Important though such topics are, the result is that historical continuities of longer standing are, as it were, defined out of existence. Soviet political institutions are seen as emanating from the doctrines of Marx and Lenin rather than, in part at least, from the country's centuries of previous political experience; and Soviet political beliefs and behaviour patterns, where they conform to the precepts of Marxism–Leninism, are taken to be the product of a successful process of political socialisation rather than a tribute to the persistence of traditional beliefs and practices which, in many important respects at least, anticipated those the Bolsheviks were subsequently to attempt to propagate. The result is an account of Soviet politics which is historically foreshortened and, in my view, seriously deficient, obscuring as it does important elements of continuity between the pre- and post-revolutionary systems.

It is the contention of this volume that the concept of political culture may help to redress some of this imbalance by allowing a greater degree of attention to be paid to the historical and national specificity of Soviet politics as well as to the similarities it shares with political systems elsewhere. Patterns of previous political experience are, of course, but one of the factors which combine to shape a nation's politics; and it would be historically unfounded as well as insulting to suggest that Russia's experience of autocracy left no other prospect than the continuation of some form of authoritarian rule, whatever government was established by the revolution of 1917. History knows probabilities but not certainties; and as I hope to make clear in this account, alternative patterns of development were always possible, right up to the experiment in limited government which took place during the final decade of Tsarist rule. It is also important not to confuse the theory of autocracy with what might, for a variety of reasons, be its very imperfect practice, and to allow for a wide range of regional and other variations. These considerations notwithstanding, there nonetheless *was* something which was distinctive about the politics of Tsarist Russia in the pre-war European context, and in this volume I have tried to suggest some of the ways in which an examination of that inheritance may help towards a better understanding of contemporary Soviet politics and of the manner in which those politics may evolve in future decades.

The concept of political culture, secondly and perhaps less novelly, allows a greater degree of attention to be paid to the dimensions of political life which extend beyond formal institutional boundaries than traditional categories of analysis have normally permitted. There has, of course, been no lack of interest in the informal aspects of politics in studies of western-type political systems in recent years. In Communist-ruled states, however, the examination of formal institutions has normally bulked larger, in part at least because of the paucity of survey and other data upon which an alternative approach might be based. The problems associated with the empirical examination of politics, in the USSR as in the other Communist-ruled states, do of course remain considerable. I hope to show in this volume, however, that difficulties of this kind may easily be exaggerated. Methodologically deficient and evasive though they may often be, the range and variety of Soviet sociological investigations into many of the informal aspects of politics has not, I think, been sufficiently appreciated in the west, and it is one of the purposes of this volume to ensure that such findings should become more widely known. The political–cultural approach, as conceived in this volume, is not in any sense a substitute for the close analysis of institutions and their workings. But it does, I think, help to supplement such analyses by directing attention towards the network of belief and behaviour patterns within which political institutions are located and by which their operation is in part determined; and more generally it may make a modest contribution towards the attempts which are presently in train to construct an adequate political sociology of the USSR and of the other state socialist countries.

This volume has been in gestation for a number of years, and in the course of its preparation I have incurred a number of debts to people and institutions which it is now my pleasant duty to discharge. My greatest debt is to Archie Brown of St Antony's College, Oxford, who first alerted me to the possibilities of the concept of political culture in the Soviet context and whose invitation to join a group of scholars preparing chapters on the political cultures of various Communist nations was the starting-point of this study. This book would have been different if he had written it himself, but without him it might not have been written at all. I am also indebted to Rene Beerman, David Lane, Mary McAuley and Bill Mackenzie for their comments upon various versions of earlier chapters; to Bernard Aspinwall, Robert A. Lewis and Warren Miller for advice and information on specific points; and to seminar and conference audiences in Cambridge, Birmingham, Liverpool and Oxford for many helpful observations and suggestions. The research upon which this study is based was made possible by the University of Glasgow and the British Council, who enabled me to make a number of extended visits to the USSR, and by the Nuffield Foundation, whose generous grant enabled me to carry out a programme of interviewing in Israel in the summer of 1976. I am grateful, finally, to the Master and Fellows of Balliol College, Oxford, for making it possible for me to spend the Michaelmas term of 1977 in their stimulating company. Many of the chapters which follow bear the marks of the opportunities for reading and discussion (though not, I hope, of the abundant hospitality) which I was able to enjoy at that time. For the errors and misjudgements that remain I am, of course, alone responsible.

August 1978 STEPHEN WHITE

For Ishbel

1

Political Culture and Political Science

Political culture may be defined as the attitudinal and behavioural matrix within which the political system is located.[1] The political culture, that is to say, both expresses and influences the patterns of political belief and behaviour within a given political system: it informs the actions of political actors; comprehends political symbols, foci of identification and fundamental beliefs and values; and generally both reflects and influences popular orientations towards the institutions and practices of government. It is a broader concept than 'operational code' or 'political style', terms which apply more properly to the actions or assumptions of a particular sub-group of a total population (and particularly to its political leadership); it is a narrower concept, at the same time, than more familiar notions such as 'national character' or 'public opinion', which have a range of reference much wider than the political system as such. In recent years the concept of political culture has been used with increasing frequency in the comparative analysis of political systems. In this first chapter we shall examine the use of the concept which has been made in the study of one such political system, that of the USSR, and then go on to consider a number of the difficulties with which the employment of the concept has more generally been associated.

The Cultural Approach to Politics

There is nothing intrinsically new in the analysis of a particular political system in terms of its socio-cultural attributes. Montesquieu, for instance, thought it appropriate to include a discussion of the 'general spirit' or 'morals and customs of a nation' in his *De l'Esprit des Lois*; Bagehot's *English Constitution* deals with both the 'dignified', or informal, as well as with the 'efficient' parts of the constitution; and de Tocqueville, in his *Democracy in America*, included an account of the habits, manners and opinions by which the members of that system were animated and to which, he believed, their democratic institutions might largely be attributed. The term 'political culture' itself can be found in the work of Herder as early as the late eighteenth century,[2] and the associated question of the assimilation of civic values or of citizenship training, a concept nowadays known more generally as 'political socialisation', is at least as old as Plato. So far as Soviet politics more particularly are concerned the term 'political culture' may be found in the writings of Lenin, and it was employed in a similar sense in Sidney and Beatrice Webb's *Soviet Communism: a New Civilization?*, a work first published in 1935.[3] The systematic employment of the term 'political culture' in comparative political analysis, however, is a product of the last twenty years.[4] At least two main explanations may be offered for the wider currency which the term presently enjoys.

In the first place, it reflects the fact that the political scientist is now concerned with both a much larger and culturally a much more heterogeneous range of political systems than those which had previously fallen within his province of inquiry. Before the end of the Second World War it was perhaps understandable that the study of politics should confine itself essentially to the institutions of government in the major states of Western Europe and North America. With the expansion in the numbers of independent states which followed in the post-war years, however, an emphasis of this kind became increasingly difficult to justify. The opinion gathered strength that the student of politics should be concerned at least in principle with the whole universe of political experience, with a 'comparative politics' which dealt on an equal basis with all the world's 150-odd nation states, rather than with the 'major foreign governments' of the industrialised western world. Practical political considerations were not unrelated to this change of emphasis. The post-war years were years in which the struggle for global hegemony moved from Europe to the more fluid situation in the newly independent countries of the Third World, and those who dispensed government and foundation support at this time were concerned—as indeed were most political scientists themselves—

that the study of politics should make some practical contribution to the preservation of these nations from Soviet and Communist influence. A good deal of research in the 1950s and early 1960s, especially that which dealt with the prospects for 'democratic modernisation' in the colonial and ex-colonial world, was related quite explicitly to considerations of this kind.[5]

As these studies advanced, however, it became clear that the forms of analysis then available within political science would be of somewhat limited value. Traditional categories of analysis related in the main to the formal structures of government of liberal democracies; they had little, if anything, to say about the socio-cultural environment within which structures of this kind might operate. The collapse of Weimar Germany, a state whose formal democratic credentials were beyond reproach, suggested that even in the developed world these self-imposed limitations might no longer be justified; a variety of circumstances, it appeared, including patterns of authority within the wider society and even particular personality types, might have to be considered in order to provide at least part of the explanation which traditional categories of analysis had so manifestly failed to supply.[6] The failure of liberal-democratic institutions in a number of the newly independent countries, however, was perhaps a more important stimulus. Elections and parliaments, it became clear, could not necessarily be transplanted successfully to these very different environments; indigenous social structures and cultures were both more different, and more resistant to modification, than political scientists had hitherto been willing to allow.[7]

To make sense of processes of this kind, to become both less specific to the institutional forms of western democracy and more sensitive to dimensions of political life which extended beyond those boundaries, the study of politics was forced to turn to disciplines in which the analysis of less developed societies—indeed in some cases stateless societies—had received a greater degree of attention. Sociology, and more particularly social anthropology, was the most important of these. The concept of political culture, in fact, may be traced to precisely such a process of cross-fertilisation, a series of meetings in the late 1950s and early 1960s between a group of politically-oriented anthropologists and a group of political scientists, among whom Gabriel Almond was the most prominent, who were dissatisfied with the traditional approaches and hoping to develop a more genuinely cross-cultural model of the political system.[8] Political culture, like 'political socialisation' and 'political communication', was one of the concepts which entered the political science vocabulary at this time. Like the others it has since been employed in the comparative analysis, not simply of the developing countries, but of developed nations as well;[9] and it has formed part of the more general movement, a movement widely but somewhat misleadingly known as 'behaviouralism', towards a more sociological and comparatively-oriented theory of the political system.

A second major impetus was the dissatisfaction which scholars in the field of Soviet and comparative Communist politics were experiencing with the 'totalitarian' model which had for some time been dominant in the study of their subject. The faults of the totalitarian model were not that it was unduly 'institutional' in character, for it emphasised ideology, terror and the mass media; nor that it was specific to a particular cultural setting, for it derived its central propositions from at least three very different societies, Nazi Germany, Fascist Italy and Stalinist Russia. It came increasingly to be recognised, however, that the totalitarian model, like the institutional model which had traditionally been employed in the analysis of political systems in the west, had become both outdated and to a large extent irrelevant to the kind of questions to which political scientists now wished to address themselves. Based upon an analysis of the Soviet system as it existed under Stalin, it was now agreed, the model had been left far behind by changes in the nature of the reality it purported to describe. The most important of these changes was probably the greatly diminished use of terror, hitherto regarded as perhaps the model's single most crucial attribute; but other changes, such as those in the size and mode of leadership of the ruling Communist party, were at least as difficult to reconcile with the original definition. A series of half-hearted revisions— 'totalitarianism without terror', 'partialitarianism', even 'totalitarianism with a human face'—attempted, without much success, to bring the model up to date. Indeed the fact that it was not abandoned altogether had arguably less to do with its scholarly merits than with its ideological attractions, equating, as it did, the Soviet system with the major Fascist dictatorships.[10]

For the student of comparative Communist politics another kind of criticism was at least as important; for the totalitarian model, whatever its other merits, had at least three major defects. It assumed, in the first place, that the Soviet system was sustained almost entirely by coercion: a proposition which may at one time have had something to recommend it but which would not now accord with the views of most scholars, satisfied by an accumulating body of evidence that many of the most distinctive aspects of the Soviet system are in fact based upon a deep and fairly widely-distributed base of popular support and do not need coercion to explain their continued existence. In the second place, the model was resistant to the comparative analysis in which students of Communist politics now wished to engage, insofar as it permitted no distinctions of substance to be drawn between one Communist or 'totalitarian' system and another, the manifest and increasing diversity among them notwithstanding. And thirdly, the model was static, in that it failed to provide a satisfactory basis for the consideration of change over time in any political system thus categorised. As Jeremy Azrael has noted:

> The onset of a period of conspicuous large-scale change in Communist systems made this deficiency seem particularly grave. Furthermore, the fact that change has proceeded in different directions in different Communist countries has suggested that the uniformity of the preceding period existed largely in the eye of the beholder—a beholder whose vision was clouded by a model that stressed formal institutions at the expense of dynamic nationally and culturally differentiated processes.[11]

These criticisms, taken together, argued the need for a more historically informed, developmentally-oriented approach to the analysis of Communist political systems. Their common 'Communism', it appeared, provided only part of the explanation of the manner in which their political systems operated; at least as important, in many cases, was what was unique or distinctive to such systems, most of which, before their respective revolutions, had had very different political experiences, levels of socio-economic development and cultural backgrounds. It is perhaps from this need to recognise the unique as well as the universal in Communist systems that the greater employment of the concept of political culture may be said in the main to derive. There is of course nothing new in the (usually highly selective) examination of the 'historical background' to a country's politics. What distinguishes the present situation, as T. H. Rigby has put it, is a 'heightened puzzlement concerning certain persistent features of Soviet reality', a puzzlement which has prompted the re-examination of a number of critical junctures in the political development of the USSR and has led to a 'renewed interest in the pre-1917 society and polity from which the Soviet system emerged'.[12] It will be the thesis of this book that questions of this kind may most satisfactorily be considered in terms of a political–cultural approach: an approach, that is to say, which stresses the historical specificity as well as the systemic similarities of Communist political systems, together with the continuing influence of that national specificity upon future patterns of political development and change.

The concept of political culture, it must nonetheless be admitted, is a problematic and by no means uncontroversial one. Some of the major points of contention will be considered later in this chapter, insofar as they relate to the manner in which the concept may most usefully be employed; we begin, however, with a consideration of some of the attempts which have previously been made to treat Soviet politics in what might be called their socio-cultural aspect, together with an examination of some of the inadequacies of such studies as they have so far been conducted.

The Psychoculturalists and Soviet Politics

One of the first attempts to apply psychocultural insights to the study of Soviet political behaviour was Nathan Leites's *The Operational Code of the Politburo*, a work first published in 1951. Based mainly on an analysis of the writings of Lenin and Stalin, both of whom were quoted at some length, Leites attempted to set out the 'rules which Bolsheviks believe to be necessary for effective political conduct'. These rules were, he thought, 'pervasive in Bolshevik calculations, whether they refer to domestic or foreign policy, propaganda, or military policy'. Leites went on to consider specific applications of each of these principles to Bolshevik policies in the conclusions to each of his chapters.[13] A further, more elaborate volume, *A Study of Bolshevism*, came out two years later; and a psychocultural study of the Moscow trials, again based upon a careful study of the Bolshevik texts and of psychoanalytical theory, appeared in 1954.[14] Leites's work, it may be noted, was more than a purely academic exercise: it was funded by the United States Air Force, and American diplomats at the end of the Korean War were apparently given copies of the *Operational Code of the Politburo* to assist them in their dealings with their Communist adversaries.[15] The outcome of those deliberations would scarcely seem to be a recommendation of Leites's work. Does it, in fact, have any enduring value?

Leites's essential thesis was that the Bolshevik leaders based themselves consistently and more or less exclusively upon the doctrine to which they formally subscribed. He believed, accordingly, that by setting out quotations from the Bolshevik classics under a variety of headings ('Organisation', 'Means and Ends', 'Violence' and so forth) it would become possible to predict the behaviour of the Soviet leadership in any situation to which those circumstances applied. This was clearly an interpretation based upon a number of somewhat arbitrary assumptions: in particular, that decisions were and could be made in Soviet Russia, contrary to experience elsewhere, upon a wholly and exclusively doctrinal basis. Leites's text reveals the force of these reservations; for while it retains a certain value as a classified directory of quotations, its contribution to our understanding of Soviet leadership behaviour and its motivation is somewhat less obvious. One need hardly have consulted the works of Lenin, for instance, to conclude that the Politburo will 'try as hard as possible to ensure success for its aims' or that its policies have been 'not only offensive, but also defensive'; nor is the Politburo unique in having 'always concentrated on specific and limited objectives, pursuing them with much energy'. The fact that the Soviet Army has attempted no territorial expansion in Western Europe since 1945, again, would seem to have little to do with the writings of Lenin in 1918; the presence of a better-armed adversary in that area is a simpler and altogether more satisfactory explanation.[16]

Leites, in a companion volume entitled *A Study of Bolshevism*, nonetheless enlarged upon these findings and related them more explicitly to psychoanalytical theory. Two basic drives, according to Leites, explained the Russian intellectual character: a preoccupation with death, and latent passive homosexual impulses. The Russian intellectual's obsession with death, he thought, found its inverse opposite in the Bolshevik feeling that death was 'empty and small and unable to interfere with life'. Indeed one might well speculate,

Leites continued, 'whether the Bolshevik insistence on, in effect, killing enemies and being killed by them is not in part an effort to ward off fear-laden and guilty wishes to embrace men and be embraced by them'. This trait was at least consistent with pervasive patterns of behaviour such as the fear of being passive and the fear of wanting to submit to an attack. 'Once one denies one's wish to kiss by affirming one's wish to kill', Leites concluded, 'this is apt to reinforce one's belief in the enemy's wish to kill by virtue of the mechanism of projection, probably heavily used by the Bolsheviks'.[17] It need scarcely be said that these are conclusions which not simply exceed the available evidence but which also attach a quite disproportionate importance to the psychological makeup of individual leaders, irrespective of situation or context, in the determination of state policy.

Leites's work was based mainly upon an analysis of published writings, political and literary. Geoffrey Gorer's *People of Great Russia*, a work in the same tradition, drew rather upon a series of interviews with former Soviet citizens and with western journalists and officials who had been able to observe Russian behaviour at first hand in the immediately preceding period. Altogether between three and four hundred such interviews were conducted.[18] Gorer, however, was also strongly influenced by psychoanalytical theory, especially its Freudian variant, and his study was virtually dominated by a concern with methods of upbringing in early childhood. The practice of swaddling seemed to him of particular importance. From the day of its birth onwards, Gorer noted, a Russian baby was tightly swaddled in long strips of material, with its legs held straight and its arms held by its sides. The baby, in fact, was completely rigid; and the better the mother, the firmer the bandages. Gorer maintained that this was simply one of the ways in which the character of adult Great Russians was formed; but in practice he concentrated upon it to the exclusion of almost all else, and his study has not unfairly been described as an 'exercise in diaperology'.[19]

Gorer, for instance, hypothesised that these periods of tight confinement, and the periods of total release which alternated with them, had important psychological consequences. When swaddled, Gorer postulated, Russian babies would find the constraints upon their movements 'extremely painful and frustrating'. They would be moved to 'intense and destructive rage' which could not be expressed physically, and which would 'typically be directed against the constraint itself rather than against those who were responsible for it'. The swaddled state, Gorer suggested, contributed to a preoccupation with the soul and its vicissitudes, since the infant thus confined could have no control over or interest in his physical movements; while the converse of this state, the total release from constraint which occurred once the swaddling bandages were removed, in turn related to the tendency of Russians towards 'maximum total gratifications—orgiastic feasts, prolonged drinking bouts, high frequency of copulation, and so on'. The swaddling/unswaddling syndrome also related to Russians' sudden and bewildering switches from kindness to cruelty, and from joy to grief; and it helped to explain why Russians saw government as 'external' to themselves. They preferred external authority to be 'firm and consistent, neither too tight nor too loose'; if it was not, it would be 'disregarded and then cast off'.[20]

A third attempt to apply psychocultural insights to the study of Soviet politics was Henry Dicks's 'Observations on contemporary Russian behaviour', first published in 1952.[21] Dicks, a practising psychiatrist at the Tavistock Institute, was given the opportunity of carrying out depth interviews with twenty-nine former Soviet citizens in post-war Germany. His conclusions were largely in accord with those of Gorer. One of the dominant and persistent conflicts in traditional and post-revolutionary Russian society, Dicks suggested, was that between the 'Russian *oral* character structure typical in many ways for the culture, and an *anal-compulsive* ("puritan") pattern characterising the elite'. There was a great deal of preoccupation with food and its acquisition and consumption, and a great deal of heavy drinking. Dicks also found the cyclical patterns identified by Gorer: fasting would be followed by feasting, and periods of gloomy abstinence would alternate with periods of bacchanalian excess. A delight in talk and song—oral communication in general—was part of the same syndrome, together with passivity and 'oral-sadistic imagery'. The cyclical pattern was particularly evident in industrial work, where there was a general preference for idleness interspersed with occasional record-breaking feats than for steady but continuous output.[22]

The whole complex of 'anal' traits characteristic of Western European society, however, Dicks found, was absent. These included traits such as a concern for the acquisition and conservation of property; orderliness, neatness and punctuality; personal hygiene; and a desire for privacy and seclusion. Only among the political elite, in fact, were these characteristics to be found to any significant extent; unlike the mass of the population they were concerned to impose control, to mould and master material, and to be rational, punctual and orderly. These characteristics derived in turn, Dicks hypothesised, from foreign (especially German) influence upon Russian society from the time of Peter the Great onwards, which had established such attributes as models of desirable elite behaviour. Lenin, Dicks noted, was a great admirer of German culture and of German social habits in general; and personal charisma would probably attach to those who, such as he, succeeded thereby in demonstrating their mastery over oral gratification needs (the first revolutionary leaders, indeed, had been 'mainly the orally frustrated'). The strain of suppressing their oral spontaneity, however, was manifest in a number of defence mechanisms: manic denial, for instance, and persecutory anxiety. The system would be able to operate at all, Dicks hypothesised, only to the extent to which these characteristics were allowed to coexist with the 'obstinate persistence of unofficial, un-Communist, but uncommonly Russian patterns of "backsliding" into fraternal, affectionate, and easy-going human relations'.[23]

There is perhaps no need to multiply further these examples of the psychocultural approach to Soviet political behaviour.[24] The capacity of those studies we have considered to generate fruitful hypotheses and insights should, at least, be apparent. Most of these studies were conducted, whatever their other shortcomings, by scholars with at least a minimum of psychoanalytic training. Their findings are to a considerable extent consistent one with another; and many have since been confirmed by other, more rigorously-conducted investigations. Inkeles, Hanfmann and Beier, for instance, administered a battery of psychological tests to about fifty former Soviet citizens and to a matched control group of Americans. Their results supported Dicks's and Gorer's at many points. Russians, for instance, were found to have a greater need for affiliation and dependence, and a stronger desire to interact with other people and enjoy affection, than the American control group. Russians scored highly on 'oral' traits, such as eating, drinking, talking and singing, but tended to lack self-control; and they also tended towards violent oscillations of mood and behaviour.[25] The parallels between such findings and the psychoculturalists' should scarcely require further emphasis.

The defects of these earlier, 'characterological' studies should at the same time not be overlooked. Interviews with emigres, in the first place, are clearly somewhat problematic; the more so when comparatively small numbers are involved. These problems are compounded when the character attributes identified, such as those of the Soviet political elite in Dicks's study, are derived not from interviews with members of the group itself but from the reported observations of others. Even investigations which have been able to gain direct access to leadership groups of this kind have reached markedly diverse conclusions;[26] and it would be surprising if many of the psychoculturalists' interpretations survived, at least in their present form, if direct access to the Soviet population itself at any time became possible (many such hypotheses, indeed, have failed to survive even a documentary mode of analysis and verification).[27] Given their small sample size, moreover, it is not surprising that the distribution and relative intensity of the character attributes identified are not clearly specified. The studies, in fact, whatever the caveats of their authors, are essentially in the 'national character' idiom, with all that that implies in terms of impressionism, unverifiability and the more or less undiscriminating attribution of all the traits identified to the whole of the national population in question. It has been one of the services of the political culture precisely to relax the assumption of homogeneity, permanency and biological determinism with which such studies have generally been associated.[28]

A further problem relates to the level of analysis which is employed; and in particular, to the tendency of Freudian-oriented psychoculturalists to extrapolate from patterns of upbringing to attitudes and behaviour, and thence to the characteristics of larger social aggregates such as classes or nations. Each of the links in a causal chain of this kind, in fact, must be empirically demonstrated; it is methodologically illegitimate to assume, as the psychocultural-ists have tended to do, that the larger social group will necessarily share all the attributes which its members may possess as individ-uals (the 'individualistic fallacy'), or conversely that the character-istics of individuals may necessarily be inferred from the characteristics of the larger group of which they form part (the 'ecological fallacy'). Dicks, at least, is aware of this problem (the danger of 'transposing concepts from individual psychology to social psychology in a manner which may be regarded as unwarranted by social scientists');[29] but most of such writings ignore the problem, and none can be said to resolve it successfully.[30] A further and related difficulty arises from the fact that psychoculturalists generally attach a quite disproportionate significance in a causal sequence of this kind to the period of early childhood. Other periods of the life-cycle tend to be ignored or neglected, and little attention is given to factors such as school and work (or indeed direct experience of the political system itself) which may intervene between early childhood and political behaviour in the adult years.[31] This general shortcoming is especially unfortunate in the analysis of Communist political systems, one of whose distinctive characteristics is the scope and intensity of the programme of political instruction and propaganda which they sponsor from the later childhood years onwards.

A third problem concerns the units of analysis which the psychoculturalists employ. Generally speaking, their propositions are held to apply to the Russian (or Soviet) population as a whole, and very little effort is made to disaggregate findings in respect of class, ethnic, religious, generational or other differences. This, admittedly, is a procedure more or less consistent with the manner in which the 'national character' concept has been used by the anthropologists among whom it was first developed; and in a small, simple and relatively homogeneous tribal community it might indeed make little sense to modify more general conclusions in respect of a series of subsidiary affiliations. In a modern large-scale society, however, with its regional variations, complex division of labour, and (especially important in the USSR) its ethnic and cultural differences, it is clearly essential to proceed beyond a series of propositions designed to refer to the national population as a whole. Gorer, among the psychoculturalists we have considered, comes closest to doing so in distinguishing between peasant, worker and aristocratic patterns of upbringing; but he largely abandons these distinctions when he goes on to speak of the development of personality, and in general his account treats this problem with something close to indifference.[32] Dicks and Leites deal with the political elite as if it were a homogeneous social group, which clearly it is not; and they make no allowance for national or ethnic differences in their respective studies notwithstanding the fact that, in Dicks's case, almost one-third of his sample were not of Russian nationality. Clearly, a more discriminating approach is required.

The final and perhaps most difficult point is that which concerns the relationship between 'national' characteristics and the socio-economic circumstances with which they are associated. To what extent, that is to say, should the observed characteristics of a particular population be attributed, not to the peculiarities of their personality or upbringing, but to determinate features of their material environment? Dicks comes closest to an awareness of this problem when he acknowledges that Russians' irregular work patterns may have their origin in nothing more complicated than the fact that theirs is a country with long winters and short intense summers in which a disproportionate part of the year's work must be performed. The attitudes he describes, he notes, may well be 'characteristic of peasants generally, with their primary producer mentality and their dependence on fitful weather and markets'.[33] This, clearly, is a concession which strikes at the heart of the psychoculturalists' case; and perhaps not surprisingly it is not developed further. Indeed the very research design employed, by dispensing with control groups and appropriate comparisons with other nations and cultures, virtually preordained that whatever character attributes the group were found to possess would be attributed, more or less exclusively, to their common nationality. This is scarcely a procedure which could recommend itself to a comparatively-minded scholarly community.

The studies we have discussed, moreover, tend also to lack an historical or developmental perspective. If Russians derive their political values and beliefs from particular patterns of upbringing in early childhood, and if those patterns remain more or less unchanged, then presumably there can be no basis for the consideration of political development and change in that society or for any attempt to relate political beliefs and values to previous political experience—that is, to examine them historically. Yet there is every reason on the face of it to relate Russians' perceptions of political authority to determinate features of that country's pre-revolutionary experience, such as the lack of developed representative institutions or of an effective rule of law, as well as to ethnic and sub-group identities, direct experience of the political system and so forth. There is clearly no need to resort to 'swaddling' hypotheses when more straightforward explanations of this kind are available;

indeed the psychocultural approach may do a positive disservice to scholarly inquiry by screening out in advance precisely those link-ages between the political system and its environment, at present and through time, which have been among the most fruitful areas of analysis in comparative politics in recent years. It will be suggested in what follows that the concept of political culture may be able to retain the merits of the psychoculturalists' approach while at the same time locating them within an explanatory framework of a broader and more satisfactory character.

Political Culture and Political Analysis

Political culture, as a concept, makes possible the consideration of political beliefs and values and their relation to continuity and change in the political system while nonetheless taking account of the valid criticisms that have been made of the 'national character' approach. It is a more discriminating instrument in at least three ways. First of all, there need be no presumption of homogeneity or unity in the political culture under investigation. Scholars normally agree that at least two levels in the political culture should be disting-uished, a 'mass' political culture applying to the population at large as well as an 'elite' political culture characteristic of the politi-cal decision-makers and other such groups (in what follows we shall be concerned primarily with the first of these categories). It is also widely agreed that, at least in Communist-ruled states, a 'regime' or 'official' political culture should be identified, to refer to the ideo-logy and practices which are prescribed and promoted by the regime; their acceptance and internalisation by the mass of the citizen body, however, must remain a matter for empirical investigation.[34] A further level, 'individual political culture', has sometimes been identified;[35] but this usage is not widely accepted and it has not been employed for the purposes of this study. The language of psychology remains the most appropriate for the actions and perceptions of individuals; the concept of political cul-ture is more properly reserved for social aggregates of the kind we have already specified.

A political culture, secondly, need be no more homogeneous 'hori-zontally' than it is 'vertically'. A political culture, on the contrary, will normally subsume a variety of political sub-cultures, each of them associated with a pattern of beliefs and behaviour in important respects different from that of the population as a whole. In the USSR the most obvious of these sub-cultures are those of a national or ethnic character; but it may often make sense to regard a particular occupation, social class, religious or regional community as constituting a political sub-culture in this sense. The extent to which the boundaries of these groups overlap, and their relation to the overall national political culture, must again be a matter for empirical investigation. The national political culture, in some cases, may be an entirely notional unit of analysis, no more than an aggregate of the political sub-cultures that constitute it. In such circumstances it may make sense to speak of a 'divided' or 'fragmented', rather than a 'unified' or 'dominant', political culture at this level.[36]

The concept of political culture, in the third place, is both more receptive to the notion of political change and more agnostic with regard to its nature and direction. Rather than postulating, in the 'national character' fashion, that a nation's political system is essentially the product of the attitudinal dispositions of its individual citizens (and therefore likely to change, if at all, only with changes in patterns of upbringing and child socialisation), the political culture approach permits socio-economic change and patterns of previous political development to be considered as of at least comparable importance in the explanation of political continuity and change. Political culture, in this sense, cannot of itself explain the existence of particular political values or patterns of behaviour, nor can it be said of itself to determine the nature and direction of change in any political system thus characterised. But it may help to account at least in part for the existence of a particular set of political beliefs and behavioural patterns, insofar as these are the product of the distinctive historical experience of the group under consideration, and it will mediate, and thus modify, the interaction between socio-economic change and the polity. Political culture, as a concept, thus argues against the reductionism inherent in attempts to equate political with socio-economic or psychological change; the political, it insists, has a degree of relative autonomy and is likely to shape, as well as be shaped by, the social, economic and psychological changes which a society may experience. Its merit, discriminatingly employed, is to identify those features of political belief and behaviour which are historically derivable, specific to a particular national or other sub-group, and likely to have a continuing influence upon its future political evolution.

The political culture approach, however, is by no means an un-problematic or non-controversial one; and in the remainder of this chapter we propose to consider three areas in which its employment has seemed particularly contentious. The first relates to the scope of political culture. Should it, in particular, be taken to refer to the behavioural as well as the attitudinal characteristics of the population under consideration? Sidney Verba, in perhaps the most widely used definition of political culture, has argued that it should be regarded as a 'system of empirical beliefs, expressive symbols, and values which defines the situation in which political action takes place. It provides the subjective orientation to politics'. The basic focus of attention, for Verba, is upon 'basic values, cognitions and emotional commitments', but not upon the formal or informal processes of interaction among political actors.[37] Lucian Pye argues similarly that political culture is a 'set of attitudes, beliefs and sentiments which give order and meaning to a political process and which provide the underlying assumptions and rules that govern behaviour in the political system', or the 'manifestation in aggregate form of the psychological and subjective dimensions of politics'.[38] There is a danger, Pye notes, that if political culture is taken to comprehend behaviour as well as beliefs it will come 'perilously close to being no more than a pretentious way of referring to politi-cal behaviour'; and as Archie Brown has noted, the opportunity will thereby be lost of attempting to explain patterns of political behav-iour, at least in part, in terms of the beliefs, values and perceptions to which they appear to relate.[39]

Most authors of this persuasion, however, appear to concede that political culture may have, at least, a behavioural aspect. Verba accepts, for instance, that one way in which one may learn about political beliefs is to observe the ways in which political structures operate. Political beliefs, he argues, 'affect and are affected by the way in which the structures operate'; there is a 'close circle of rela-tionships between culture and structure'.[40] Pye goes somewhat fur-ther in referring to political culture as embracing the 'political ideals and operating norms of a polity', a definition which would appear at once to concede that the concept should have a behavioural as well as an attitudinal dimension; and writing more recently he has indeed explicitly included patterns of political behaviour, as well as beliefs and sentiments, within his definition of political culture.[41]

Verba similarly accepts that although the relationship between political beliefs and behaviour may vary, 'it is clear that they are never irrelevant to each other. Inconsistencies between belief and belief or between belief and action have significant implications for a political system'.[42]

A number of other writers are less concerned to draw this distinction. Jowitt, for instance, regards political culture as the 'informal organization of the state', or as a 'set of informal, adoptive postures—behavioural and attitudinal—that emerge in response to and interact with the set of formal definitions—ideological, policy, and institutional—that characterize a given level of society'.[43] Rosenbaum, similarly, defines political culture as a 'conceptual shorthand for feelings, thoughts and behaviours we note, or infer, from watching men living out their civic lives'; while David Paul, who addresses this problem more directly, regards political culture as an 'observable configuration of values, symbols, orientations and behaviour patterns' which, when observed in historical perspective, can 'shed more light on a society's political culture than can the best attitudinal data'.[44] This broader definition, moreover, finds a good deal of support in the sociological and anthropological literature, in which culture is typically defined as the 'total way of life' of a social group or as an 'abstraction from behaviour and the products of behaviour'. It was from these sources that the concept of political culture was in the first instance derived; and to at least one of the scholars most prominently associated with the political cultural approach, Robert Tucker, a departure from traditional usages of this kind has not seemed desirable.[45]

To subsume a behavioural as well as an attitudinal dimension within the definition of political culture has at least two further advantages. In the first place, it avoids the problem of circularity which arises when political beliefs are inferred from political behaviour and then used in turn to explain that behaviour (or vice versa);[46] and it avoids the related and thorny problem of attempting to assess the extent to which political beliefs may actually be said to have influenced behaviour—beliefs may be internally contradictory, some may be more 'actionable' than others, and so forth.[47] There is, in any case, no getting away from the problem of the manner in which political beliefs are formed in the first place. Unless they are to be regarded as genetically determined (in which case, presumably, they must be more or less unchangeable, evidence to the contrary notwithstanding), we must permit at least the possibility that they may relate to or be modified by direct experience of the political system in the later childhood and adult years, a concession which in turn makes it difficult to argue for the causal primacy of beliefs. In reality the reciprocal influence of one upon the other, both in childhood and in the adult years, will be such that any attempt to establish a causal relationship between them will be well-nigh impossible.[48]

A second problem concerns the relationship between beliefs and behaviour and the performance of a political system. To some extent this may be expressed in terms of the relationship between the first two modes of political orientation identified by Almond and Verba in *The Civic Culture*, the cognitive (knowledge of the political system) and affective (feelings about the political system), and the third, or evaluative orientation (judgements and opinions about political objects).[49] Although Almond and Verba are fully aware of the extent to which evaluations of the outputs of a political system may influence emotional attitudes towards it (the importance of direct experience of the political system, they write, has been 'seriously underemphasized'),[50] it is probably true to say that they gave rather less attention to the manner in which political beliefs might be modified and influenced by such experiences than to the relationship which operated in the reverse direction from political beliefs to behaviour.[51] The emphasis which Almond and Verba thereby gave to the interpretation of political culture has had at least two unfortunate consequences. In the first place, it has obscured the extent to which a given set of political beliefs and values may be a reaction to, not an explanation of, the manner in which the political system operates. The deferential attitudes identified in many surveys of working-class opinion, for instance, may simply reflect a realistic scepticism as to the ability of the mass public to influence the making of political decisions in their society; of genuine value consensus, at any rate, there appears to be little unambiguous evidence.[52] In the Italian political system, similarly, differences in the practice of politics north and south may be accounted for more simply in terms of the benefits which local elites derive from existing arrangements than in terms of 'moral backwardness', 'subject-participant orientations' and the rest.[53] It is more than sixteen years since we were urged to abandon the 'oversocialized conception of man';[54] the moral, it appears, can still bear repetition.

Looking, further, towards the future, it is clear that existing patterns of supportive political beliefs need provide no guarantee as to the continuance of such support in years to come, whatever the performance of the political system or the evaluation by its citizens of that performance. The recent political experience of the USA is particularly instructive in this regard. The emergence of a series of acute and intractable domestic difficulties in the middle of the 1960s, it appears, has been accompanied by a sharp erosion of generalised popular trust in government, precisely one of the key values on which, at the end of the 1950s, the USA scored so highly in the Almond and Verba survey. Between 1958 and 1964, for instance, more than three-quarters (77 per cent) of those who were polled by the Institute for Social Research of the University of Michigan were prepared to say that they trusted the national government 'most of the time' or 'always'. By 1966, however, this proportion had dropped to just over two-thirds (68 per cent), and by 1970 it had fallen still further, to not much more than half (55 per cent) of those surveyed, and was still in decline. In 1958, similarly, some 81 per cent of those polled were prepared to state that the government was basically run in the interests of all; but by 1970 this had become a minority view, a majority (55 per cent) inclining rather towards the opinion that it was 'pretty much run by a few big interests'.[55] These, clearly, are considerable movements of opinion; and it would be surprising if they were not related, at least to some degree, to the experience which ordinary citizens had acquired of government over this period in terms of stability, employment, prices and so forth. In turn they point up the need to incorporate this reciprocal link between performance and political beliefs into any adequate political-cultural analysis.[56]

This brings one to the third and final point which must be given at least preliminary consideration at this stage, the question of the causal status of the political culture approach. Clearly we cannot argue, as some have been prepared to do,[57] that a country's political culture provides a necessary and sufficient explanation of the manner in which its political system operates. We should then be unable to account for the fact that political systems, in a variety of cases, have changed with a rapidity greatly in excess of that of any conceivable change in the political culture which underlies them; nor should we be able to explain the fact that apparent similarities in political culture, such as (if we are to believe Almond and Verba) in Britain and the USA, should give rise to political systems of a rather different character. We should equally be unable to account for any changes in the political culture itself; certainly, any reciprocal link between polity and culture would have to be excluded. The reverse of this position, however, that the political culture is wholly capable of explanation in terms of the manner in which the political system actually operates, has equally little to recommend it. We should find it extremely difficult, on this basis, to explain the marked differences in the manner in which Communist political systems have tended to operate, despite the great similarity among them in terms of formal institutional structures; and we should find it equally difficult to explain the sources of development and change in a political system, explicable as they in many cases are only in terms of a country's previous political experience and the attitudes and expectations which derive from that experience. Political culture, in fact, must be regarded as both 'causing' and 'caused': as a variable which mediates between the political system and its environment, providing a framework within which patterns of political belief and behaviour, historically considered, can be located, and as a factor which will influence and constrain—though not determine—future patterns of development in a political system.

The relationship may helpfully be conceptualised in dialectical terms. The political culture, we may suggest (at any rate in the broader, more 'concrete' terms in which it has here been considered), may be regarded as in some sense an approximation to the 'superstructure' of a political system, with the economic and institutional environment constituting its 'base'. As in Marxist theory, the base will ultimately determine the 'superstructure' (the parallel, it should be stressed, is not exact and is employed for heuristic purposes only); the political culture or superstructure, however, should not be seen as simply the reflection of that material base but as a complex of ideas and practices, relatively autonomous in their existence, which are in turn capable of influencing and modifying the base in a complex pattern of interaction over time. Both 'base' and 'superstructure', thus considered, will have a certain amount of autonomy; changes in the one will not be explicable simply in terms of the other, or vice versa.[58] It is, I believe, the merit of the political culture approach that, conceived in these terms, it makes possible a concentration upon the specificity of political beliefs and practices in a given political system while nevertheless locating them within an explanatory framework of a broadly materialist character. This, at any rate, is the spirit in which the present inquiry has been conducted.

2

The Imprint of Autocracy

Soviet political culture is rooted in the historical experience of centuries of absolutism.[1] Since at least medieval times the country has typically been ruled by a succession of strong, autocratic monarchs; and countervailing institutions—parliamentary, legal, or whatever—have remained weak and undeveloped. The country's geography no doubt predisposed towards a pattern of development of this kind. The lack of natural boundaries, which might have provided a secure defence against invasion, has tended to place a premium upon central control and unity; the country was isolated from the major trade routes and developed no powerful commercial oligarchy to rival those of medieval Europe; and adverse climatic and other conditions inhibited the development of a strong and autonomous landowning class whose political ambitions might, as elsewhere in Europe, have limited and constrained the prerogatives of monarchy. Whatever the explanation, it is at least clear that the government of Russia has been regarded for some time, and not without justification, as a despotism more Asiatic than European in character. 'If there is one single factor which dominates the course of Russian history, at any rate since the Tatar conquest', as Hugh Seton-Watson has put it, 'it is the principle of autocracy'.[2]

This is not to suggest that such a pattern of development was in any way inevitable or preordained. The country's early political development, on the contrary, was characterised by the emergence of popular assemblies (the *veche*) which were comparable in many ways to those which existed at the same time in Western Europe, and which similarly placed not inconsiderable constraints upon the exercise of princely rule. The *veche*, which existed in Kiev and in the other major Russian towns of the twelfth century and later, was a deliberative assembly of the town's freeman population; it decided questions of justice and administration, was responsible for the declaration of war and peace, made laws and issued charters, and elected officials (the *posadnik* and the *tysyatskii*) who were in turn responsible for the implementation of decisions and the leadership of the local militia. More important for our purposes, it elected a prince and concluded a contract (*ryad*) with him, designed to specify and limit his powers with respect to taxation, the distribution of military obligations, and the allocation of territory. A prince was unable to rule in a 'free town' without an agreement of this kind.[3]

The *veche* was not a fully-developed, representative or sovereign assembly. As in city states elsewhere, the urban patriciate had generally a preponderant influence upon its deliberations; and through its control of the agenda of meetings and of the implementation of decisions it could usually ensure that no policies inimical to its interests were pursued. Cases of bribery and intrigue were not unknown; and the term *veche* itself could cover a wide variety of phenomena, from full assemblies of the populace to consultations between the prince and his principal subordinates.[4] Meetings of the *veche* in the former, more normal, sense, however, were by no means always the occasions for violence and demagoguery that some sources have suggested. Particular places and forms of meeting came gradually into existence; decisions appear generally to have been taken in an organised manner, probably by a form of balloting; and those who were present at such meetings were generally seated upon benches provided for the purposes not, it has been noted, a practice which would suggest a riotous or disorderly assembly.[5] Social tensions certainly existed; but at least in Novgorod, where civic self-government of this kind was most fully developed, a reasonably stable political order evolved, and the city avoided the degeneration into tyranny which befell so many Italian city-states in the same period. The *veche*'s authority, moreover, was by no means nominal; princes and their families were required to reside outside the city walls and forbidden to acquire land within the territory over which it ruled, and they could be, and sometimes were, expelled if they violated their obligations towards the townsfolk. At least in Novgorod such expulsions bore the character of a public trial.[6]

The Tartar invasion of the thirteenth century, however, brought this pattern of development to an end in most Russian towns; and the expansion of the Muscovite principate (where *veche* institutions had not developed) in the fifteenth and sixteenth centuries led to the termination of city self-government in its last remaining outposts, Novgorod (in 1478) and Pskov (in 1510). The term *veche* itself did not immediately disappear;[7] and in the Baltic area 'estate' institutions (the *landtags*) continued to meet into modern times, in a manner broadly similar to that of the evolution of representative institutions elsewhere in Europe.[8] In Russia proper, however, the basis had now been laid for that distinctive impress of autocratic institutions upon the fabric of social life which forms so central an element in the country's political culture. We propose in what follows to examine that inheritance more closely under three broad headings: structures of government, perceptions of government, and the style and scope of government.

Structures of Government

A central characteristic of the Muscovite state was the absence of political institutions in any way constraining the exercise of monarchical power. The monarch (called, from 1547, the Tsar), it was true, did discuss matters of legislation and taxation with his principal aristocratic subordinates in an institution known as the Boyar Duma.[9] The Duma controlled the local administration, took decisions on the organisation of the army and landholding, and received foreign consuls. Its role in the conduct of foreign relations was perhaps the most impressive of its formal functions; but a legal code of 1550 described the Duma's authorisation as an essential part of the legislative process, and some have gone so far as to describe it as a 'legislative' or 'supreme controlling organ'.[10] The growing influence of the Tsar, however, allowed him to reduce its influence; and from about the middle of the sixteenth century an 'inner Duma' came into existence, composed of the more amenable of the Tsar's nobles, to which important matters of state were increasingly directed. The Tsar began to legislate on his own authority, in the form of decrees or *ukazy*; and although the Boyar Duma survived until the end of the seventeenth century, it was as a body much reduced in membership and dwindling in significance.[11] Even at the height of its powers, moreover, the Duma had been in no sense a body with a legal standing independent of that of the Tsar, even when, as was sometimes the case, it met by itself. Its purpose was simply to execute the instructions of the Tsar, who appointed its members. It had no area of competence of its own, its composition and size were extremely unstable, it maintained no records, and it had no fixed procedures. It was an advisory, not a representative institution.[12]

The *Zemskii Sobor*, which met from the mid-sixteenth until the mid-seventeenth century, more closely resembled an institution of an embryonically parliamentary character.[13] The *Sobory* were essentially periodic gatherings convened by the Tsar whenever he wished to discuss a particular issue 'with all the land'; their membership, accordingly, consisted of the principal social estates— the clergy, boyars and gentry—together with the townsfolk and (at least on one occasion) the peasantry. In full session it could be a body of by no means inconsiderable proportions. Some 400 people attended the *Sobor* of 1598, for instance, while that of 1613 (at which Alexis Romanov was elected Tsar) had as many as 700 or 800 members. This was the period in which the *Zemskii Sobor* had its greatest degree of influence; and for the first decade of the new dynasty its sessions were virtually continuous. Thereafter, however, it came to be summoned more rarely, and to be concerned more or less exclusively with matters of foreign policy. From about the middle of the seventeenth century its membership became less and less inclusive and representative in character; finally, in 1722, the *Sobor* was deprived of its right to elect to the throne and fell altogether into desuetude.[14]

Even before this time, however, the *Zemskii Sobor* had not been a body which placed any effective limitation upon the prerogatives of the monarch. The Tsar, on the contrary, decided when assemblies were to be convened; and he also decided in what manner representatives were to be elected to it, in some cases simply nominating them himself. The *Sobor*'s decisions, moreover, were effective only when the monarch chose to agree with them.[15] Klyuchevsky's verdict that the *Sobor* of 1566 was a 'consultation of the government with its own agents', it has been suggested, may fairly be applied to its other meetings as well. The *Sobor*'s participants were considered to be performing a state service, for which they were reimbursed by the treasury, rather than exercising a right; and although the participants could state their grievances and petition for redress, the monarch retained full and unchallenged powers of decision and action. Both the *Sobor* and the Boyar Duma, it has been argued,

> . . . may best be viewed as expedients necessary to the state until such time as it could afford an adequate bureaucratic apparatus. The Duma provided a link between the crown and the central administration, the Assembly (*Sobor*) a link between the crown and the provinces. As the bureaucratic apparatus improved, both institutions were quietly dropped.[16]

It was not until the early twentieth century, in fact, that political institutions of an even remotely 'parliamentary' character made their appearance in Russia. Wrung in the course of the revolutionary events of 1905 from a reluctant Tsar, the State Duma was always a vulnerable body whose powers were constantly in danger of curtailment by a jealous monarch. Formally, however, those powers were extremely extensive. The Duma had the right to enact and amend legislation; it could appoint and dismiss government officials; it had the right to consider the national and departmental budgets; and it had general supervisory rights over the apparatus of state control. It had the right, moreover, to address questions to the chairman of the Council of Ministers (the newly-established 'Cabinet') and to individual ministers; it supervised the administration of the state railways and of private companies; and it could examine in addition any question which the Tsar might invite it to consider. Without the consent of the Duma, promised the Tsar's manifesto of 17 October 1905, 'no law can come into force'.[17]

The Duma's powers, as defined by subsequent legislation, proved in fact to be rather more modest. The Duma's rejection of a budgetary proposal, it emerged on 8 March 1906, would not in fact prevent its enactment. The Duma, moreover, had no right to alter expenditure connected with the Army or Navy, foreign loans, the affairs of the imperial household, or many matters within the competence of the Ministry of Internal Affairs (some two-thirds of government expenditure was thus removed from its control). The Duma's control over the executive was also extremely limited. Ministers were responsible to the Tsar, not to the Duma, and the Tsar alone had the right to appoint or dismiss them. Ministers could be questioned on the floor of the house, but they could refuse an answer or else provide one at whatever later date they found convenient.[18] The Duma could vote its dissatisfaction with ministerial statements of this kind, but such votes were of no constitutional import. Indeed it almost seemed, wrote the liberal historian and Cadet leader, Paul Milyukov, that 'the more a minister succeeded in antagonising the Duma, the more reliable he was considered to be [by the Tsar] in that contest between the old regime and the Russian democracy'.[19]

The Tsar's position in any case remained a virtually impregnable one. He nominated just over half the members of the second legislative chamber, the State Council, which had the right of veto over all the proposals which the Duma submitted to it. (The remainder of its members were elected by the landed nobility, the Holy Synod, educational institutions and merchants.) Under the terms of the Basic Laws of the Russian Empire, moreover, which he alone could amend, the Tsar remained the ultimate source of legislative authority, an 'autocratic and unlimited monarch' whose commands his subjects were enjoined to obey by 'God Himself'.[20] The Tsar could endorse or reject legislative proposals, determine when the Duma should sit and when it should be dissolved, and, if he chose to do so, he could promulgate decrees on his own authority which had the force of law. Legislation of this kind was supposed to take place only in 'extraordinary' circumstances, and it had subsequently to be presented to the Duma and State Council for their consideration. It became general practice to resort to procedures of this kind, however, especially for particularly reactionary pieces of legislation, and Duma sessions were sometimes arbitrarily terminated in order to provide for it. The Tsar additionally retained exclusive control over declarations of war and peace, over relations with foreign states, and over the armed forces.[21]

The Duma's influence over the conduct of government, these restrictions notwithstanding, seems to have been steadily increasing in the years before its eventual dissolution. Norms and procedures of a more or less parliamentary kind were gradually evolving (it was Duma pressure, for instance, which led to the dismissal of four ministers in 1915, the most notable success the Duma had yet achieved), and it is arguable that these powers of influence might have developed into full-blown legislative sovereignty had war and revolution not supervened.[22] This, however, must remain a matter for conjecture. So far as the facts are concerned, it is clear that the Russian Empire was governed, as late as the early twentieth century, by a scarcely-modified autocracy, and that it was the only major country of which this could still be said (Table 2.1).

TABLE 2.1   *Political institutions by country, 1815–1914*

	Russia	UK	France	Germany	Austria–Hungary	USA
Selection of effective executive by direct or indirect election	no	yes	1848–51; 1871–	no	no	yes
Complete or incomplete parliamentary responsibility	no	yes	1815–48; 1873–	no	no	yes
Partial or full legislative effectiveness	no	yes	1815–47; 1861–	1867–	1863–	yes
Elective legislature	1906–	yes	yes	1867–	1863–	yes

SOURCE   A. H. Banks (comp.), *Cross-Polity Time-Series Data* (Cambridge, Mass., 1972).

The point is not simply, or even mainly, the absence of constitutional checks upon the exercise of monarchical authority (the Queen, after all, to this day retains impressive *formal* powers in Britain). It is more important for our purposes to note that popular links with such representative institutions as existed were extremely tenuous, both in terms of levels of participation in the political process and, more 'subjectively', in terms of knowledge and of attachment to those institutions among the mass of the citizen body. The franchise, in the first place, was a restricted and highly unequal one. The right to vote was confined to males over the age of twenty-five; and within that category there were further exclusions in respect of the armed forces, students, itinerants and foreigners. Provision was also made for further, more or less arbitrary, individual exclusions.[23] Those who remained eligible to vote were divided into three (later four) electoral colleges, at which point a further series of biases came into operation. The result was to accord representation as follows: one member of the landlords' electoral college represented 2000 voters, one member of the urban college represented 4000 voters, one from the peasant college represented 30,000 voters, and one from the workers' college represented 90,000 voters.[24] In all, only about $3\frac{1}{2}$ million citizens were admitted to the franchise, a proportion of the population no greater than had been the case in Britain a century earlier, and an extremely low one in comparative terms, as Table 2.2 makes clear.

TABLE 2.2 *Franchise and parliamentary representation by country (percentages)*

	Russia	UK	France	Germany	Italy	USA
Electorate as a proportion of population:						
circa 1870	0.0	7.9	27.1	19.4	2.3	22.4
circa 1910	2.4	17.9	28.9	22.2	23.4	26.3
Parliamentary representation circa 1910:						
aristocracy/nobility	51.0	15.4	11	12.9	16.5	n.d.
middle class/bourgeoisie	24.2	67.3	68	55.6	77.6	n.d.

SOURCES *Die Wahl der Parlamente* (Berlin, 1969); T. Mackie and R. Rose, *International Almanac of Electoral History* (London, 1974); D. Marvick (ed.), *Political Decision-makers* (Glencoe Ill., 1961); P. N. Milyukov, *Russia Today and Tomorrow* (New York, 1922); E. N. and P. R. Anderson, *Political Institutions and Social Change in Continental Europe in the Nineteenth Century* (London, 1967); G. Sartori *et al.*, *Il Parlamento Italiano* (Naples, 1963); and US Bureau of the Census, *Historical Abstract of the United States from Colonial Times to 1957* (Washington DC, 1960).

The results, in terms of the representation of social groups within the institutions of state, were as might have been expected. A careful examination of contemporary press and archival sources has established that the social composition of the First Duma was as follows: out of 498 deputies, 180 (36.1 per cent) were members of the nobility; 231 (46.4 per cent) were peasants; 48 (9.6 per cent) were engaged in trade and manufacture; 93 (18.7 per cent) represented the legal, medical and educational worlds; and a mere seven deputies (1.4 per cent) were industrial workers. The biases implicit in a pattern of representation of this kind became even more marked in the Third and Fourth Dumas, which were elected under the revised and more restrictive legislation of 1907. The landed gentry increased their representation to 51 per cent, while the proportion of peasant deputies (who had proved rather less biddable than the government had expected) fell to 22.4 per cent, and that of the working-men deputies to less than 1 per cent of the total.[25] These results are compared with those for a number of other European countries in Table 2.2; the over-representation of the nobility in Russia compared with other countries, and the under-representation of less privileged social strata, emerge reasonably clearly.

The point is again not simply, or even mainly, that workers and peasants were less well represented in the institutions of state in Russia than they were in other countries. At least as important, the new representative body disappointed even liberals and moderates, precisely those groups which were increasing their parliamentary representation in other countries at this time and which might have been able to maintain and even extend the limited powers with which the Duma had originally been entrusted. Trading and manufacturing circles, in particular, were notably under-represented. Of a total membership of about 425 in the Third Duma, it has been established, only 24 (5 per cent) were directly involved in business activities of any sort, and only five deputies were engaged in what could be called large-scale industrial activity.[26] The 'liberal bourgeoisie', indeed, appear on the whole to have regarded the Duma with indifference or even suspicion. The Duma, in their view, was composed of landed notables who were poorly informed of the needs of industry and commerce and of their importance to the national economy; and they were generally more concerned to establish strong and autonomous economic associations outside the representative system altogether than to maximise their influence within it. The business world took a somewhat greater interest in the Third and Fourth Dumas than in their predecessors; but the longer they continued to meet the more it became apparent that landlord-reactionary rather than liberal-bourgeois views predominated within them, and the greater became their disillusionment.[27] The result was that representative institutions in Russia lacked not simply the constitutional powers of corresponding bodies in Western Europe; more crucially, they drew upon an altogether more restricted range of social support.

Perceptions of Government

One consequence of the weak articulation of representative institutions was a highly personalised attachment to political authority, and in particular to the person of the Tsar. It has frequently been noted, for instance, that the popular uprisings which periodically convulsed Russian society in the seventeenth and eighteenth centuries were almost never directed against the Tsar himself. Their target was much more frequently the boyar aristocracy, who were typically supposed to have removed the Tsar from effective control of the nation's affairs and from whose maleficent attentions the rebels generally proposed to deliver him. In Stenka Razin's rising of 1670–71, for instance, a careful distinction was always drawn between the boyars, who were massacred as traitors to the Tsar, and the Tsar himself, to whom the rebels offered to submit after every reverse. The rebels even went so far as to claim that the Tsarevich Alexis, the Tsar's eldest son and heir to the throne, had eluded the boyars and was marching with them, although the Tsarevich had died in 1670.[28] Pugachev, a century later, more boldly declared that he was himself the rightful sovereign. There were more than twenty such pretenders in Russia during the seventeenth century, and more than forty during the eighteenth century (the unfortunate Peter III was rescued from the dead on at least sixteen occasions).[29] The myth of a 'just Tsar', as Avrich has noted, played a major part in virtually every popular uprising during this period, and it was clearly deeply ingrained upon the popular consciousness. As late as 1917 Sir George Buchanan, the British Ambassador to Russia, was convinced that it was not the Emperor but the government of which the nation had grown weary. 'Oh yes, we must have a Republic', a soldier told him, 'but we must have a good Tsar at its head.'[30]

The tendency to conceive of political authority in personalised terms was reflected also in the widely-used term 'Batyushka Tsar' (or 'little father Tsar'), emphasising the personal nature of the bond between the Tsar and his subjects, and in popular proverb and folklore. Some of the proverbs which were collected by Dal' in the middle of the nineteenth century, for instance, ran as follows: 'Without the Tsar the land cannot be ruled'; 'God in the sky, the Tsar on earth'; 'Without the Tsar, the country is widowed'; 'The people are the body, and the Tsar is the head'; and 'No-one is against God or against the Tsar'.[31] Popular folk-tales emphasised different but related aspects of his political authority. The Tsar, it was said, used to travel around incognito among his people, working beside them in farm and workshop and learning of their needs at first hand. Many saw him as the 'godfather of the peasant', christening their children and supporting the poorest among them (it was sometimes said that the Tsar was himself of humble origin). Popular folk-songs spoke similarly of Ivan the Terrible as a wise leader and brave commander who had crushed the treachery of the boyars and established a stern but just social order (*poryadok*), and of Peter the

Great as a friend of the people, considerate and just, who was at the same time a merciless foe of aristocratic or ecclesiastical intrigue. If such a monarch were to deny the popular will it could be only because he was an imposter or because, as the popular proverb put it, 'The Tsar is willing but the boyars resist' ('*Tsar' khochet, a boyare ne dayut*'). Between the real Tsar and his people no such conflict of interest was conceivable.[32]

The personified nature of political authority is apparent also in the words used to refer to entities such as 'the state' and 'government'. The Russian word for state, *gosudarstvo*, for instance, is simply a derivation from the word for lord or ruler, *gosudar'*. *Gosudar'* is in turn a word of ancient origin, the original meaning of which was that of a lord or master (*dominus*) whose powers extended over both people and things (occasionally it could even mean 'slaveowner'). From the mid-fourteenth century it came to be used, in much the same sense, to connote political authority.[33] The closest English equivalent of the word *gosudarstvo*, the power exercised by such a ruler, might be 'dominion' or 'patrimony'; either term, at least, would better convey the notion that the state was not simply a legal expression but essentially the private property of its ruler. Several other words—*gospodar, godpodin, obladetel', volodetel'*—similarly implied both ownership and rule, and Russian has always lacked the distinction between these two which was introduced in the west through the agency of Roman law. The word for an administrative sub-unit of the state, *volost'*, for instance, derives from the old Slavonic word *vlast'*, connoting power or force rather than legally-defined and limited authority.[34] It is this wider conception of the nature of political authority which informs contemporary Soviet usages such as 'state power' (*gosudarstvennaya vlast'*) or 'the authorities' (*vlasti*).

Russians, moreover, appear generally to have had little knowledge of or attachment to the political institutions by which that central state authority was mediated. The Russian experience of representative democracy, as we have seen, was in any case a limited one; and the government took care to limit the diffusion of even this modest experience among the population at large by restricting the reporting of Duma meetings, impeding meetings between deputies and their constituents, and limiting the number and range of activities of political parties.[35] Comprehension of party programmes and political institutions, in consequence, appears to have been fairly rudimentary. Peasants, for instance, appear from contemporary inquiries to have been poorly informed of the existence of the Duma and of the parties represented within it; not infrequently they deliberated together and then cast their votes as a group, or asked to be told how to do so. The inhabitants of one village, deciding they had made a mistake, even complained to the authorities that they had not been sent instructions. 'Why weren't we, dark and ignorant people, told for whom to vote?', they demanded to know.[36] Even in the towns a knowledge of democratic procedures was no more securely founded. In the elections to the Third Duma in 1907, for instance, employers sent their clerks and husbands their wives to vote for them, and some voters left in indignation when the polling clerks refused to tell them for whom to cast their vote. Voters thrust letters, petitions, insurance policies, passports and even bad verse into the ballot boxes in some cases, rather than the voting slips they were supposed to have brought with them.[37]

Levels of attachment to representative institutions were correspondingly low. Voters often did not take the trouble to make use of the rights with which they had been entrusted, and the proceedings of the Duma appear to have been followed with no great attention (many were simply unaware of its existence).[38] The dissolution of the First Duma by the Tsar met with little popular opposition; and when a number of its members withdrew to Vyborg and issued a manifesto calling for the nation to rally to its defence, the appeal, in the words of one of its authors, 'fell flat' (its only practical consequence was that the opposition was deprived of some of its most effective debaters, who were arrested and excluded from participation in future sessions).[39] Even by 1918, when Russia's short-lived 'constitutional experiment' came to an end, there was no greater attempt to defend the Constituent Assembly, which the Bolsheviks dissolved in that year as soon as it had met.[40] The liberal bourgeoisie, as we have seen, were somewhat sceptical of the value of such institutions, and it is difficult to resist the conclusion that formal bodies and procedures of this kind played little part in the attitudes towards government which characterised most other Russian citizens at this time.

This is not necessarily to suggest that these low levels of knowledge of and attachment to the formal institutions of state implied any lack of political interest and opinion in a more general sense, or a predisposition towards absolutist forms of government in particu-

lar. The patterns of political belief and behaviour of which we have
been speaking, in the first place, were characteristic primarily of
central Russia. Elsewhere in the Empire, such as in Poland and
Finland, there was a greater experience of and attachment to the
forms of representative government, and in Siberia, the north and
the Cossack lands, where serfdom had been less firmly established
and with which communications were in any case often difficult, a
set of more independent-minded attitudes and values appears to
have prevailed. Even in central Russia, moreover, a series of savage
and bitterly-fought peasant revolts, and rather later the establishment of Soviets, suggested that deference towards the central authorities might not be without its limits. That deference was also in
decline, and in the end it was manifestly not sufficient to sustain the
monarchy which supposedly rested upon it. Opinion is divided as to
when popular faith in the Tsar might be said to have disappeared;
some, following Lenin, have put it as late as Bloody Sunday, 22
January 1905, when the St Petersburg police fired upon a crowd of
unarmed demonstrators who were approaching the Winter Palace
with icons and the Tsar's portrait to beg for help and the redress of
grievances. At all events it is clear that by the late Imperial period
popular trust in the institution of monarchy had been considerably
attenuated, and that even before this date the passive obedience
of the Russian peasant could coexist quite happily with what Milyukov termed his 'indifferent scepticism . . . towards any actual
power'.[41]

The life of the local community, moreover, carried on at the same
time as, and largely unaffected by, political events at the centre of
the Empire, and at this level a rather different set of orientations
prevailed. Robert Tucker has described this phenomenon as the
'image of dual Russia'. Since at least the eighteenth century, he
points out, there was a consciousness, largely inarticulate but none
the less real for that, of Russia as a dual entity, composed of the
state and 'official Russia' on the one hand—the Tsar, the court and
their agents in the localities (*vlasti*)—and of the people and the
society on the other (*obshchestvo, narod*), separate from the first and
with a life and a set of values and priorities of their own. Tucker
quotes Herzen on this point:

> On the one hand, there was governmental, imperial, aristocratic
> Russia, rich in money, armed not only with bayonets but with all

the bureaucratic and police techniques taken from Germany. On the other hand, there was the Russia of the dark people, poor, agricultural, communal, democratic, helpless, taken by surprise, conquered, as it were, without battle.[42]

Any discussion of the traditional Russian political culture must take account of the disjunction between these 'two Russias', as Herzen described them. Popular orientations towards government, the first of these, were largely personalised, acceptive of the Tsar as the 'central knot' by which the kingdom was preserved from anarchy and destruction, and little concerned with procedures or institutions by which his power might be limited and held periodically to account. They co-existed, however, with a rich and democratic community life, with which all but the political elite more closely identified. As the proverb put it, 'God is high above and the Tsar is far away'.

The Style and Scope of Government

The tendency to conceive of political authority in personal and unmediated terms was in turn related to the regime's centralised and bureaucratic governing style. The establishment of a quasi-Cabinet in 1905, in the form of a reconstituted Council of Ministers, appeared to presage a more limited and constitutional role for the monarch. The Council was empowered to oversee major decisions; it met regularly, with a formal agenda and prior circulation of ministerial memoranda, and a 'prime ministerial' figure, rather than the Tsar himself, presided. The Council, however, like the Duma, had no authority to consider the activities of the ministries of the Army or the Navy, the Court or the Department of the State Controller; and individual ministers were responsible to the Tsar himself rather than to the Council or, singly or collectively, to the Duma. The apparatus of state, moreover, was repeatedly changed, militating against the formation of established procedures or institutional *esprit de corps*; and the Tsar's personal chancellery continued to perform important governmental functions. One of its sections, for instance, regularly reviewed legislative proposals and occasionally drafted measures on its own initiative. Another, the celebrated Third Section, kept a constant watch upon the activities of revolutionary movements and the press; collected information on counterfeit money, and on religious and commercial associations; and exercised general supervision over the administration of justice in urban areas. These sections were dissolved in 1880 and 1882 respectively; but the section that remained was by no means a negligible institution, retaining responsibility, in particular, for the appointment and dismissal of senior governmental officials, and the Third Section continued to make its influence felt through the Ministry of the Interior, to which its apparatus had been transferred intact.[43]

The Tsar had additional powers with regard to the conduct of government in the country as a whole. He appointed the *gubernatory*, the representatives of central government in the localities, and also the governors-general, whose considerable powers included the right to report in person to the Tsar whenever they thought it appropriate to do so. The powers of governors were also extensive: they could prohibit meetings, forbid the sale of newspapers and journals, order arrests and dismissals, and transfer any case they wished to a military court. Their powers were somewhat attenuated by the reforms of the 1860s, which set up elective local councils known as *zemstvos* and provided for a degree of urban self-government; but a further recentralisation took place towards the end of the nineteenth century, and in any case the *zemstvos* had always been a somewhat anomalous addition to the state structure, their autonomy unrecognised in the administrative theory of the time and their proto-democratic character inconsistent with the overall structures of absolutism.[44] Indeed given the absence of institutional checks upon the exercise of governmental authority, it might often appear that the only effective defence of local autonomy lay in the venality of the bureaucracy and the absence of reliable communications between Moscow and the provinces. As late as the early twentieth century it took fifteen days for a letter to get from Moscow or St Petersburg to Khabarovsk, and letters to places off the main railway lines could take 'months' to reach their destination.[45]

Russia differed from its principal western neighbours in its scope as well as in its style of government. This is apparent, first of all, in Russia's lack of autonomous sub-group activity. Trade unions and strikes, for instance, were illegal until 1905. Strikes, for economic purposes only, were legalised in December 1905, and the formation of trade unions and other associations became possible in March 1906. There were heavy penalties for industrial action in government offices, state-owned enterprises and the public services, however, and regular attempts were made by the police to infiltrate and undermine the union leaderships (not to speak of the formation of bogus 'trade unions' and the employment of *agents provocateurs*). Unions were also closed, or denied registration, as the authorities found appropriate.[46] Employers were subject to a similar degree of detailed government regulation of their affairs through the factory inspectorate and the police. Their presence was generally welcomed by the employers, as they were normally willing to arrest particularly recalcitrant workers at the employers' request. Sometimes, however, they used their influence to compel factory managers to make concessions rather than withdraw them, in order to reduce pressure upon the government for reforms of a more straightforwardly political character;[47] and in general their presence made for a highly controlled and bureaucratic, rather than autonomous and self-regulating, economic sub-system.

The legislation of 1906 which legalised the existence of trade unions also provided for the formation of associations of other kinds. Their establishment, however, required the approval of the appropriate minister or official, and their operation was subject to a large number of restrictions. No society or body could be formed, for instance, if its aims or objectives were considered to represent a threat to public morals or social order, or if it had a political character and was directed from abroad; and the Minister of Internal Affairs could dissolve any association if he deemed its activities to be a threat to public order. No meetings could be held in hotels, restaurants, inns or educational institutions, or near public buildings; and any meeting of any kind could be prohibited by the head of the local police force if he decided accordingly. The police attended all meetings, and had the authority to close them at any point if they departed from their advertised subject or if their proceedings appeared likely to 'incite hostility between one section of the population and another'.[48]

It was difficult, moreover, to defend such civil liberties as did exist through autonomous judicial institutions. The distinction between government and the courts was not recognised in the political practice of medieval Russia, and as late as the nineteenth century the courts were termed, with only slight exaggeration, 'extensions of the administration and the police'.[49] The legal reforms of 1864 did lead to some changes (even the rich and powerful were dissatisfied with the delays and complexities of the old system):[50] court hearings became open and public, judges were declared independent of the administration, and a system of advocates was introduced. The aim, in the words of the statute, was to provide for a 'swift, just, merciful [and] equal' legal system, to increase the authority of the courts, to give them a greater degree of independence and 'generally to strengthen popular respect for the law'.[51] A number of provisions were soon retracted, however, and in 1881 a system of extraordinary courts came into existence whose operations still further reduced the scope of the rule of law. Originally intended to remain in force for three years but regularly extended thereafter, the new legislation conferred virtually unlimited powers upon the governors-general to arrest, fine or exile any citizen, to ban any meeting, even of a private character, and to close any commercial or educational institution or any newspaper or journal. Trial by jury in political cases had already been suspended three years earlier.[52]

Lying behind these practices and related to them was the fact that in Russia, unlike Western Europe, the familiar liberal distinction between actions (which were quite properly subject to due process of law) and beliefs (which were a matter for the individual alone and could be no legitimate concern of the government) was not widely understood or appreciated. In Russia, on the contrary, it was considered entirely proper that the state should assume responsibility for all aspects of a citizen's welfare, moral as well as material, and that it should establish such rules as it saw fit for this purpose. One aspect of this 'paternal' conception of the nature of state authority was the censorship system. In Russia, under the legislation of 1882, any newspaper which had been three times 'warned' by the censor would henceforth be obliged to submit the text of each succeeding issue to the censor in advance of publication. A Special Conference, composed of the ministers of Education, Justice and the Interior and the Supreme Procurator of the Holy Synod, was empowered to suppress any periodical and forbid its publisher or editor from editing or publishing any other paper in future.[53] A number of liberalising changes were introduced in 1905–6; and it is true that censorship varied in its scope and intensity and was by no means as successful in achieving its objectives as the authorities presumably intended (indeed so far from hindering the circulation of advanced theories of politics and religion, it was noted at the time, the censorship was actually 'directly responsible for the circulation among the public of the strangest and most compromising reports as to the dealings and intentions of the court and the high governmental circles').[54] It was nevertheless clearly the most illiberal system of any major European country at this time.

It was also of importance that the religious faith of the overwhelming majority of the population, Russian Orthodoxy, was never as independent of the state as was generally the case elsewhere in Europe. The Orthodox Church, on the contrary, had been so closely linked to the state since the time of Peter the Great (and even earlier) that it has frequently been termed a department of state. Church affairs were regulated by the Holy Synod, established in 1721, with a membership selected by the Tsar and operating under the general supervision of one of his officers. The Orthodox Church was in turn represented upon the Council of Ministers and upon local councils in the provinces; it received financial support from the government; and it enjoyed a monopoly of religious propaganda, including religious education within the schools and the right to carry out missionary work. It was not actually a crime to leave the Orthodox faith; but the Criminal Code required that anyone who did so be sent to the clergy, who would advise him to return to his former belief, and that in the meantime measures should be taken to prevent him from influencing his children. The Criminal Code also provided that those who had induced someone to give up his faith should be sent to Siberia or sentenced to hard labour; and it required that the children of marriages in which one partner was Orthodox should be brought up within that faith.[55] There was clearly no suggestion, in any of this, that the religious faith or beliefs of its citizens could be no proper concern of government. Indeed it was in many ways this close association between belief, nationality and citizenship—expressed in the celebrated formula *Samoderzhavie, Pravoslavie, Narodnost'* (Autocracy, Orthodoxy, Nationality)—which was the most distinctive contribution of the old regime to the political culture of the Soviet government which succeeded it.

3

The Social Fabric of Absolutism

In the previous chapter it was suggested that the 'traditional' Russian political culture had a number of features which served to distinguish it fairly sharply from most other European states of the same period. Political institutions, especially those which might aggregate popular demands and constrain the exercise of monarchical power, were weak and poorly articulated; government was highly centralised and unusually extensive in scope; and the political attachments of the majority of the citizen body were predominantly to the Tsar himself, rather than to the institutions within which popular sovereignty might be said to have reposed or to the parties which competed for representation within them. These, indeed, were features of the Russian scene with many centuries of history behind them, and they were reflected in a series of travellers' accounts which from the sixteenth century onwards drew attention, with scarcely varying unanimity, to the tyrannical powers with which the Tsar had been endowed compared with those of his counterparts elsewhere in Europe. It was perhaps not surprising in the circumstances that many of them should have concluded that Russians might be constitutionally incapable of sustaining a set of political arrangements of a less despotic character.[1]

If our initial examination of the concept of political culture has any validity, however, we should be chary of accepting explanations which rest upon assumptions of an unchanging and inherently authoritarian 'national character' of this kind. The pattern of attitudes towards and expectations of government which may be regarded as characterising the 'traditional' political culture seems, on the contrary, to be much more simply explicable in terms of the distinctive social structure by which it was sustained and by which, we have argued, a political culture will always be conditioned. In this chapter we propose to examine that social structure more closely, noting the extent to which it underlay and reinforced popular orientations to government and the extent to which, at the same time, it diverged from the developing social structures of other major European countries at this time. Developments in Western Europe should not, of course, be regarded as the 'norm' in this connection; on the contrary, a variety of investigations have established that institutions such as competitive elections, a rule of law and developed civil liberties may well be highly specific to such nations, and their offshoots overseas, in whose development an essential and perhaps unrepeatable contribution may have been made by feudalism and by the liberal-capitalist society which succeeded it.[2] This uniquely 'western' pattern of development is nonetheless central to the differences in political culture between Russia and its major western neighbours with which we are principally concerned in this study. In this chapter we shall examine the social structure upon which the 'traditional' Russian political culture was based under three broad headings: crown and nobility, state and economy, and the structure of peasant society.

Crown and Nobility

The earliest Russian social group to which the term 'nobility' can properly be applied is the boyar aristocracy, a social group which made its appearance in the eleventh century as a result of the coalescence of the courtly retinue of the Kievan principate with the indigenous Slavic aristocracy.[3] The boyars were expected to perform the same duties as their courtly predecessors: they retained an obligation to serve in the prince's armed forces, and they continued to offer counsel to the prince in the conduct of state affairs. Increasingly, however, as it became too expensive for the prince to maintain a retinue at court, the boyars were provided with grants of land upon which to provide independently for the upkeep of themselves and their military serving-men. Unlike their counterparts at this time in Western Europe they received their land as an outright grant rather than as a benefice conditional upon continued military service, and they were permitted to retain it even if they chose to leave the prince's service and enter that of another. It was the senior members of the prince's retinue who were first to do so, and the land with which they had been endowed, the *votchina*, formed the basis of the powerful and relatively autonomous position which they occupied at this time. Well before the end of the twelfth century, it appears, private ownership of large landed properties had become relatively commonplace at the upper levels of Kievan society, and some of these estates at least amounted to substantial rural economies.[4]

Until at least the sixteenth century there appear to have been no restrictions upon the right to own land, and peasants, artisans, priests, merchants and even slaves appear in the sources as landowners as well as the landowning nobility. With the extension of the principate of Moscow in the fifteenth and sixteenth centuries, however, these rights began gradually to be attenuated. From about the late fourteenth century, for instance, it became established that the boyar's right of departure from a prince's service could be exercised only under certain conditions, and that the right of the repurchase of land within the same family must be exercised within a specified period.[5] Much more important, the granting of land upon conditional or service tenure became more common, eventually altogether superseding the earlier practice of granting outright and inalienable landholdings. The earliest extant reference to the granting of a benefice of this kind appears to be in a will made by Ivan I of Moscow in 1328. It became increasingly common thereafter, and by the sixteenth century, following a substantial extension in the territorial dimensions of the Muscovite state, the practice had become widespread.[6] Part of the newly-conquered lands were retained by the Tsar (as he was now called) for himself; but the major part of it was distributed upon service or *pomest'e* tenure to the nobility, either to the original residents or to those who had been resettled from elsewhere. By the late sixteenth century it had been established that the tenure of land was in all but exceptional circumstances conditional upon the provision of military service to the Tsar.[7]

The boyars might be thought to have gained some compensation with the increase in their powers over the tenants on their own estates which took place at the same time, a process which reached its culmination in the final and definitive enactment of serfdom in the Law Code (*Ulozhenie*) of 1649. But this would be to overlook the further and more direct assault upon the position of the boyars which was undertaken by Ivan IV in the late sixteenth century, apparently provoked by the reluctance of his senior counsellors to endorse his marriage to a bride of non-royal stock and by the refusal of his closest associates to swear allegiance to his infant son when the Tsar thought he was dying.[8] Ivan IV, like his predecessors, responded with a policy of wholesale confiscation and resettlement; but he added to them a more personal campaign of pillage and extermination based upon a new territorial administration which he set up in 1564, known as the *oprichnina*. The depredations of its members, the *oprichniki*, fell not only on the upper nobility; other social groups, indeed whole towns and villages, were put to the sword if their loyalty was thought to be in doubt. The boyar aristocracy, however, was the principal intended victim of this process, and it bore most heavily upon them—contemporary estimates of the number who had been killed ranged from 400 to 10,000 and even more.[9] The Tsar, with the lesser gentry from whom the *oprichniki* had been recruited, had triumphed; the boyar aristocracy had been crushed and in most cases liquidated. The rank itself had ceased to exist by the end of the sixteenth century.[10]

The analogies between social institutions in Russia at this time and those in contemporary Western Europe have given rise to a long and at times passionate debate about whether Russian society during this period may properly be regarded as 'feudal'.[11] Economically, at least, there could be little doubt that a form of society existed in which a privileged social group, the landowning aristocracy, were sustained by the rent and other forms of tribute with which they were provided, under coercive sanction, by the peasants who lived on their estates. Feudalism in this sense, defined as the existence of a class of serfs rendering tribute to those who owned the land on which they worked, may be said to have existed in Russia from about the fourteenth century until the abolition of serfdom in 1861 (and probably in many other societies as well).[12] There was also a connection between military service and the possession of land, albeit not a hereditary one, and a variety of legal and administrative institutions existed which recalled those of feudal societies elsewhere.

Feudalism, however, at least in its 'classic' European form, was also a complex network of reciprocal and relatively evenly-balanced rights and obligations, of monarch to landowner and of landowner to serf as well as vice versa, within an overall framework which was defined by contract and regulated by the courts. In this latter respect, at least, it is clear that feudalism in Russia is scarcely to be compared with that which existed elsewhere. The landowning nobles, in particular, were far more dependent upon the monarchy than was the case elsewhere in Europe, and they lacked those enforceable rights as against their sovereign which elsewhere were to develop into the rule of law.[13] Estates were not granted in perpetuity, and the political privileges and immunities of the nobility, though considerable, did not (at least within the period we are considering) become heritable. The nobles, accordingly, were unable to develop into minor but independent barons as in France or Germany, and by the fifteenth and sixteenth centuries they had been completely subordinated, economically and politically, by the central state authorities.[14] We have already noted that a close connection has widely been agreed to have existed between the existence of feudalism and the subsequent development of representative government in the west; in Russia, however, there was clearly no social basis upon which an equivalent pattern of development could take place.

The Russian nobility of the more modern period, the *dvoryanstvo*, came into existence in the second half of the sixteenth century, and was formally constituted as an estate at the beginning of the eighteenth century.[15] The *dvoryanstvo* was composed of those boyars who had survived the depredations of the earlier period, together with the lesser nobles and gentry who had received estates upon *pomest'e* or service tenure at the same time or earlier; its membership was codified, and unified with a number of those who owed their position to service rather than heredity, by the Table of Ranks, which was introduced by Peter the Great in 1722 and which survived, with some modifications, until 1917. The Table of Ranks was designed to provide a steady flow of eligible recruits into the imperial military and civil bureaucracies, and to establish the principle that rank was in all cases dependent upon service to the state rather than upon ancestry. It provided for fourteen parallel grades or *chiny* within the military, civil and imperial court administrations (the term itself, like many others at this time, was borrowed from contemporary bureaucratic practice in Germany). All new recruits were supposed to begin their careers at the lowest rank or *chin* in the service which they had entered; promotion from this point was supposed to depend upon merit and length of service alone. Hereditary nobility attached to specified upper points in this hierarchy.[16]

These reforms, on the face of it, should have completed the subordination of the nobility to the state which Peter's Tsarist predecessors had initiated. In the event, however, it seems rather to have accelerated their crystallisation into a single entity with common interests and privileges, and thus to have increased their corporate identity and self-consciousness (the nobility had not previously existed as a single and unified social group, and its internal divisions had been deep). The century which followed saw this newly-formed social group both consolidate and extend its powers. The obligation upon the nobility to provide armed service to the crown was first limited, and then abolished altogether in 1762; and in 1785 Catherine the Great conceded a Charter of the Nobility, which both confirmed the privileges which had already been won—exemption from military service and taxation, freedom to dispose of property as they saw fit, and immunity from corporal punishment—and added further powers with regard to provincial administration and justice. The conditions which a section of the nobility attempted to impose upon the Empress Anne on her accession in 1730 showed that at least some members of nobility were already capable of conceiving of interests they might share in common;[17] and the success which the nobles enjoyed in securing the restitution of their privileges and perquisites under Alexander I at the beginning of the nineteenth century, after his predecessor had reduced or withdrawn them altogether, showed at least an implicit capacity for political action. Why did the nobility nonetheless fail to establish some permanent institutional expression of their common self-interest, and some lasting limitations upon the exercise of monarchical power in favour of those corporate interests, as their counterparts in Western Europe had been able to do?

Insofar as an explanation can be offered, it would appear to consist of three elements. In the first place, the Table of Ranks, while it did formally constitute the nobility as a social estate and thereby laid the basis for the formation of a collective self-consciousness, nonetheless introduced an element of fluidity and thus insecurity into its ranks by providing for the possibility of administratively-decreed inclusions and exclusions. Those who served with particular distinction in the ranks of the imperial bureaucracy were now enabled to enter the nobility and to obtain hereditary rank, while those who failed to serve with sufficient distinction, or who failed to

attain a specified level of education, might be excluded from the
nobility or at least be prevented from attaining heritable status
within it.[18] The first half of the nineteenth century saw a particularly rapid 'dilution' of this kind with the establishment of a
ministerial system, the development of a huge civil service and the
formation of the largest standing army in Europe. Since officer
status and all but menial administrative positions automatically
endowed the holder with noble status (until 1845), this process
resulted in a considerable numerical increase in the ranks of the
nobility, quite apart from the tendency towards such an increase
which derived from the territorial conquests of the same period and
the incorporation of the local aristocracies in such areas.[19] The
nobility was able to achieve some degree of security, these processes
notwithstanding, by securing the heritability of estates held upon
service or *pomest'e* tenure in the seventeenth century (the difference
between this and freehold tenure was formally abolished in 1714),
thus providing at least some kind of guarantee of wealth and social
position which was independent of the dispositions of the crown.
The ownership of estates did not, however, of itself confer noble
status, and the acquisition of large estates by state servants, court
favourites and wealthy merchants still further reduced the connection between extensive landownership and heritable nobility which
formed the basis of the aristocracy elsewhere. The Russian *dvoryanstvo* was thus a less secure and rather less cohesive social group
than its counterparts elsewhere in Europe.

Even the landed estates, moreover, provided a less reliable foundation for aristocratic position than might otherwise have been
supposed. The continuous cycle of confiscations, dispossessions,
grants and resettlements deprived the Russian nobility of those
long-standing ties with particular parts of the country which many
of its European counterparts possessed; indeed in most cases estates
were scattered over many different parts of the country and were
difficult to unite into a single coherent whole, let alone to exploit
profitably. This encouraged the tendency which the nobles had
already manifested to reside in the capital for all but a few months
of the summer, thereby reducing their local ties still further. These
fissiparous tendencies were reinforced by the laws of inheritance,
which, apart from one brief interval (1714–31), provided for the
division of estates upon death to all those eligible to inherit rather
than for their transmission undivided to a single heir. The Russian

aristocracy's lack of princely castles and of territorial titles, such as existed elsewhere in Europe, was a reflection of these circumstances.

The nobility, thirdly, continued to require the material support of the state to retain possession of their estates and privileges in the face of the passive and sometimes active opposition of the mass of the population over whom they ruled. It is a common misconception to suppose that Russian aristocrats were universally wealthy. Some, such as the Sheremetyevs, the Yusupovs and the Golitsyns, undoubtedly were; but many more were relatively impoverished, deeply in debt and possessed of only modest quantities of land and labour. It has been established that in 1858-9, for instance, the richest 5 per cent of serf-owning nobles held more than 40 per cent of all serfs, but that the poorest 75 per cent held less than 20 per cent of the total. Substantial numbers of nobles had in fact been compelled or had decided to give up their serfs in the pre-reform era, and many of those who retained them lived a life distinguishable in little but legal status from those who worked the land in their service.[20] The seventeenth and eighteenth centuries saw a series of bloody and stubbornly-pursued peasant *jacqueries*, and in the nineteenth century, in the years before the abolition of serfdom, there was a steadily rising incidence of rural disorder. Most nobles, however assuming their position in legal terms, were in no position to resist such a challenge; they had perforce to depend upon the protection of the monarchy if they were to sustain their accustomed position in life. They were accordingly the less likely to seek to undermine its authority.

Whatever the merits of these explanations, there can at least be no doubt about the outcome: an aristocracy which was defined in terms of service to the state, which varied a great deal internally in its values, wealth and geographical origins, and which depended upon the monarchy as the ultimate guarantor of its economic position and privileges. This was scarcely an aristocracy which was likely to bind the monarchy to a series of constitutional limitations upon its power such as its counterparts had achieved elsewhere in Europe.

State and Economy

It appeared no more likely that a successful assault upon the monarchy would be launched by Russian merchants and manufacturers. Industry was slow to develop in Russia; it was hampered by a lack of capital (for a disproportionate share of the resources which were available were diverted to military purposes), by a lack of internal demand (for which serfdom and the rural economy were largely responsible), and by the competition of states which had been earlier to industrialise. Although Russia had become the world's fifth industrial power by 1914, therefore, with relatively well-developed mining, textile and metallurgical industries, it was still a backward country in most other respects. Industry contributed no more than a fifth of the national income and employed a still smaller proportion of the total labour force; agriculture, on the other hand, contributed almost half the national income and employed almost two-thirds of the country's population. Almost three-quarters of the value of Russian exports to other countries was accounted for by foodstuffs and other agricultural semi-manufactures, similarly, while imports were composed disproportionately of machinery and other finished manufactured goods.[21] The differences in occupational structure between Russia and a number of other major western states at this time are set out in Table 3.1. Calculations of national income for the same period are difficult to compute and must necessarily be approximations; by any estimate, however, there was a large gulf in living standards between Russia and most

TABLE 3.1   *Occupational structures of selected countries,* circa *1900 (percentages)*

	Russia (1897)	France (1901)	Germany (1907)	Italy (1901)	UK (1901)	USA (1900)
Agriculture, forestry and fishing	58.6	43.4	28.4	54.2	12.0	37.6
Extractive industry	0.6	2.1	6.4	0.6	8.0	2.6
Manufacturing industry	13.2	24.0	32.0	21.2	35.2	21.8
Construction	2.3	4.4	10.2	7.0	10.5	5.7
Commerce, finance	4.1	6.8	6.7	4.4	5.2	9.5
Transport and communications	2.3	4.7	5.3	3.5	12.2	7.2
Services	17.2	14.8	10.3	8.4	9.1	13.2
Other	1.6	—	0.6	0.6	7.7	2.3

SOURCES   Adapted from B. R. Mitchell (comp.), *European Historical Statistics 1750–1970* (London, 1975), and US Bureau of the Census, *Historical Statistics of the United States* (Washington DC, 1960).

other European states at this time, and in the immediate pre-war period it appears if anything to have been increasing.[22]

Another indicator of Russia's relative economic backwardness was the prominent place which foreign interests had assumed in the country's financial and economic life. Foreign capital, for instance, is estimated to have accounted for about 44.1 per cent of the total capital of Russian joint-stock banks in 1916, and for 45 per cent of the total capital of the ten largest. Foreign capital was particularly prominent in the major banking concerns of St Petersburg, which have not unfairly been described as 'Russian in appearance [but] foreign in resources' at this time.[23] Foreign companies, in which the major banks had often a controlling interest, were estimated to have accounted for about a third of the total share capital of all Russian joint-stock companies during the same period; and in a number of sectors, particularly those connected with natural resources or advanced technology, the proportion was even higher. About half the capital invested in Russia's chemical industry, for instance, was held abroad, together with nearly half of that invested in the metallurgical industries; and in the mining industry as much as 91 per cent of the total share capital was foreign-owned.[24] The Russian bourgeoisie, such as it was, remained largely outside these more 'modern' sectors, a trading rather than a manufacturing group and relatively small in numbers. Two features of its development are of particular importance for an understanding of the origins of the traditional political culture: its dependence on the state, and its political inertia.

Russian industry—largely, no doubt, because of its relatively 'late' development—was unusual in the extent to which it depended upon the protection of tariff barriers. The levels at which such imposts were fixed tended to vary; but in the late nineteenth century, at a time when Russian industrial development was beginning to accelerate, import duties had reached an average level of almost 30 per cent. In 1891 this was increased to an average level of 33 per cent, a level much higher than that which existed in most other European countries at this time (in some cases the tariff was a prohibitive 100 per cent or more); and by 1902 it had increased still further to an average level of 40 per cent on all imports.[25] One result of this policy was that the prices of goods in Russia were higher, for quality which was often inferior, than was the case elsewhere; manufacturers who depended upon imported raw materials or machinery were penalised, and the ability of the population to buy their products, or more generally to sustain an adequate standard of living, was adversely affected. A result which was less immediately apparent was that Russian manufacturers became less entrepreneurially-minded, preferring to seek their fortunes by intriguing for a revision of tariff levels or an occasional exemption rather than by technological innovation or capital investment. The regular provision of state subsidies and grants, together with the provision of lucrative contracts for work to be carried out in the public sector, bound business even more closely to government tutelage.[26]

The government itself, moreover, was an active rather than a passive participant in these proceedings. The links between the Ministry of Finance and the major banking houses, for instance, developed, in the words of its most authoritative historian, 'to an enormous extent and to a greater extent in Russia than in any other country'. The Ministry assumed responsibility for the banks' liquidity, it regulated their issue of share capital, and it nominated directors (who tended to be former civil servants with little aptitude for their task) to their boards of directors. By 1914 this interpenetration had reached its maximum extent.[27] The Ministry of Trade and Industry similarly established a close working relationship with the major industrial syndicates. The links established went beyond the provision of contracts and the regulation of trading arrangements in the country as a whole; they extended to the details of company affairs, their articles of association, share issues and ownership, the nomination of directors, and their trading activities generally.[28] The government regulated prices, controlled profits, decreed which raw materials might be used, and fixed freight charges. Its agents, indeed, assumed a more or less controlling role in private capitalist affairs, attending industrial conferences and sitting on the boards of all joint-stock companies, banks and syndicates, and exercising influence within them in a manner which often owed little to ordinary commercial considerations.[29]

A particularly important agency of government control was the State Bank, founded in 1860. Formally the equivalent of national state banks such as the Bank of England or the Bank of France, the Russian State Bank was in fact an enterprise of a rather different character. The former were essentially private banks, whose public responsibilities were limited to the regulation of the volume of money in circulation and the administration of the national debt.

The Russian State Bank, in contrast, was a political as much as a commercial institution, functioning (with a brief interval between 1896 and 1898, when an attempt was made to turn it into a central bank on orthodox western lines) as a department of the Ministry of Finance.[30] The Bank, in terms of its working assets, was the largest in the world. It was used to set up subsidiary banks, such as the Peasants' Land Bank and the Land Bank for the Nobility, and it extended assistance to private companies and associations, frequently upon the basis of the political acceptability of their owners rather than the economic viability of their proposals.[31] The Bank also controlled the country's savings banks and credit associations, it held treasury balances and the current accounts of government enterprises such as the railways, and it had important interests in banks in the Far East and Persia which were used to finance Tsarist foreign policy adventures.[32] The Bank functioned generally as a 'regulator of the whole industrial and commercial life of the nation'; its role was constantly increasing and had reached its maximum extent by 1913.[33]

The state, moreover, was a considerable entrepreneur in its own right. It owned extensive collieries, oilfields, goldmines and sealing-grounds, as well as industrial enterprises and more than two-thirds of the entire railway network. The state was in fact the largest single entrepreneur engaged in mining and metallurgy.[34] There was also a special category of peasant known as the 'state peasant', whose status was different from and in many respects superior to that of the serfs who were employed on the estates of private landowners. With the expansion of the national territory the 'state peasants' grew more rapidly in numbers than did the serf population generally, and by the time of the emancipation there were in fact more state peasants than there were serfs in private ownership.[35] The extent of the Russian government's involvement in the economic life of the nation was greater than it was in other autocratic states, such as Prussia; at this time, indeed, it appears to have been without an obvious parallel anywhere. The 'predominant activity of the state in every sphere of economic life, not only as an administrator but as an actual undertaker of the various processes involved', it has justly been remarked, was a 'central fact' of Russian economic life.[36]

All of this may help to explain why the Russian bourgeoisie was, by common consent, the most backward class politically at the beginning of the twentieth century—more backward even than the peasantry and the proletariat.[37] Lenin repeatedly commented upon its 'amazing, almost unbelievable powerlessness'; and other Soviet writers have frequently remarked upon its relatively limited influence upon the conduct of state affairs and its lack of that moral-political authority which characterised the bourgeoisie in the west.[38] This was not to say that its influence upon governmental decision-making was altogether non-existent. From at least the end of the nineteenth century Russian merchants and manufacturers did acquire a 'behind the scenes "consultative" influence' upon commercial and industrial policy, and for a time under the prime ministership of S. Yu. Witte (1903–6) this began to acquire a regular institutional form.[39] The 1891 tariff legislation, for instance, was worked out in close collaboration with 'those best acquainted with the matter at issue' (that is to say, with substantial business interests); and business firms and associations had a direct influence upon the introduction and reform of company legislation in the early twentieth century through their correspondence and direct intercession with the government departments concerned.[40] The Association of Industry and Trade, the country's main industrial association, was normally given an opportunity to examine and comment upon relevant legislation before it was sent to the Duma; and businessmen were also able to bring some influence to bear upon government through special commissions, on which business interests were normally represented, and through private contacts.[41]

Russian businessmen had no formal or institutionalised right to participate in such consultations, however, and their influence does not generally appear to have been predominant within them.[42] Outside these restricted circles, moreover, there was only a limited amount of influence which Russian businessmen could bring to bear upon public matters that concerned them. An attempt to establish a political party to represent the whole of Russia's industrialist class collapsed in 1905 in the face of their inability to agree upon a common programme;[43] and although business interests subsequently acquired some degree of influence within the Octobrist party, so called because it accepted the constitutional settlement of October 1905, it drew its support from liberal opinion within the administration as well as from the business world and can scarcely be considered to have been a 'businessmen's party' in the ordinary sense of the word. The formal representation of business interests in political life, as we have noted, was in fact extremely limited. Its organisational base was the industrial association or congress, some 175 of which had come into existence by 1914, rather than the political party or section of a party; but even industrial associations received less than whole-hearted support. A proposal to establish a new organisation to represent the interests of Russian traders and manufacturers as late as June 1917, for instance, met with an unenthusiastic response and was taken no further; and legislation to establish chambers of commerce on Western European lines was similarly abortive. A speaker at a conference of Russian factory-owners, held in Moscow in December 1917, complained bitterly that so far as their self-organisation was concerned Russian merchants and manufacturers had been 'far outstripped' by the working class.[44]

The Russian bourgeoisie, in any case, was not a large or well-developed social formation. The mercantile 'estate' (*soslovie*) is estimated to have had about a million members in 1914; the bourgeoisie, more broadly defined, may have amounted with their families to about 6 million people at this time, out of a total population of about 160 million. Of these no more than perhaps 3000—members of commercial dynasties such as the Putilovs, the Morozovs and the Tretyakovs—represented substantial industrial interests.[45] Even this relatively small group, moreover, was heterogeneous in character and internally divided, above all between Moscow and St Petersburg, the cities in which most of its members were resident. The St Petersburg bourgeoisie was older, larger and economically more developed than that of Moscow. It was, however, to a greater extent a trading rather than a manufacturing bourgeoisie; it was more closely linked with foreign capitalist interests; and it depended more heavily upon the material support of the imperial court and government, a circumstance no doubt not unconnected with its relatively greater political docility. The Moscow-based bourgeoisie, on the other hand, was more indigenous, more independent and more 'progressive' in its views. Its leaders were more united (although both camps contained major differences of interest and opinion), it succeeded to a greater extent in gaining support from liberal landowning circles for its cause, and as the First World War developed it appears to have established a degree of relative ascendancy among merchants and manufacturers in the country as a whole.[46] Generally speaking, however, the Russian bourgeoisie was a class whose interests were still relatively weakly articulated by 1917; its typical representative, a few more enlightened employers apart, was an old-fashioned master or *khozyain* with a relatively limited and short-term conception of how his interests might best be advanced.

We seem justified in assuming, with Max Weber, a more than coincidental relationship between the weakness and political passivity of the Russian capitalist class and the lack in Russia of those liberal constitutional freedoms which had by this time become relatively firmly established elsewhere in Europe.[47] It is certainly consistent with such an interpretation to find that it was foreign employers, rather than Russian ones, who were generally the most active in promoting trade unions and collective bargaining among their local workforces, some even going so far as to give discreet encouragement to their struggle against the autocracy (they were rewarded with a more moderate and economistically-minded workers' movement than that which their Russian counterparts faced elsewhere).[48] It is also consistent with such an interpretation to find that it was precisely the most independent and industrially-based section of the Russian bourgeoisie, that based in Moscow, which was the most forceful in urging liberal economic and constitutional reforms upon the government in the years before the First World War. The interests of industry, a group of Moscow industrialists wrote to the government, were connected in the 'closest possible manner' with a stable legal order, individual liberty and freedom of scientific inquiry. The absence of such freedoms, they argued, was provoking periodic upsurges of labour unrest which might otherwise find a peaceful and legal means of expressing themselves; they urged an extension of the franchise, equal representation, and a more powerful legislative Duma.[49]

The liberal bourgeoisie, however, were as yet in no position to do more than request the adoption of such reforms; and the shock of the revolutionary events of 1905–6, and later the temptation of wartime super-profits, seem to have choked off even this tentative interest in reform, leaving the majority of industrialists to return to the alliance with the nobility and autocracy with which they had earlier been content. The Russian bourgeoisie, in other words, was ultimately no more successful than the Russian aristocracy had been in limiting the exercise of monarchical power and compelling the adoption in Russia of liberal constitutional forms which had by this time been fairly widely adopted elsewhere in Europe. In this respect also, as in that of the relationship between the crown and the nobility, the Russian autocratic state found deep roots in the pre-revolutionary economy and social structure.

The Structure of Peasant Society

The relative underdevelopment of industry in Russia found its converse in the much more agrarian nature of Russian society compared with its major western neighbours. According to the 1897 census, the last to be completed before the revolution, nearly three-quarters of the total population were employed in agriculture but only about 10 per cent were employed in industry, much of it of a home handicrafts or part-time character. In European Russia proper, excluding Poland, the agrarian nature of society was even more marked.[50] Russia was not unique in having a majority of its labour force employed in agriculture at this time; it did, however, have a larger proportion of its population thus engaged than any of its principal western neighbours, and its industrial labour force was also the smallest (Table 3.1). Far fewer people, also, lived in towns. Only 12 per cent of the population of European Russia did so in 1897, according to the census of that year, and by 1913 the proportion had risen to no more than 15 per cent, a level again rather lower than that of most other European states at this time. Even this relatively low proportion of urban residents somewhat overstated the real position, moreover, for many who were nominally urban residents retained an occupation which would have been more characteristic of residence elsewhere. In 1897 nearly 10 per cent of urban residents gave their occupation as agriculture, for instance, a higher proportion than was accounted for by the army and administration put together, and even in major cities like Moscow and St Petersburg the proportion of the population employed in agriculture remained considerable.[51]

Many urban residents, indeed, had only recently arrived from the countryside, and they tended to retain strong links with the village and its seasonal economy. In 1902, for instance, only about a quarter of the population of Moscow had actually been born within the city, and nearly a third had been living there for five years or less. An analogous situation existed in St Petersburg.[52] Many of these new residents, according to an investigation in 1910, continued to maintain close ties with the village they had recently left; as many as two-thirds of the factory workers of St Petersburg were estimated to have retained ownership of some village land, for instance, and nearly a fifth returned to the village every summer at harvest time. Many more sent regular remittances to their families in the village, and retained partial ownership of a cottage or other property there.[53] Russia before the First World War, then, was an overwhelmingly agrarian society, with a relatively small urban population which, though rapidly growing, was still closely linked with the rural economy, and with the great majority of its population employed in agriculture. In the final section of this chapter we propose to consider a number of ways in which this agrarian society, standing in many respects apart from 'official' Russia of government, the courts and bureaucracies but accounting for the vast majority of the country's population, underlay or contributed to the 'traditional' political culture as we have described it in the previous chapter.

A discussion of this kind must necessarily begin with some account of the peasant commune, or *mir*, within which most Russian peasants lived. The *mir*, sometimes also called the *obshchina*, was the name for an organisation of village-based peasants, and it was also the name for an assembly of village householders which met periodically to discuss and reach decisions upon a variety of matters of common concern.[54] It performed a wide range of functions, of which perhaps the most important was the periodic redistribution of the land in whose ownership the *mir*, rather than the individual householder, was vested (householders did, however, retain a small amount of land for their personal use, and neighbouring meadow and forest lands were held in common). The commune was also responsible for the collection of taxes, both those which it itself levied and those of the government (for which it was collectively responsible until 1903, under an arrangement known as *krugovaya poruka*).[55] It was responsible for the despatch ('frequently of its less popular members')[56] of recruits to the armed services; and it undertook a variety of legal duties concerned with the issuing of passports, exile and banishment, the interception of fugitives and (at least until 1861) the prevention of the disappearance of its members. The administration of communal responsibilities of this kind was undertaken by a village elder (*starosta*) and a number of other officials, who were elected, usually for a three-year term, at the village assembly (*skhod*). It was the peasant commune with its elected officials which functioned as the lowest level of the Tsarist administrative structure; it was responsible for matters such as road and bridge maintenance, fire brigade and police duties, care of the aged and infirm, education, the accommodation of visiting officials and so forth, as well as for the payment of the redemption dues which arose as a result of the emancipation of 1861.[57] It was, thus, the basic unit of the social world for most Russian peasants beyond their own immediate family and household.

The repartitional peasant commune was not a universal institution in pre-revolutionary Russia. Communal land ownership was predominant in European Russia, particularly in the central agricultural areas, but in the Ukraine and White Russia private landholding was more common, and in the Baltic area communal landownership did not exist at all.[58] The structure of peasant society, even in European Russia, was also changing rapidly in the late nineteenth and early twentieth centuries under the impact of the abolition of serfdom and of the reforms that followed it. The most important of these were the Stolypin land acts of 1906–11, a comprehensive series of legislative measures designed to strengthen individual peasant proprietorship for more or less explicitly political reasons (a prosperous class of private landholders, it was thought, would provide a social base for the autocracy more secure than any it had yet been able to establish). Members of communes in which land was not regularly redistributed were simply to receive their holdings in private ownership; while members of repartitional communes were to be entitled to do so, if possible in a single consolidated landholding, if at least a fifth of the members of the commune decided accordingly. The commune could itself be abolished by a two-thirds vote of those concerned.[59] The reforms, however, were pursued with something less than vigour (Stolypin himself was assassinated in 1911), and their impact in the years before the First World War should not be exaggerated. Fewer than a quarter of householders are estimated to have obtained private ownership of the land on which they worked by this time, and no more than 10 per cent of them established the single consolidated farm units which the reforms had been intended above all to encourage.[60] The repartitional commune remained, as in the past, the dominant institution in the social and economic life of the Russian countryside.

Decision-making in the *mir* was by no means always the idyllic exercise in direct democracy that nineteenth-century Slavophile writers have generally depicted.[61] Communal meetings seem often to have degenerated into prolonged drinking-bouts, and at election meetings the most successful candidates were frequently those who had bought the most drinks. The richer peasants tended not to seek office themselves (the duties of a *mir* official were onerous and not usually in demand), but their economic leverage over voters and their officials normally ensured that no policies inimical to their interests were pursued. Bribery and extortion seem to have been fairly widely practised, aided by the fact that in many communes the account books were in a state of some disorder and illegal transactions were therefore less readily identifiable; and the commune could exercise petty tutelage as well as beneficent guidance over the personal affairs of its members.[62] The *mir*, nonetheless, was formally an institution of an extremely democratic character, its periodic meetings providing an informal forum at which any villager could speak (though only heads of households could vote), with the entire commune participating in the making of most decisions. It would be surprising if it failed to reinforce the dispositions of its members to resolve their affairs in a collective, consensual and broadly egalitarian manner.

Collectivist predispositions of this kind may well have been strengthened further by a number of other aspects of the economy and society within which most peasants lived. Male migrant labour, for instance, particularly in mining, bricklaying, freight handling and other trades, was normally based upon a labour co-operative known as the *artel'*. This was a group of men, usually between ten and twenty strong, who contracted with each other and collectively with an employer to work at a fixed rate in cash and perquisites and to share the proceeds equally.[63] Co-operatives were also fairly widely distributed, particularly by the early years of the twentieth century.[64] It was of importance, too, that the structure of the peasant household was itself of a broadly collectivist character. The head of the household (*bol'shak, starshii*) exercised patriarchal authority; he represented the household in the village assembly, handled all legal transactions on its behalf and generally acted as its representative in all external dealings. He enjoyed no right of private ownership, however, at least until the era of the Stolypin reforms, and in legal terms it was the household itself, rather than any of its individual members, in which the ownership of land and movable property was vested.[65] All the members of the household normally lived within the same large room, moreover, sometimes three generations together, and all contributed their labour and earnings to the 'common kettle' and took their meals from the 'common bowl'. The Russian peasant household was thus a physical as well as a legal and economic collectivity (it is perhaps indicative that the Russian language contains no word for 'privacy').[66]

The rural community was bound together by two further influences, the religion to which the majority of its members subscribed and the suspicion of outsiders which peasants in Russia seem to have shared with their counterparts elsewhere. There can clearly be no place at this point for an extended discussion of the distinctive but at the same time amorphous doctrine to which members of the Orthodox church subscribed.[67] It is of some importance, however, to note that a central element in that body of doctrine was the concept of *sobornost'*, of a living and unitary community of all believers in whose association love, truth and freedom were all located. John Maynard has put it as follows:

> At the very root of the Russian conception of religion lies the idea of a brotherhood of the faithful, in whose mutual love resides the revelation . . . What excommunication is to the pious Catholic, that, to the Orthodox, is separation from the congregation of the brethren, in which truth and love alike reside. He must seek restoration by the adjuration of all errors and the confession of all sins. Outside of the congregation he cannot be right.[68]

Varying views have been taken of the piety of the Russian peasantry at this time, and it would certainly be going too far to suggest that the outward signs of devotion—icons, benedictions and so forth— were necessarily in proportion to the peasant's inward state of grace. The existence of a sense of identification with a community of fellow-believers, however, which was what the concept of *sobornost'* essentially expressed, has not seriously been disputed; and it would be surprising if the organised religion of the majority of Russians did not, through concepts such as *sobornost'*, to some degree rein- force the collectivist orientations which appear to have characterised the majority of Russian peasants at this time.

What Lenin called the peasant's 'instinctive, primitive democratism'[69] emerges perhaps most clearly in the literature of this period. In Chekhov's 'The Malefactor', for instance, a peasant, brought to court for stealing a nut from a railway track to weigh down his fishing tackle, completely fails to understand his guilt, and in accounting for his activities constantly refers to them in terms of 'we', the people from his locality. 'We make sinkers out of nuts', the peasant explains to the magistrate who is investigating the case. There was nothing as suitable as a nut for a sinker, it being heavy and having a hole in it; and how could one possibly fish without a sinker? The magistrate explained that, because of his action, a train might leave the track and people might be killed. The peasant replied:

> God forbid, your honour! Do you think we are wicked heathen? Praise be to God, kind master, not only have we never killed anybody, we have never even thought of it! Holy Mother preserve us and have mercy on us! . . . For how many years has the whole village been unscrewing nuts, and not an accident yet? If I were to carry a rail away, or even to put a log across the track, then perhaps the train might crash, but a nut—pah! . . . We understand, so we don't unscrew them all; we always leave some; we do it carefully; we understand.[70]

Chekhov was involved in a good deal of legal work throughout Russia in his capacity as a doctor; this incident, and many others like it in his stories, may therefore be reasonably true to life.

This is not to suggest that the pre-revolutionary peasantry were necessarily possessed of all those sterling virtues with which they have sometimes retrospectively been endowed. Their habitual collectivism was as much the product of necessity and circumstance as it was of an instinctive kinship with all men; the collective ownership of land could co-exist with the fiercest individualism in its cultivation; and the reverse side of the peasant's simple communalism could be meanness, cruelty and apathy. Gorky, seeking out in his youth the 'kindly, contemplative peasant, the indefatigable searcher after truth and justice' which his reading had led him to expect, found only a 'harsh and cunning realist, well able to act the simpleton when it suited him'. Reformers were greeted with cynicism and derision; truth was held in no high regard ('Truth will not fill your belly'); and any opportunity to make a profit out of the adversity of others was invariably exploited. The decisions of the collective commanded no great respect ('The *muzhik* is not stupid, but the commune is a fool'), and the sufferings of fellow peasants elsewhere left him relatively unmoved. 'They don't weep in Ryazan' for a harvest failure in Pskov', as Gorky was told; or as an old man from Novgorod put it, 'People die, the road is made smooth for us'. Even in foreign countries, Gorky pointed out, there was a more sympathetic public response to natural calamities of this kind.[71]

The peasantry, moreover, for all their apparent conservatism and respect for patriarchal authority, were also capable of rising in revolt, sacking the landlords' mansions and putting the Tsar's agents to the sword. It was true that their devotion to the Tsar himself seems to have remained intact for most or all of this period, and that if any legislative act gave them less than they considered rightly to be theirs, such as the emancipation of 1861, the peasant's instinctive reaction was to blame the Tsar's corrupt subordinates rather than the Tsar himself. But the correlate of this was that they were prepared to accept as legitimate only those decisions which accorded with their own interests; and when those interests incorporated a belief that the land belonged to the peasant who worked it, whatever lord or crown might represent, it was clear that the peasants' naive monarchism might not be without its limitations. There were certainly subversive implications in the doctrine by which the Tsar was supposed to have the people's best interests at heart, but which held that if he did not act in accordance with those interests he must be an imposter and need not necessarily be obeyed.[72]

Implicitly conflicting beliefs of this kind could perhaps have co-existed as long as they did only in a state as loosely integrated as was the Russian Empire at this time. The world of government and the world of the peasant village, as we have seen, were in fact two separate worlds for most practical purposes. This was partly a question of legal status; not until 1905, for instance, did peasants receive full juridical equality with other Russian citizens, and even after this date they remained largely outside the framework of formal legal institutions and subject to a variety of further disabilities.[73] Levels of literacy were also low, and the practice of open and consensual decision-making must in part have reflected the fact that alternative procedures based upon written rules and records would simply have been unworkable. In 1897, for instance, no more than 28.4 per cent of the population aged between nine and forty-nine were literate, and although some improvement had been achieved in the years before the First World War the level of literacy in Russia (and especially in the countryside) was still considerably below that of most other European nations.[74] The provision of public libraries and the circulation of printed matter were also less than they were in most other Western European countries at this time.[75]

Communications, however, were probably the factor which contributed most powerfully to the phenomenon of a 'dual Russia' which these social distances expressed. The total railway network, for instance, expanded very quickly in the late nineteenth and early twentieth centuries, for strategic as much as for any other purposes; but the level of provision and use per head of population remained far below those of Russia's major western neighbours, as Table 3.2

TABLE 3.2   *Communications in selected countries,* circa *1870 and 1910*

	Russia	France	Germany	Italy	UK	USA
Total railway network (km)						
circa 1870	10,731	15,544	18,876	6,429	21,558	85,170
circa 1910	66,581	40,484	61,209	18,090	32,184	387,580
Railway network (km per 10,000 population)						
circa 1870	1.3	4.8	5.2	2.5	8.3	21.3
circa 1910	4.1	10.4	9.4	5.3	7.9	41.9
Passengers per head of population						
circa 1870	0.3	2.8	4.4*	0.8	12.4	4.2*
circa 1910	1.2	12.6	23.7	2.9	30.9	10.5
Items of mail per head of population						
circa 1870	1.4	17.9	11.3	8.6	41.0	n.a.
circa 1910	12.1	96.5	87.4	42.2	131.3	160.7
Telegrams per head of population						
circa 1870	0.0	0.2	0.2	0.1	0.5	0.2
circa 1910	0.2	1.3	0.7	0.5	2.2	0.8

SOURCES   Calculated from B. R. Mitchell (comp.), *European Historical Statistics 1750–1970* (London, 1975), and US Bureau of the Census, *Historical Statistics of the United States* (Washington DC, 1960).
* Estimated.

makes clear. The circulation of postal items and of telegrams again reflected the extent to which most Russians remained outside a unifying national network of communications of a kind which existed in most Western European countries at this time. The liberal historian and politician Paul Milyukov, writing in 1922, summed up this disjunction between 'state' and 'society' as follows:

For centuries the state power remained in Russia what it was when the northern Vikings first came: an outsider to whom allegiance was won only and in the measure of its utility. The people were not willing to assimilate themselves to the state, to feel a part of it, responsible for the whole. The country continued to feel and live independent of the state authorities.[76]

4

The Making of
New Soviet Man

The new Soviet regime inherited a large, heterogeneous and backward Empire from its Tsarist predecessors. It also inherited a distinctive and deeply-rooted pattern of orientations to government, which we have termed the 'traditional Russian' political culture. It may be helpful at this point briefly to recall some of its essential features. Representative institutions, as we have noted, were weakly articulated and ineffective; levels of popular participation were low; and governing style was centralised, bureaucratic and authoritarian. Popular political attachments, in consequence, were highly personalised; and political knowledge and experience, outside an extremely limited circle, was virtually non-existent. The scope of government was unusually broad: it extended not only to those spheres of life in which other governments of the time were active, such as public order and taxation, but also into economic entrepreneurship and control, religion and morals, and the detailed administration of justice. It was based, finally, upon a society of a highly 'traditional', *gemeinschaft* character, in which there was a strong tradition of group solidarity together with its converse, a suspicion of outsiders; a greater degree of reliance upon face-to-face relations than upon anonymous procedures; and in which it was accepted that every aspect of the life of the community, from agriculture and military service to beliefs and behaviour, should be subject to the regulation of the community as a whole.

There was clearly much in an inheritance of this kind which the Bolsheviks could adapt to their purposes. A centralised political system was one to which a party based on 'democratic centralism' could accommodate itself without difficulty; public ownership and regulation of the economy was a Bolshevik goal as much as it had

been, to an extent unusual among contemporary states, a characteristic of Tsarist Russia; and the broadly 'collectivist' character of
social and political life, with its direct concern for the moral as well
as the material well-being of citizens, was again not inconsistent
with Bolshevik objectives. The difficult circumstances under which
the new regime came into being may well have reinforced these
continuities further. The new Bolshevik government was scarcely
likely to relinquish the extensive controls of its predecessor when
the lives of its leaders were in danger and its very existence was at
stake; and the economic chaos of the time, a consequence of revolution and civil war, may well have encouraged a more extensive
degree of centralised planning than would otherwise have been con-
templated. To this extent, at least, an emphasis upon the continuity
of Tsarist and Soviet institutional structures would not seem to be
misplaced.

There was much in the traditional inheritance, at the same time,
to which the new Soviet government could not but take exception.
The class system, in the first place, hindered the adoption of much-
needed social and educational reforms and provided a basis for
political opposition; there was a high level of at least overt religios-
ity; and there was little knowledge of or interest in political institutions and doctrines, in any but more especially in their Bolshevik
variety. Partly, of course, these were aspects of traditional society
which any reforming government would have wished to change; the
Provisional Government, in its few brief months of office during
1917, had indeed already begun to do so. But the Soviet government's objectives stemmed also from the more far-reaching purpose
to which it was committed, the establishment of a socialist society
radically different from any that had previously existed. It was to
overcome those aspects of the traditional political culture which
stood in the way of such objectives that a comprehensive programme of political propaganda and education was developed: a
programme, probably unprecedented in its scope and intensity,
whose ultimate objective was the establishment of a Communist
society and the creation of a 'new Soviet man' to inhabit it. It is to
an examination of this programme, at present and as it has
developed over time, that the present chapter is devoted.

Political Socialisation: the Development of a Programme

It appeared initially as if the imminent success of the world revolution might make any effort of this kind redundant. Writing in the first issue of the Communist International's new journal in May 1919, Georgy Zinoviev, the chairman of its executive and a senior Bolshevik leader, noted that the International had already gained three Soviet republics as its main base, Soviet Russia and the Soviet republics of Hungary and Bavaria (which had just been established). But 'nobody would be surprised', he added, 'if by the time these lines appear in print we have not three, but six or more Soviet republics'. In a year, he confidently forecast, they would 'already be beginning to forget that in Europe there was a struggle for communism, for in a year all Europe will be communist'. Only in England and the United States was there a possibility that capitalism might survive for another year; but this would be 'beside a wholly communist European continent'.[1] Even the normally more cautious Lenin, in his address to the Comintern's founding congress in March 1919, appeared convinced that the victory of the proletarian revolution was inevitable and that the formation of the international Soviet republic was at hand. All the comrades present who had seen the establishment of the Communist International and of the Soviet Republic, he assured them, would also see the formation of the World Federation of Soviets. That July, he wrote four months later, would be the 'last difficult July'; the 'next July we will see the victory of the international Soviet republic—and that victory will be complete and final'.[2]

The new party programme adopted by the VIII Party Congress in 1919 reflected these optimistic assumptions. The October revolution, it declared, had 'begun to lay the foundation of a communist society'; the development of the revolutionary and Soviet movement in other countries now 'proved that a new era has begun—the era of the world-wide proletarian communist revolution'. The programme decreed the supersession of bourgeois by proletarian democracy; the ending of the actual as well as of the formal inequality of women; the establishment of entirely new principles of justice, administration and defence; and the participation of 'all the working masses without exception . . . in the work of state administration'. The realisation of these and other measures, declared the programme, 'will carry us in advance of the Paris Commune, and the simplification of the work of administration, together with the raising of the level of culture of the masses, will eventually lead to the abolition of the state'.[3] 'What Marx prophesied is being fulfilled before our very eyes', wrote Bukharin and Preobrazhensky in their *ABC of Communism*, a popular exposition of the new party programme which made its appearance at this time. 'Everywhere the workers are advancing towards revolution and towards the establishment of Soviet rule.'[4] The long tradition of utopian thought had influenced many Bolsheviks;[5] for some months at least, as European capitalism tottered in the balance, it seemed as if their dreams might well be realised.

The Soviet republics in Bavaria and Hungary, however, soon foundered, and with the apparent re-establishment of political stability elsewhere in Europe it became apparent that these early forecasts might require some modification. Zinoviev admitted to the Second Congress of the Comintern in the summer of 1920 that he had been over-enthusiastic in his prediction that the whole of Europe would become Soviet within a year; two or even three years, he thought, might now be required.[6] This forecast had itself to be revised in its turn. There had been a time, Zinoviev later reflected, when the Bolsheviks had believed that 'only a few days or even hours remained before the inevitable revolutionary upsurge'; but these optimistic forecasts had not been borne out.[7] On the whole, Zinoviev told the XIII Party Congress in 1924, they had correctly estimated the objective tendencies of development. 'But the factor "time" we did not judge altogether precisely. This is now abundantly clear to us.' There could now be no doubt that the victory of socialism in the European countries was a 'question not of three months, but of a far longer period'.[8] Lenin, writing in his last published work, 'Better Fewer, but Better', in 1923, had to take comfort in the fact that the revolutionary movement was beginning to develop in some of the countries of the east, and that these, together with Soviet Russia, constituted 'in the final analysis' the 'overwhelming majority of the world's population'. In the major capitalist countries, he acknowledged, the pace of development had been much slower than they had expected, and they could 'not at present gamble that it will accelerate'.[9]

The Bolshevik leaders had always accepted that Russia was far from the mature capitalist society in which the transition to socialism was supposed to take place. They believed, however, that the

Russian revolution would precipitate a process of revolution in other and more developed European states, and that with their assistance it would thereafter move rapidly towards a more prosperous and self-administering, albeit somewhat 'backward', Communist society.[10] With the failure of the revolution in Europe it became apparent that these expectations were unlikely to be realised, at least within the short or medium term, and the difficulties involved in attempting to establish socialism in Russia itself became rather more obvious. Bureaucracy was one of them. 'You can throw out the Tsar, throw out the landowners, throw out the capitalists', Lenin told a congress of miners in January 1921. 'We have done this. But you cannot "throw out" bureaucracy in a peasant country, you cannot "wipe it off the face of the earth". You can only *reduce* it by slow and stubborn effort.'[11] He went on to observe:

> The more backward the country in which the zigzags of history cause [the socialist revolution] to begin, the more difficult is the transition from the old capitalist relationships to the new relationships of socialism. As well as the tasks of destruction there are other tasks, infinitely difficult: those of organisation.[12]

These were tasks, he warned, which could not be accomplished simply by legislation; they required a 'great and lengthy labour', and any further advance towards Communism would be dependent upon the extent of their success in resolving them.[13]

Some impression of the task the Bolsheviks now confronted may be gained from a series of sociological studies which were carried out at this time in the Russian countryside. An inquiry in Voronezh province, for instance, found that newspapers were scarcely ever received there, and that even Communist Party members read them no more than once a week (this was regarded as 'frequent'). No-one could identify Georgy Chicherin, the People's Commissar for Foreign Affairs; and when a newspaper was read out aloud, it was found that half the words it contained were incomprehensible (the sentence 'Chicherin sent a note', for instance, was thought to have a musical rather than a diplomatic significance). A list of forty-six words frequently encountered in the local press, such as 'project', 'memorandum' and 'intrigue', was read out; not one respondent knew what all the words meant, and the best could manage no more than 70 per cent correct replies.[14] A group of peasants in a village north of Moscow, in another inquiry, were found to have heard of Lenin, Trotsky and Kalinin, the Soviet President, but of no other political leaders of note.[15] Inquiries elsewhere found a generally favourable attitude towards the new regime but little conception of how it operated at all but the local level; and even members of the party were found to have a 'very weak grasp' of Communist theory and to be 'generally little interested in this question'. The most salient local attitude was simple apoliticism.[16]

The beginnings of an attempt to alter this state of affairs was made in the immediate post-revolutionary years, generally in a somewhat improvised manner and in connection with the struggle against internal and external opponents in which the Soviet government was then engaged. In April 1918, for instance, it was decided that all monuments to the Tsar and his associates should be removed and replaced by a series of monuments to figures of revolutionary, literary or scientific eminence. The first of these, a bust of Karl Marx, was unveiled in September 1918; memorials to Robespierre, Stenka Razin, Plekhanov, Engels and others were unveiled soon afterwards.[17] A series of 'agitational points' was established at the same time, generally in railway stations or other places in which large numbers of people congregated; and a series of 'agitational trains' and 'agitational ships' came into existence, charged with carrying the party's message to the farthest corners of the land.[18] Agitational campaigns were also initiated: in May 1918 a 'Karl Marx week' was celebrated to commemorate the centenary of his birth, and a 'week of the front' and a 'transport week' were both celebrated early in 1920. Nor did the leaders of the revolution refrain from a more direct contribution to the success of their cause: most of them were skilful mass orators, and Lenin, for instance, according to incomplete data, made as many as 216 speeches in the period 1918–20.[19]

These, however, were 'mass-agitational' measures only; the development of an informed political consciousness could not be achieved so simply, and the new regime began to devote an increasing amount of attention to it as the civil war drew to an end. The elimination of illiteracy was clearly a first prerequisite. In 1920, for instance, less than half the population aged between nine and forty-nine could read or write, and although these levels later increased dramatically they remained for some time a serious constraint upon the party's propagandist efforts. The level of literacy within the party compared favourably with that for the population as a whole; but even in the party the problem was not unknown, particularly in certain areas and among certain nationalities. In 1927, for instance, the illiteracy rate among party members in the Central Asian republics varied from 27 to 46 per cent, and as late as 1933 more than a fifth of all members in the area were still illiterate. 'While such a thing as illiteracy still exists in our country', Lenin had written, 'one cannot speak of political enlightenment'; its elimination, largely accomplished by the late 1930s, was a political task as much as it was an educational one.[20]

Political education in a general sense was the responsibility of the Commissariat of Enlightenment, headed by A. V. Lunacharsky, and more particularly of *Glavpolitprosvet*, its Chief Committee for Political Education. The primary function of *Glavpolitprosvet*, which was established in 1920, was to provide political education for the mass of the non-party population, although it bore some responsibility also, in conjunction with the Communist Party apparatus, for the political education of party members. *Glavpolitprosvet* was also associated with the campaign against illiteracy and with the general conduct of atheistic propaganda, and it undertook some work in connection with the propagation of advanced agricultural methods in the countryside. The Committee maintained a network of village reading-rooms, of which some 21,500 were in existence by 1925; and it maintained a large and growing number of clubs, libraries and other cultural institutions in the countryside, whose overall membership was approaching a million by the end of 1925. For the whole of its existence (until 1930, when it ceased to exist as a separate department within the Commissariat) the Committee was headed by Lenin's wife Krupskaya.[21]

Glavpolitprosvet maintained a network of elementary political schools throughout the country, which were attended by both party and non-party members. By 1925 there were more than 8000 such schools, with a total enrolment of 265,000.[22] The X Party Congress resolved in 1921, however, that the political education of party members should be primarily the responsibility of the Party's own agitation and propaganda department.[23] Repeated complaints made it clear that there was much here to occasion disquiet. 'The largest group of workers and peasants who have entered the party since February–October 1917', a conference of leading party secretaries pointed out in 1921, 'does not possess elementary political knowledge.' At the X Party Congress in the same year Preobrazhensky complained of the 'immense gap' which had opened up in the party between the 'communistically mature element' and those, generally the younger party members, who had 'not the patience to read *Capital* and other fundamental works'. D. B. Ryazanov, the director of the Marx-Engels Institute, remarked similarly that the 'percentage of comrades who have had a fundamental Marxist schooling' was growing 'smaller every day'.[24] The XI Party Congress resolved in 1922:

> In the next year or years the RKP must unconditionally devote its attention not so much to an increase in the number of its members as to an improvement in its qualitative composition . . . The stormy years of civil war did not allow sufficient attention and sufficient resources to be devoted to raising the standard of Marxist education and the cultural level of rank-and-file members of the party. The next years must be dedicated to this task of first-class importance.[25]

A number of party schools had already been organised among the Bolsheviks in exile, and the need to organise a comparable system in Russia itself was voiced by a delegate to the VI Party Congress as early as the summer of 1917. The circumstances of the time prevented its realisation; but in August 1920 it was decided in principle to establish a network of schools of this kind, and a more elaborate system was worked out at a conference at the end of the following year. Second-grade schools offering a nine-months' course to prepare students for either propaganda or Soviet and party work were to be set up in the provincial capitals; and first-grade courses offering an elementary three-months' course 'to raise the political consciousness of the masses' were to be established in county capitals. The lengths of both courses were later extended, and their conditions of admission made more restrictive. Neither these, however, nor the elementary 'schools of political literacy' which were established in 1921, made any attempt to restrict their admissions to either party or non-party applicants; both were regularly admitted to virtually all such institutions and courses.[26] By 1927 it was reported that 40.8 per cent of party members had attended a party school at some level; by 1929–30 the total number of students for the first time exceeded a million, and by 1933 the total had reached more than $4\frac{1}{2}$ million. Complaints nonetheless persisted about the low level of attainment of many new and existing party members.[27]

The party educational system was completed by a number of institutions of national or higher educational designation, most of them based in Moscow. These included the Communist (originally the Socialist) Academy, established in 1918 and according to its statutes the 'highest All-Union academic establishment for the study, on the basis of Marxism and Leninism, of problems of the social and natural sciences and also of problems of socialist construction'; the Institute of Red Professors, founded in 1921, which was intended to provide politically reliable staff for the institutions of higher education; the Communist Universities, headed by the Sverdlov Communist University in Moscow, which prepared candidates for service within the party administration; and the Communist Universities of the Toilers of the East and of the National Minorities of the West, which provided political education for promising radicals from the countries concerned. The total number of students attending these universities in the middle 1920s was about 6000.[28] The Marx-Engels Institute was founded in 1920, and the Lenin Institute in 1924; they were merged into the Marx-Engels-Lenin Institute in 1931, with responsibilities which included the collection, preservation and publication of the works of Marx, Engels and Lenin; the maintenance of the party's records; and academic research in the fields of Marxist-Leninist theory and party history. The Institute is known today as the Institute of Marxism-Leninism.[29]

A major function of party and non-party educational institutions was to further atheist work among the population, in association with the other organisations which were charged more specifically with this task. The church was widely regarded as having compromised itself by its close association with the old regime in Russia, and among the first acts of the new government was a decree separating church from state, nationalising all church-owned property, and prohibiting ecclesiastical ownership of property and the public provision of religious instruction. Churches were to be able to hire out such buildings and objects as they required for their religious services; but they were not permitted exclusive use of the buildings they occupied, and lectures, concerts, cinema shows, dances and even anti-religious meetings could take place there as well. Priests, described as 'servants of the bourgeoisie', were disfranchised by the 1918 constitution and subjected to discriminatory rates of taxation; and church marriages and divorces were denied legal recognition. There were ritual warnings from the central authorities against pressing the anti-religious campaign too far and thereby strengthening the very prejudices which it was designed to remove; and the constitution did continue to provide the right of religious, as well as of anti-religious, propaganda. The church was nonetheless already under strong pressure as the 1920s drew to a close.[30]

The new decade saw a renewed offensive against the churches' remaining influence. Hundreds of places of worship were closed by decree; thousands of priests were exiled or executed; and churches and seminaries were requisitioned and used as sanatoria, schools or asylums. Anti-religious departments were established in universities and technical colleges, and an All-Union Anti-Religious University was opened. An atheist newspaper, *Bezbozhnik*, came into existence in 1922; its supporters formed themselves into a 'Society of Friends of the Paper *Bezbozhnik*' and then, in 1925, into a 'League of the Godless'. Renamed the 'League of the Militant Godless of the USSR' in 1929, the League claimed to have as many as $5\frac{1}{2}$ million members by 1932. Anti-religious museums were also opened: in 1929 in Moscow, and in 1932 in Leningrad, in the former Kazan Cathedral. More than forty such museums were in operation by this date.[31] Under an amendment to the constitution in 1929, moreover, the church and its members were deprived of the right to carry out religious propaganda which they had earlier enjoyed, retaining only the formal right to religious worship. A number of concessions were made to the churches in later years: the clergy were given back the right to vote, their taxation was restored to the same level as that of other citizens, and during the Second World War there was even a modest detente in relations between church and state. The Khrushchev years, however, saw a renewed attack upon religion and its practitioners, and despite the somewhat more judicious tone of his successors there can be little doubt that between the objectives of the churches and those of the party-state authorities there remains a basic incompatibility.[32]

The new regime, finally, from the first displayed an awareness of the importance of ensuring that the educational and cultural environment of its citizens was consistent with the objectives which it sought more directly to pursue through the system of political instruction. Schooling, for instance, was required at an early stage to devote itself to the preparation of students who were 'armed with the theory of Marxism' as well as with more conventional forms of academic knowledge; music, painting, literature and the arts in general were gradually compelled to subordinate themselves to political orthodoxy; and the developing media of film, radio and later television were harnessed to the task of transmitting the party's message to the widest popular audience.[33] The popular press was similarly expanded, particular attention being devoted to the Marxist classics. Between 1917 and 1923, for instance, the *Communist Manifesto* was published in no fewer than fifty-eight separate editions; and by 1937 the publication of the works of Marx, Engels and Lenin had exceeded a total of 147 million copies.[34] The newspaper and publishing industry has expanded steadily ever since within the framework of a system of censorship which, though introduced on a 'temporary and extraordinary' basis in 1917, has continued to function in its basic essentials down to the present day.[35] The gradual development of this network of political communication since 1913 is set out in Table 4.1.

TABLE 4.1   *Political communications in the USSR, 1913–76*

	1913	*1940*	*1960*	*1976*
Library books and journals per head of population	0.3	2.7	8.9	16.6
Clubs per 1,000 population	1.3	608.0	605.5	528.7
Number of cinema visits a year per inhabitant	0.7	4.6	16.7	16.5
Number of radio receivers per 1,000 population	—	5.8	128.6	240.7
Number of television sets per 1,000 population	—	0.0	22.1	225.4
Number of books published per inhabitant	0.6	2.4	5.7	6.8
Number of journals published (copies per inhabitant per year)	0.7	1.3	3.6	12.0
Number of newspapers published (copies per inhabitant per day)	0.0	0.2	0.3	0.7

SOURCE   Calculated from *Narodnoe Obrazovanie, Nauka i Kul'tura v SSSR. Statisticheskii Sbornik* (Moscow, 1977).

Political Socialisation Today

Of the scale and vigour of the present programme of socialisation there can be little doubt. It embraces, first of all, a system of formal political instruction presently organised at three main levels. At the primary level (Elementary Political School) students study the biography of Lenin, the fundamentals of political and economic knowledge, and current questions of party policy. The normal period of study is five or six years, and the method of instruction is by lecture and discussion (*beseda*) within groups of perhaps 10–25 persons. At the intermediate level (Schools of the Fundamentals of Marxism-Leninism) the subjects of study are the history of the CPSU, political economy, Marxist-Leninist philosophy, and the fundamentals of scientific Communism. Tuition is by independent study and discussion over a period of six to eight years, and students are expected to engage at the same time in a form of practical political activity related to their studies. At both levels, in addition, students are required to study the new Constitution of the USSR and the speeches of party and state leaders in connection with its adoption and with the sixtieth anniversary of the revolution. These materials will eventually be incorporated into existing courses.[36]

At the advanced level the programme of study is both more varied and more vocational in emphasis. Students enrolled in the Universities of Marxism-Leninism, for instance, one of the forms of party education at this level, study the history of the CPSU, political economy, dialectical and historical materialism, scientific Communism and current party policy, as well as the particular sphere of practical activity (economic management, propaganda or whatever) in which they propose subsequently to engage. Students enrolled in the Schools of the Party *Aktiv*, another form of party education at the advanced level, study current problems of the theory and practice of party policy, economic management and party propaganda, especially as these concern the local or regional party committee to which the School is attached. Tuition lasts for two years or, for those without a completed higher education, four years. Students enrolled in 'theoretical seminars', a further more general form of party education at the advanced level, study problems of the history of the CPSU, party development, economic theory, atheism, aesthetics and so forth, usually for one or two years in the case of each topic chosen. The study year begins on 1 October and lasts until the following June at all levels.[37]

When the present system was first introduced in 1965–6 there were 11.1 million students engaged within it at various levels. There has since been a steady expansion and the total now stands at over 20 million, more than 8 million of whom are not party members (Table 4.2). Particularly noteworthy is the greater than proportionate increase in the numbers engaged in study at the intermediate and advanced levels of the system: these have increased substantially since 1966, as Table 4.2 makes clear, while the numbers engaged in study at the primary level have steadily declined. There has been a further process of specialisation within each category: in the Universities of Marxism-Leninism, for instance, fewer than 10 per cent of students are now enrolled in the general faculty rather than either of the two other faculties which are oriented more specifically towards particular aspects of party work.[38]

TABLE 4.2   *The party educational system*

	Number of participants (millions)		
	1966–7	*1970–1*	*1976–7*
System of party study:			
primary level	5.2	2.3	2.4
intermediate level	3.0	6.7	8.0
higher level	5.3	6.3	10.4
total:	13.5	15.3	20.8
of which party members:	9.6	10.3	12.4
System of Komsomol study	3.2	6.2	7.0
System of economic education	—	13.8	35.0

SOURCE   *Partiinaya Zhizn'*, no. 10 (1976) p. 23; and no. 21 (1977) p. 42.

A number of further changes were introduced into the party education system by the XXV Party Congress in 1976, prompted by what were stated to be the rising level of education and consciousness of the Soviet people, advances in science and technology, and favourable changes in the international situation. The main element of the new changes was to be the introduction of a series of courses based upon the reports and materials presented to the Congress, this being 'one of the prerequisites for the undeviating implementation' of its discussions. From 1976 onwards, accordingly, courses have been introduced at the primary level on 'current problems of the policies of the CPSU'; at the intermediate level on 'the policies of the CPSU—Marxism-Leninism in action'; and at the advanced level on 'current problems of the theory and policy of the CPSU in the light of the decisions of the XXV Party Congress'. The introduction of these new courses was to be completed by 1978. In future years, the Central Committee decree has indicated, additional new courses will be introduced, dealing, at the primary level, with the elements of Marxist-Leninist social teaching; at the intermediate level, with the fundamentals of Marxism-Leninism; and at the higher level, with the theory and practice of developed socialism, with the economic, agricultural and social policies of the party, with the socialist way of life, and with international relations and Soviet foreign policy.[39]

Party education classes are conducted by 'propagandists', of whom there were over 1.3 million in 1975. Their numbers in 1969 and 1975, and their distribution by relevant social categories, are set out in Table 4.3. The proportion of propagandists with a higher education, it will be noted, has steadily increased and presently accounts for over 87 per cent of the total; in urban areas, and among those responsible for the advanced level of party study, it comes close to being universal. The proportion of propagandists

TABLE 4.3   *Party propagandists, 1969 and 1975*

	1969	%	1975	%
Total (thousands):	1097.1	100	1316.9	100
of which with complete or incomplete higher education	875.9	79.8	1149.8	87.3
Party, Soviet, trade union and Komsomol officials	40.3	3.8	93.5	7.1
Directors of enterprises, state and collective farms and organisations	133.5	12.2	202.9	15.4
Scientific and technical staff, agronomists, economists, doctors etc.	377.9	34.4	662.3	50.3
Teachers, lecturers and researchers	296.5	27.0	257.7	19.6

SOURCE: *Partiinaya Zhizn'*, no. 21 (1977) p. 43.

with a specialist knowledge of particular areas of economic and social life has also increased considerably. Propagandists receive their initial training in the propaganda faculties of the Universities of Marxism-Leninism; thereafter they are encouraged to extend their knowledge and improve their skills by participation in the seminars and short-term courses which are organised for this purpose. Many seminars and 'methodological conferences' of this kind are held in the local House or Room of Political Enlighten-ment, of which there are presently more than 7000 throughout the USSR. These serve as the main organisational base of propaganda work, providing equipment and other aids for lecturers as well as library resources, facilities for group discussion and (in some cases) qualified 'consultants' to advise upon materials and methods.[40]

The carrying of the party's message to the population at large, a function described as 'mass-political work', is the responsibility of the party's apparatus of agitation and propaganda. At the apex of this structure stands the Propaganda Department of the Central Committee of the CPSU, first established as such in 1920; beneath it and under its general supervision come the Departments of Agita-tion and Propaganda at the republican and regional levels, headed by a member of their respective secretariats; while further down again come the Departments of Agitation and Propaganda of the district or town party committees, headed again by a member of their secretariat. Departments of this kind are concerned with such matters as the political education system within their locality; the work of the lecturers who undertake mass-political work at farms, factories and other institutions within their area; and the overall direction of the 'voluntary' bodies which carry out work of relevance to the party's objectives in this field, such as atheistic propaganda. The local Department of Propaganda and Agitation also exercises a general supervision over the work of the local press and over educational institutions in the area. The work is normally carried out by a head of department, one or two deputies, and from two to seven 'instructors'.[41]

Mass-agitational work at the local level is conducted by 'agita-tors', 'political informers' and 'lecturers'. 'Agitators' (*agitatory*), of whom there were 3.7 million in 1976, are supposed to be concerned with the affairs of the local workgroup and especially with economic matters such as the fulfilment of production targets; but all kinds of other questions, from the layout of the local 'red corner' to the personal affairs of members of the workgroup, also come within their competence. Agitators normally work in groups (*agitkollektivy*) in carrying out these duties, but they are supposed to be members of a local workgroup and their characteristic method of work is the talk or discussion (*beseda*) with one or a number of its other members. The agitator 'is always among his workmates', as a *Pravda* editorial has put it, 'connected with them by the same interests and problems, exercising constant ideological and moral influence upon those around him and closely relating the clarification of general political questions with the daily affairs of the workshop, section, link or brigade'.[42]

The 'political informer' (*politinformator*), in contrast, is not necessarily a member of the local workgroup, and his responsibilities are both more general and more specialised than those of the agitator. The *politinformator* will normally concentrate upon a particular area, such as economic, political, cultural or international affairs, and his lecture (*politinformatsiya*) will normally deal with its chosen topic at greater length and in more detail than an agitator would normally devote to his *beseda*. Political informers, as these requirements might suggest, are expected to be better educated than agitators and to be in a position to give an intellectually satisfactory exposition on any topic within their field of competence. They work, like agitators, in groups, and normally come under the control of the party bureau of a major factory or institution or of a district party committee. There were 1.8 million *politinformatory* in 1976.[43] Lecturers (*dokladchiki*) are engaged in the same kind of work at a still more advanced level, and their membership is accordingly drawn mainly from local academics and white-collar workers as well as, for especially important occasions, from senior party and state officials attached to the lecturers' group of the regional or republican party committee. There were 300,000 such lecturers in 1976. Agitators, *politinformatory* and lecturers, like party propagandists, are provided with a series of seminars, methodological conferences and other opportunities to discuss their problems and experiences, and party committees are supposed to keep them regularly informed about the progress of their work.[44]

This carefully differentiated system, like so much else in Soviet life, looks rather more impressive on paper than its actual performance might suggest. There is no shortage of evidence, for instance, that the distinctive functions supposedly entrusted to each of these varied groups of activists are not always carefully observed in practice, or even fully understood by the party committees nominally responsible for their management.[45] These problems occur particularly frequently with agitators and *politinformatory*, whose respective spheres of operation do overlap to some degree and who may in some cases even be the same people. The functions of agitators and *politinformatory* may indeed have been intended to overlap, as the reason for the introduction of the *politinformatory* in the middle 1960s was apparently in order to allow the agitators to be replaced by lecturers who would be able to carry out their work at the higher and more sophisticated level which better-educated Soviet audiences were now believed to require.[46] Present policy, however, is that both have a distinctive function to perform, and that both, together with the *dokladchiki*, should continue to carry out their respective individual duties.

A further important contribution to party propaganda is made by an organisation which, while nominally 'voluntary', nonetheless comes under the overall direction of the party: the All-Union 'Knowledge' (*Znanie*) Society. Founded in 1947 and known until 1963 as the All-Union Society for the Dissemination of Political and Scientific Knowledge, the Society took over the functions that had previously been discharged by the League of the Militant Godless and is presently one of the most important centres of atheist propaganda in the country. It organises question-and-answer sessions, arranges for broadcasts on relevant themes on the radio and television, and publishes a variety of books and pamphlets (more than 58 million in 1976) as well as a number of journals, including the monthly atheistic journal *Nauka i Religiya* (*Science and Religion*). The Society has over 3 million members at present, and in 1976 they presented over 24 million lectures to a total audience in excess of 1245 million.[47] Although the promotion of atheistic propaganda is the Society's original and most distinctive function it is engaged in other areas as well: in 1975, for instance, more than 20 per cent of the lectures delivered under its auspices were concerned with Soviet or party history, and another 20 per cent were divided equally between international affairs and medical matters.[48] Most of the Society's members work as teachers, lecturers or white-collar workers, with a small admixture of party, state and trade union officials; the fact that leading industrial workers and collective farmers are not well represented has been commented upon adversely.[49]

In addition to these efforts, and together with the programmes of political and economic study organised under Komsomol and trade union auspices (the numbers engaged in which are shown in Table 4.2), an important place is given to 'visual agitation'—posters, slogans, 'Boards of Honour' and so forth—designed to reinforce the party's efforts at the place of work, in public parks and town squares, on major public buildings and elsewhere. The original emphasis of such measures was upon the citizen's place of work and public places generally; but since the early 1960s, and especially since the introduction of the five-day week in 1967, it has been increasingly recognised that this will tend to leave housewives, pensioners, and the very young outside the ambit of the party's propaganda, together with employed members of the labour force on their days off. The organisation of political work in residential areas has accordingly received a higher priority in recent years, and it forms an important part of the responsibilities of the local party Department of Agitation and Propaganda. An area will normally be divided into a number of 'microdistricts' for this purpose, in each of which a 'council for work among the population' will be established with responsibilities which include the preparation of a plan for political work within the area in question. A typical scheme for a 'microdistrict' of this kind might embrace sporting and cultural activities, the preservation of public order and play facilities for children as well as political lectures, atheistic propaganda and the maintenance of visual displays, 'red corners' and the like.[50]

A great deal of attention is similarly devoted to anniversaries and events of note, such as Lenin's birthday (22 April), May Day (1 May), and the anniversary of the October revolution (7 November). The adoption of the new Soviet Constitution in 1977 was the occasion for a particularly vigorous campaign of this sort. In Moscow, for instance, more than 400,000 lecturers and agitators were involved in explaining the preliminary draft version to the population and mobilising support for its adoption; agitational and 'consultation points' were opened by local party committees to provide information and advice for interested parties; and the columns of the local and national press were made available for correspondence and discussion as well as for authoritative party pronouncements.[51] Altogether more than 140 million Soviet citizens had taken part in the discussion of the draft Constitution, Brezhnev told a special session of the Supreme Soviet on 4 October 1977, or more than four-fifths of the country's adult population; the discussion had shown 'once again how firm and creative is the unity of all classes and social groups, all nations and nationalities, and all generations of Soviet society around the Communist Party'.[52] More regular events, such as local or national elections, the gathering of the harvest or the adoption of a Five Year Plan, are treated with an equal degree of seriousness. The electoral campaign, for instance, is planned in some detail; for at least the two previous months a series of appropriate articles will appear in the press, visual propaganda will be stepped up, agitators will call at people's homes and a series of meetings will be held at *agitpunkty* or 'electors' clubs' in the constituency, pointing out the achievements of the previous period and the tasks which await completion in that which succeeds it. The conduct of campaigns of this kind is an important part of the responsibilities of a local party organisation in this field.[53]

Special care is taken to ensure that youth is brought up in the revolutionary tradition. Schoolchildren are enrolled at the age of seven in the Young Octobrists; then, at the age of ten, in the Pioneers; and finally, between the ages of 14 and 28, in the Komsomol, the 'trusty ally of the party', as Brezhnev described it to the XXV Party Congress, 'its immediate and militant reserve'.[54] Young people are engaged through these organisations in forms of political activity and instruction appropriate to their years. Regular meetings are held with veterans of the civil and second (Great Fatherland) wars, for instance, and with Old Bolsheviks. Schoolchildren are encouraged to collect information about historical figures and events, and expeditions are organised to nearby places with military or revolutionary associations. Figures or events of particular importance are commemorated by obelisks, memorials, plaques and street-names; and the places of birth or residence of major political figures are often turned into 'house-museums', with a regular programme of lectures, exhibitions and visiting school parties.[55] The education system itself makes a further contribution: party orthodoxy influences both the curriculum and the teaching of individual subjects, and the social organisation of the school itself, by breaking up pupils into small self-regulating groups of ten or more each, further strengthens the values of co-operation and collective responsibility which the party seeks more generally to promote. Patterns of child-rearing in the pre-school years may reinforce these predispositions further.[56]

Finally, and perhaps most obviously, the mass media are not ignored. 'In the major and complicated task of the formation of the new man, in the ideological struggle with the capitalist world', the XXIV Party Congress was told, 'the means of mass information and propaganda are a powerful instrument of the party—newspapers, journals, television, radio and the information agencies.'[57] Their output, accordingly, has steadily increased. The daily print of all newspapers was 7 million in 1925; by 1950, however, it had risen to 36 million, and by 1976 it had reached over 169 million copies a day or 66 copies per 100 inhabitants, a level of saturation which compares with or exceeds that of most other industrial nations.[58] About a third of this total is accounted for by the major central dailies, such as *Pravda* (10.6 million copies daily) and *Izvestiya* (8 million copies daily); a further quarter represents publications intended specifically for younger age-groups, such as *Komsomol'-skaya Pravda*, which had a circulation in 1976 of nearly 10 million, and *Pionerskaya Pravda*.[59] In the same year nearly 4 million copies of the works of Marx and Engels, and nearly 17 million copies of works by Lenin, were published.[60] Television is an institution of relatively more recent origin; already, however, it is received by 80 per cent of Soviet households (or 98 per cent of those families within its transmission area), and there are plans to extend this coverage still further in the near future. Much of the emphasis of programme-making is upon entertainment (39.7 per cent of the output of the first national network in 1972, for instance, fell within this category) but social and political themes are also important (they accounted for 11.7 per cent of total output in the same year). Radio programmes reflect a similar emphasis.[61]

This, then, is a programme of political socialisation of considerable scope and intensity, and it would be surprising if it failed to have some kind of effect upon the population which is subjected to it. In the two chapters which follow we shall consider this question more closely, looking first at mass political values and behavioural patterns and then secondly at the extent to which more specifically Marxist-Leninist values appear successfully to have been inculcated. To the first of these themes we now turn.

5

The Contemporary
Political Culture

Political culture has been defined in this volume as the 'behavioural
and attitudinal matrix within which the political system is located'.
We shall be concerned in what follows, therefore, with changing
patterns of political behaviour as much as with the political beliefs
and values associated with them. This is not to suggest that the two
will necessarily be in exact accordance. Certain forms of political
behaviour, such as strikes and demonstrations, are effectively prohibited in the USSR and no conclusions can therefore be drawn
from their relative infrequency; while others, such as the affirmation
of support for each new Five Year Plan or change in party policy,
are in practice so close to obligatory that little can be inferred from
their generally unanimous character. Not all forms of political
behaviour, however, are equally regimented; and in some, such as
the complex of activities known as 'socio-political activity', a degree
of discretion is permitted which allows at least provisional conclusions to be drawn from the widely varying rates of participation
which do in fact emerge. The fact that a particular form of political
behaviour may be effectively prohibited, moreover, does not in fact
prevent all citizens from engaging in it, as the activities of a well-
publicised group of 'dissidents' has in recent years made clear; while
even more or less compulsory forms of political behaviour, such as
participation in national elections and referenda, themselves constitute part of the pattern of regular and repeated interactions by
which the political culture may be characterised at the behavioural
level.

An emphasis upon political culture as comprising a behavioural
as well as an attitudinal component has the additional merit of
conforming to the criteria which the Soviet authorities have them-

selves accepted as the most appropriate for measuring the political consciousness of their society. 'The measure of the success of the political upbringing of the masses', as Brezhnev told the XXV Party Congress in 1976, 'is of course concrete action. Communist consciousness is a combination of knowledge, convictions and practical activity.'[1] Lenin had argued that the advance from the lower to the higher phase of socialism was possible only when all took part in the administration of the state; Brezhnev, similarly, has stated that the advance towards Communism will depend upon bringing workers ever more closely into the direction of state affairs, economic and political life generally.[2] People were still to be found, Brezhnev told the XXV Congress, who 'know our policies and our principles but do not always follow them in practice, who do not struggle for their realisation and are unconcerned about violations of the norms of our socialist community'. The most advanced ideology, he had earlier pointed out, 'becomes a real force only when, having been absorbed by the masses, it impels them into action, determines the norms of their daily behaviour'.[3] The party, therefore, has attempted to change patterns of political behaviour as well as the values and beliefs which underlie them; an examination of the extent of its success must necessarily embrace both.

Patterns of Political Behaviour

It may be best to begin with the language which Soviet citizens employ to describe their political and social activities more generally. Not all the terms which Soviet citizens presently employ, of course, may be regarded as evidence of a shift in political allegiance. Many, such as 'comrade', 'demonstration' and 'internationalism', had already entered the Russian language before the revolution (though their use was confined to a relatively limited circle), and many other 'Sovietisms', though authentically post-revolutionary, refer simply to changes of administrative designation or to new socio-political institutions, such as 'Komsomol', 'All-Union' and 'Five Year Plan'.[4] A number of other terms which have become obsolete as a result of changes in social forms, however, may perhaps be more legitimately regarded as illustrative of changes in social attitudes. Words such as *gospodin* (gentleman), *barin* (baron) and *prisluga* (servants), for instance, have now lost all but an ironic or specifically capitalist connotation, and a number of forms of deferential address which were fairly widely used in pre-revolutionary Russia, such as *blagovolite soobshchit'* (be so kind as to tell me) and *milosti proshu* (you are welcome), have now virtually disappeared from everyday speech.[5] Deferential forms of address such as these have, of course, lost currency in other countries also over the same period, and their gradual disappearance can only somewhat arbitrarily be identified with a developing commitment to Soviet socialism. Changes in linguistic usage over the whole Soviet period, however, do appear to provide some evidence of a gradual democratisation of social values in a manner broadly acceptable to the party-state authorities.

Linguistic changes of a more specifically political kind have also occurred in the choice of personal names in the USSR, although the evidence on this point is again not altogether conclusive. The practice of naming children after revolutionary leaders and institutions, for instance, became quite widespread in the 1920s and 1930s. Boys were given names such as 'Vil' (from the initials V. I. Lenin), 'Marlen' (Marx and Lenin) or 'Rem' (Revolution, Electrification, Mechanisation); girls rejoiced in names such as 'Ninel' (Lenin spelt backwards), 'Oktyabrina', or even 'Traktor' and 'Pyatiletka' (Five Year Plan). In the town of Kostroma more than two-thirds of the children born in 1930 were called by new-style names such as 'Avangard' and 'Kommir' (Communist World); and in urban centres elsewhere, though less so in the country, the new names were widely utilised.[6] There was a decline in the popularity of the new-style names thereafter, however (names such as 'Zikatra' (Zinoviev, Kamenev, Trotsky) and 'Lentrozin' (Lenin, Trotsky, Zinoviev) were obviously something of a liability), and today they appear to be relatively uncommon. Parents in Kostroma used as many as 139 names in the 1930s, for instance, but only 57 in 1961 and only about a dozen at the end of that decade; and figures elsewhere record a parallel decline.[7] Tempting though it might be to argue a process of political disenchantment from such figures, however, the inference would be illegitimate: the original adoption of the new-style names was part of a more general fashion for innovation and modernity as much as it reflected a commitment to party policies, and the party itself sponsored the subsequent return to more traditional usages from the 1930s onwards, in personal names as in other matters. Neither linguistic changes nor changes in personal nomenclature, in other words, appear to offer unambiguous evidence of a shift in political allegiances.

We are upon somewhat firmer ground in examining the nature and extent of political participation within the USSR over the period in question. Voting, admittedly, is not nowadays an entirely voluntary affair. Ballot boxes are carried on long-distance trains and on Soviet ships in foreign waters; they are taken to the sick in their beds and to shepherds in distant pastures; and even cosmonauts are provided with facilities for recording their votes in the appropriate constituency on earth. There is no choice of party, nor even of candidate; and electoral commissions, in their enthusiasm to record the highest possible turnout, have resorted to irregularities too frequently for the results to be taken entirely at face value.[8] It is in fact extremely difficult not to vote, and since the late 1930s no more than about 1 per cent of the electorate has ever managed to avoid doing so.[9] But this was not always the case, as Table 5.1 makes clear, and the ability the regime presently manifests to secure the participation of virtually the entire adult population in the electoral process is an aspect of the contemporary political culture whose importance should not be minimised. It may not in itself constitute evidence of ideological commitment on the part of the citizenry, as Soviet spokesmen, for instance, have frequently represented.[10] It does, however, at least serve as evidence of the regime's increasing ability to mobilise the population and to integrate them into the political system, which 'for any state—particularly one in the beginning stages of development—is a very important achievement', one tending to 'create both an identity between party, state and citizen, and tighter bonds within the society as a whole'.[11] The regime has also shown an increasing ability to involve wider sections of the population, such as women and young people aged under 30, in the work of party and state institutions generally (Table 5.1).

Membership of the Communist Party, again, is not an entirely voluntary matter: membership is by the recommendation of existing members only, it is highly selective, and it can be withdrawn in the course of a 'purge' or a more limited exercise such as the changeover of party cards in 1973–4, when some 347,000 of the party's existing members were not permitted to re-enrol.[12] The motives for joining, equally, may vary: some will presumably be committed to the party's long-term objectives, but a large and perhaps increasing proportion may have been motivated by the belief that their career

TABLE 5.1   *Some indicators of political participation, 1917–77*

	1917	1926	1939	1959	1977
Party membership (members and candidates per 1000 population)	0.2	7.3	19.6	39.5	62.0
Komsomol membership (members per 1000 population)	0.1*	11.9	48.4	90.2	138.0
Trade union membership (members per 1000 population)	16.6*	62.8	n.a.	258.5	440.1
Electoral participation (country or local Soviets, per cent poll)	22.3†	48.9	99.1	99.9	99.9
Female membership of the CPSU (per cent of total)	7.4§	12.2	14.8	19.7	24.7
Female representation in country or local Soviets (per cent of total)	1.0†	9.9	33.1	38.3	49.0

SOURCES   *Partiinaya Zhizn'*, no. 21 (1977); *Narodnoe Khozyaistvo SSSR za 60 Let. Statisticheskii Sbornik* (Moscow, 1977); *Bidrag till Oststsforskningen*, vol. 4 (1976); *Sovetskaya Istoricheskaya Entsiklopediya*, vol. 13 (Moscow, 1971); *Itogy Vyborov i Sostav Deputatov Mestnykh Sovetov Deputatov Trudyashchikhsya 1975g* (Moscow, 1975); *Izvestiya* (25 June 1977).
* 1918; † 1922; § 1920.

prospects would be improved as a result (Brezhnev, certainly, saw fit to warn at the XXV Party Congress that only those who wished to join 'not for the sake of some kind of privileges but for dedicated work for the benefit of communism' could be accepted as members).[13] Party membership, these restrictions notwithstanding, has nonetheless expanded threefold over the past 30 years; it presently embraces some 6 per cent of the total population or 9 per cent of the adult population, and still higher proportions of men, the better educated, those aged between 30 and 60, and urban residents.[14] Membership of the Komsomol and the trade unions is much less exclusive, and their growth in membership has been correspondingly more spectacular (Table 5.1). Again, it is difficult to attach an unambiguous significance to such increases: a variety of motives is involved, and a variety of pressures to join or not to join. But it is at least clear that the lack of popular involvement in political life which was characteristic of Tsarist Russia has been largely overcome, and the simple fact of these relatively high levels of participation, whatever its 'meaning' to individual members, is an aspect of the contemporary political culture of some importance at the behavioural level. Formal or not, the USSR is now a society with levels of membership of political and other mass organisations which bear comparison with those of most other western industrial societies.[15]

A more discriminating indicator of participation, more discriminating because it is to a greater extent a voluntary or elective form of activity, is participation in socio-political activity (*obshchestvenno-politicheskaya rabota* or *deyatel'nost'*). Socio-political activity of this kind has been defined as 'self-motivated participation in the construction of socialist [Communist] society without the consideration of material reward';[16] it embraces such forms of activity as attendance at meetings and conferences, membership of a factory or trade union committee, the editing of a 'wall newspaper' at one's place of work, lecturing within the party educational system and acting as an unpaid police auxiliary (*druzhinnik*). A good deal of such activity, again, is not entirely voluntary, and party members in particular must discharge the obligation placed upon them by the Party Rules to 'take an active part in the political life of the country, in the administration of state affairs, and in economic and cultural development' (Art. 2). Even for party members no precise requirements are made, however, and for the mass of the population such activity is indeed voluntary and is in fact engaged in to a widely varying extent. It seems reasonable to regard such activity as both an important aspect of the contemporary political culture, considered simply at the behavioural level, as well as an indicator of the distribution of political opinion within the society of somewhat greater value than non-competitive elections.[17] In what follows we shall consider both the overall level of participation of this kind, at present and as it has developed over time, and also the changing distribution of the kinds of activities which are included within it.

It is clear, first of all, that overall levels of socio-political activism have increased very considerably over the total period of Soviet rule. The earliest studies which lend themselves to a comparative analysis of this kind were conducted by S. G. Strumilin in the early 1920s. Strumilin found that the average male worker spent about 2.9 hours a month engaged in socio-political activity, and that the average female worker spent about 1.42 hours a month thus engaged. Only about 3.3 per cent of the workers who were polled at this time regarded themselves as engaged in such activity.[18] Studies which were published in 1928 and 1932 showed that these levels of activity had increased somewhat, although levels of activism in the countryside still tended to lag behind those in the town.[19] Studies in more recent years have shown further increases, to between 1.5 and 6 hours a week in the case of a male worker and between 0.9 and 3.5 hours a week for women.[20] The average amount of time devoted to such activities over the whole period of Soviet rule is estimated to have increased almost seven times, and the proportion of working people engaged in them is reckoned to have increased as much as eighteen times.[21] The proportion of the population presently engaged in such activities varies widely: at a collective farm in central Russia, for instance, only about a quarter of the working population were involved, while at a Kishinev tractor factory, on the other hand, almost three-quarters of the workforce were thus engaged.[22] Generally, however, levels of participation tend to vary very little from about half of the group considered. The average level of participation among industrial workers in Kalinin and Kalinin province, for instance, was 53 per cent; at a factory in Krasnoyarsk it was 52.5 per cent; at two factories in Novosibirsk it was reported to be 47.8 and 56 per cent respectively; and among a stratified sample of some 17,000 workers in the Urals the overall level of participation was 58 per cent. These, in comparative terms, are relatively high figures.[23]

There have been considerable changes also in the content of socio-political activity. In the 1920s, according to Strumilin's survey, some nine-tenths of the time spent by the average worker on such activity was devoted to relatively 'passive' forms of activity such as attendance at meetings and demonstrations, and only about 7 per cent of the total time was devoted to more 'active' forms such as organisational work in a trade union or factory committee.[24] By 1966, in a study in the Urals designed to provide data comparable to those which Strumilin had earlier obtained, these proportions had changed considerably. The amount of time devoted to attendance at meetings and demonstrations had dropped to three-tenths of the total, while the carrying out of social commissions (*obshchestvennye porucheniya*) and other more 'active' socio-political functions now accounted for seven-tenths of the total.[25] The changes which have taken place in the structure of socio-political activity over this period are set out in Table 5.2. Of the time the average worker now devotes to socio-political activity, approximately 20

TABLE 5.2   *Participation in socio-political activity, 1922–3 and 1965–6*
(*percentage of workers*)

	1922–3	1965–6
Reading of newspapers	43.0	87.0
Socio-political work in organisations	3.3	51.0
Attendance at meetings and demonstrations	66.1	95.0
Attendance at lectures and talks (*besedy*)	24.3	71.6
Attendance at political study circles and seminars	12.0	48.0
Total socio-political activity (hours/minutes per month)	0.27	5.0

SOURCES: *Obshchestvennyi Interes i Lichnost'* (Sverdlovsk, 1967) p. 43;
E. M. Kuznetsov, *Politicheskaya Agitatsiya: Nauchnye Osnovy i Praktika*
(Moscow, 1974) p. 281.

per cent is accounted for by attendance at meetings, seminars and
conferences; 3.5 per cent is accounted for by the preparation and
delivery of lectures, reports and so on; and about 75 per cent is
devoted to the carrying out of social commissions.[26] Clearly there
has been a substantial change, not only in the time expended upon
socio-political activity by the average worker but also in the content
of such participation, with mainly 'active' forms increasingly pre-
dominating over rather more 'passive' forms of such activity.

Similar changes have occurred in the nature and extent of socio-
political participation among a group of particular importance
from the regime's point of view, young people under the age of 30. A
study of the involvement of young people in the carrying out of
social commissions, for instance, found that 46.3 per cent of those
who were asked were presently thus engaged, compared with 22.6
per cent in a similar survey conducted in 1929.[27] Another survey
found that only 20–22 per cent of Komsomol members had taken
any part in socio-political activity in the earlier year, but that 56.4
per cent were thus engaged in 1966.[28] The conclusions of the most
detailed of these investigations so far to have been conducted, a
study of collective farm youth designed to provide results comparable with those obtained by an earlier investigation in 1938, arrived
at broadly similar conclusions (Table 5.3). On almost all the
relevant indicators, it will be seen, the involvement of young people
in socio-political activity was greater, and sometimes considerably

TABLE 5.3   *Socio-political activity of collective-farm youth, 1938 and 1969 (percentage of respondents thus engaged)*

	1938	1969
Membership of the Komsomol	23.4	61.9
Membership of the CPSU	0.5	16.4
Involvement in regular socio-political activity	11.3	57.2
Possess works of Lenin	10.2	10.6
Make use of library	55.7	83.5
Have read basic Marx and Lenin texts	6.8	11.6
Regularly read newspapers	70.3	72.7*
Attendance at lectures:		
1–3 times a year	52.5	65.9
4 or more times a year	47.5	34.1
Attendance at museums and exhibitions:		
1–3 times a year	80.5	75.4
4 or more times a year	19.5	24.6

SOURCE   V. E. Poletaev (ed.), *Sotsial'nyi Oblik Kolkhoznoi Molodezhi po Materialam Sotsiologicheskikh Obsledovanii 1938 i 1969 gg* (Moscow, 1976) pp. 20–32.
* Regular readership of newspapers and journals.

greater, in 1969 than in 1938. The proportion of those who had attended more than four lectures a year had admittedly fallen, and in a number of other cases the proportion of young people involved in 1969 was only slightly greater than it had been in 1938. On the most important indicators, however, such as Komsomol membership, party membership and participation in socio-political activity, there had been considerable increases. Again, whatever the motives of those involved, the fact that an increasing and, in comparative terms, relatively large proportion of Soviet young people take a regular part in socio-political activity must be accounted an aspect of the contemporary political culture of some importance.

We may note, finally, that levels of religious observance have shown a marked and continuous decline over the whole period of Soviet rule. Formally, of course, the church is separated from the state, and the principle of freedom of conscience is enshrined in the Soviet Constitution (Art. 52). But there can be no doubt that the party authorities, these provisions notwithstanding, nonetheless regard religion as inimical to the 'scientific world outlook' which they seek to propagate, and the elimination of religious influence has occupied a prominent place in the campaign of agitation and propaganda which they have sponsored ever since 1917. In terms of formal religious observance, at least, their efforts would appear to have been relatively successful. In the working-class families surveyed by Kabo in 1928, for instance, 75 per cent of heads of families and their wives had attended church before the revolution, but only 26 per cent did so in 1924. The baptism of children had similarly become less common; all of those surveyed had done so between 1918 and 1922, but fewer than three-quarters still did so in 1924. Expenditure on religious purposes fell by more than half over the same period.[29]

Comparisons between the levels of religious observance of these years and those of the more recent period reveal a continuing process of decline. Comparing the results of investigations conducted in the 1920s and 1930s with those obtained in more recent years, for instance, V. D. Kobetskii has shown that present levels of religious observance have fallen to approximately one-fifth of their level in the earlier period. The proportion of families giving their children a religious upbringing was found to have fallen by about three-quarters over the same period; while the proportion of young people who could be regarded as religious had fallen to almost a tenth of its earlier level, from between 12 and 22 per cent in the 1920s and 1930s to only 1–3 per cent in the more recent period.[30] Contemporary estimates of the level of religious observance tend naturally to vary, depending upon which area, social group, age or nationality is considered. Overall, however, there appears to be substantial agreement that average levels of religious observance have fallen continuously over the whole period of Soviet rule, and that remaining active believers are concentrated disproportionately among the old, the less educated and those resident in the countryside.[31]

It would be unwise to take such findings as evidence of a corresponding decline in the level of belief, however, particularly in the case of a tenacious and deeply-rooted value such as religion. It shall be noted, first of all, that it has simply become more difficult to practise: the number of churches available for religious use has declined by more than two-thirds since the revolution, and attempts to celebrate religious rites elsewhere have in recent years been repressed with especial vigour. The churches have also found it increasingly difficult to produce and distribute religious literature, and to engage in those activities in which churches in other countries engage as a means of maintaining and extending their influence. Believers, moreover, have found that their careers will be adversely affected if their religious convictions become known, and particular fields of employment, such as those concerned with the care of the young, appear effectively to be denied to them. Social pressures such as these, together with the physical unavailability of churches, suggest that the level of religious observance in the USSR may be a considerable understatement of the level of religious belief in that country.[32] There is no reason to assume, further, that a decline in levels of religious observance and belief need be only and exclusively the result of the successful propagation of a 'scientific world outlook' by the party-state authorities. Other countries, even those in which organised religion receives the formal or informal support of the state, have also experienced a decline; and it may be that the urban, industrial way of life, with its attenuation of family and neighbourhood affiliations, has more to do with such a process than secular propaganda in itself. This would certainly be consistent with the present distribution of religious observance in the USSR, substantially higher levels of which are recorded among housewives, pensioners and rural residents than among those engaged in modern industrial occupations.[33]

There is little evidence, finally, to suggest that the mass of non-believers have in fact become conscious and committed materialists, as official values would require. Both believers and non-believers, on the contrary, appear to have strikingly amorphous and often self-contradictory views about the whole question of their religious faith or lack of it. Almost all those surveyed in a recent investigation at a garment factory in Kuibyshev, for instance, whether they regarded themselves as 'believers' or not, lacked a knowledge of the Scriptures. Only a third of the believers thought that one could not lead a good life without a belief in God; while almost half of the non-believers thought that man could not live without a belief in some kind of God, and almost the same proportion were unwilling to support a campaign against religion and its remaining influence.[34] Among rural believers in particular, it has been noted, there is 'considerable confusion about some of the most basic aspects of belief'; many believers fail to practice their religion, have an extremely nebulous conception of the principles of their faith, and in some cases even favour the conduct of atheistic propaganda and attend atheistic lectures.[35] Other investigations have found that many ostensibly non-religious families continue to display icons in their homes and to observe religious festivals, and that few of them attach importance to the upbringing of their children in an explicitly non-religious atmosphere. The formation of an atheist consciousness in the Muslim areas of the USSR, where religion, nationality and culture are so closely intertwined as to be virtually inextricable, has proved to be a task of particular difficulty.[36]

The evidence which we have so far reviewed, in other words, although it may accurately describe the patterns of social and political behaviour of which a society's political culture is in part constituted, may be an imperfect guide to the beliefs and values with which those patterns of behaviour are associated; and a disjunction of this kind may be particularly great in the case of values which, such as religion, are prevented from finding overt expression by a variety of formal and informal mechanisms. The behavioural evidence, that is to say, can embrace only part of the 'attitudinal and behavioural matrix within which the political system is located'; it must be supplemented by further and independently derived evidence regarding political beliefs and values. To this our next section is devoted.

Political Beliefs and Values

The student of Soviet political beliefs and values starts with the undeniable handicap that direct access to the population he is studying is restricted in a variety of ways, and that the conduct of a systematic survey-based investigation into attitudes towards and expectations of government similar to those which have been conducted in a number of other countries is in present circumstances impossible. In the absence of such findings a variety of other sources must be employed, most of which will be drawn upon in the discussion which follows. The first of these, and perhaps the most important, is emigre evidence: evidence, that is to say, based upon surveys of Soviet citizens who for one reason or another find themselves abroad and are there available for an investigation of this kind. Emigre evidence, of course, is subject to a number of biases: the emigre will normally have chosen to leave the political system in relation to which he is being interviewed and may therefore be expected to be more than normally antipathetic towards it; the samples available are generally less than representative in terms of their ethnic, social and occupational characteristics; and the size of sample available is generally too small to permit other than the most approximate consideration of the impact of educational, generational and other factors upon the distribution of political opinion within the group as a whole. Not all such studies are subject to these shortcomings, however, and the most substantial of them so far to have been conducted, a study by a team from Harvard University under the direction of Alex Inkeles and Raymond Bauer, was able to draw upon the large numbers of Soviet refugees in Western Europe at the end of the Second World War to provide a sample which was both fairly large (more than 2700 respondents completed questionnaires and a further 329 submitted themselves to extended life-history interviews) and reasonably representative of the population of the USSR at the time in terms of its party membership and other relevant characteristics. The findings of this study, *The Soviet Citizen*, have widely been accepted as the single most authoritative source of information on the political values and beliefs of the Soviet mass public which is presently available.[37]

Studies conducted more recently with Soviet emigres in Israel and the USA do not generally rest upon so ample an empirical foundation. The new group of emigres, some 150,000 of whom have left the USSR since 1971, do nonetheless represent a reasonably wide range of ages, occupations, and places of origin; and the careful use of this source does make possible both a variety of insights into Soviet political opinion of a kind not available elsewhere as well as a means of checking upon the continued validity or otherwise of the earlier findings. It may further be noted that, whatever their other shortcomings, these and earlier emigre data can provide at least a reasonably firm negative indication of the distribution of political opinion within the larger population (if those who have left the USSR are found to favour any aspect of its social or political system it may fairly be assumed that the Soviet population itself would be at least as likely to do so); and they may also provide at least a provisional basis for the assessment of within-group differences, on the assumption that whatever factors bias the sample as a whole will operate relatively uniformly as between one sub-group and another and that their interrelationship will therefore be approximately the same as that within the larger national population.[38] Emigre sources of this kind obviously require careful handling, and it would be unwise to accept a conclusion upon this basis if it were either implausible or inconsistent with findings derived from other sources. Discriminatingly employed, however, they may provide both a good deal of interesting information of a kind which is not otherwise available as well as a body of evidence which, in conjunction with other sources, may be of considerable value in an investigation of Soviet political beliefs and values. It is on this basis that such evidence has been employed in the present study.

Apart from emigre sources, a variety of other bodies of information may be drawn upon for our purposes. Soviet sociological literature, for instance, may be employed when it bears (usually indirectly) upon the subject in question; the reports of long-term western residents and journalists, a number of valuable examples of which have recently appeared, are also useful; Soviet fiction, which has a long tradition of devoting itself to socio-political issues and may frequently be more illuminating than an equivalent non-fiction account, should be consulted; memoirs and autobiography are important, particularly for changing generational values; and finally behaviour itself, whether in the form of riots, demonstrations, corruption or other 'negative' phenomena, may provide both an indirect commentary upon political values and a useful check upon findings derived from other sources.[39] Each of these sources is subject to a variety of shortcomings, and no great weight should be attached to findings which depend exclusively upon any one of them. Literature, for instance, may convey atmosphere but be unduly 'impressionistic'; while Soviet sociological research may be subject to a variety of methodological defects as well as to biases and distortions of a more straightforward character. When a number of sources independently converge upon a particular conclusion, however, it would seem unreasonable not to grant that conclusion at least a limited measure of validity.[40] What then do our results suggest?

Government and the Economy

A variety of investigations have found that most Russians, even when disposed in a hostile manner towards the system as a whole, nonetheless favour many of its most distinctive institutional attrib utes. Most of the displaced persons who were interviewed by Inkeles and Bauer, for instance, decisively rejected two of the most central institutions of the USSR at that time, the secret police and the collective farm. There was widespread support, however, for public ownership of the economy, at least of heavy industry and communications, and for an extensive measure of state planning and control. A clear majority within each social group, as well as of the group as a whole, favoured state planning and control of the economy under a set of hypothetical 'ideal conditions'. Only 14 per cent supported the establishment of a capitalist system under such circumstances; four-fifths preferred an essentially socialist system, with extensive public ownership and control over most areas of economic life. Support for state ownership and control was strongest in basic sectors of the economy, such as heavy industry and transport and communications; more than 85 per cent of respondents were in favour of both of these principles, with little variation between one social group and another, and respondents who had lived for a year in the United States were at least as likely to favour them as those (the vast majority) who had continued to live in Europe. There were very few, similarly, who spontaneously cited the public ownership and control of industry as a feature of the system which they would be anxious to change if the Soviet government were overthrown and a different kind of government established in its place.

There was much less support for the collective farm system, however, nearly all respondents believing that it should be abolished and the land redistributed to the peasants, and for the public ownership of light industry, where the existing Soviet system met with less than universal approval. Only among collective farmers, in fact, was there majority support for state ownership of light industry; three-quarters of white-collar workers and almost two-thirds of industrial workers were opposed to it, and respondents who had taken up residence in America were even more emphatic in their opposition than those who had remained in Europe. Most respondents, nevertheless, remained committed to a broadly collectivist economic system, and the NEP system which existed in the USSR in the 1920s, under which banking, foreign trade and most industry had been in the hands of the state but small-scale private trade had been permitted, was supported by the overwhelming majority. 'We lived poorly before the revolution; only under NEP was it easier', was one typical explanation. Another commented: 'Under the NEP life was better than even under the Tsarist regime. You could buy everything you wanted, and there was no unemployment'. One respondent even claimed: 'The standard of living of the workers and peasants at that time, the period of the NEP, was higher than in any other country of the world'. Inaccurately though they may have perceived it, it was clearly a system of this kind which corresponded most closely to the mind of society in which most respondents would ideally have liked to live.[41]

Interviews with a more recent generation of former Soviet citizens confirm the impression that the state is expected by most Russians to play a rather more prominent role in economic life than would normally be the case in the west. Most respondents in an investigation in Israel conducted by the present author, for instance, favoured state guarantees of full employment (although many were careful to point out that this had not in fact been achieved in the Soviet Union, declarations to the contrary notwithstanding), and most also favoured the principle inscribed in the (then) Soviet Constitution, 'He who does not work shall not eat'. There was less agreement about the extent to which a state might be justified in taking action to reduce inequalities and to limit differences in income and material circumstances. Inequality, if this simply meant differences in individual talents and endowments, was considered to be a normal and perfectly healthy feature of any society; and there was also a case for some differences in remuneration in order to provide incentives for people to work harder and improve their qualifications (which is in fact how such differences in the USSR are presently justified). But it was widely agreed that extremes of income inequality should be avoided, together with inequalities of power and status which might stem from such differences, and there was overwhelming agreement that the state had a right and a duty to limit such inequalities and to secure a basic and satisfactory standard of living for all its citizens. One respondent identified 'distributive justice' (in English) as the approach which best accorded with his preferences in this matter, and specifically rejected the 'American system'. It was widely agreed at the same time that 'artificial attempts' to bring about total equality should be avoided, not least because they were likely to have the opposite effect to that which had apparently been intended.

Most respondents also favoured an extensive degree of public ownership of the economy. More than 86 per cent, for instance, favoured state ownership and control of heavy industry, and many specified the inclusion of light industry as well (one commented simply: 'Everything should be in the hands of the state'). There was universal agreement, on the other hand, that agriculture should be returned to private hands, or perhaps organised on some kind of co-operative basis (the Soviet system was widely agreed to have been a lamentable failure in practice), and it was also agreed that handicrafts and services (*remeslo*) should be returned to the private sector, though perhaps under some form of state supervision and control. There was virtually unanimous support for a 'mixed economy' system, neither wholly state-owned nor wholly private, and again it was the New Economic Policy of the 1920s, with its toleration of a reasonable amount of private initiative within a largely state-owned framework, which accorded with the preferences of most respondents. There was also substantial agreement that transport and communications should be publicly owned and controlled, together with education and medicine and the social services generally (although some were willing to permit the existence of a parallel private sector in these fields, perhaps under some form of overall state guidance, and there was fairly general concern that state control over education should not be allowed to extend to the detailed determination of the curriculum, as is presently the case in the USSR). Again, these are responses which accord quite closely with those that the Harvard team had obtained a generation earlier.[42]

State and Society

The broadly 'collectivist' bias of responses to questions concerned with the role of the state in economic life emerges also in attitudes towards the role of the state in social and cultural affairs. The Harvard investigators, for instance, found a 'deep-rooted expectation among Soviet citizens that their government and society will provide extensive social welfare benefits, including job security, universal education, medical care and other securities and guarantees', an expectation which showed almost no variation from one social group to another.[43] The two aspects of the Soviet system which received the strongest spontaneous support were the educational and medical services, both of which a clear majority in all social groups wished to retain even if a change of government made it possible to do otherwise. It was features of the Soviet welfare system such as these which respondents were most likely to favour, and which appeared to accord most closely with the kind of society in which they would ideally have liked to live. Respondents who had lived in the United States, with its predominantly private health and welfare services, were even more emphatic in their support of these aspects of Soviet life than those who had remained in Europe. It was again the achievements of the Soviet government in these fields which respondents were most likely to credit to its favour, their overall hostility towards the system notwithstanding; and it was the inadequate implementation of the principles of Soviet social welfare, rather than those principles in themselves, which accounted for most reservations. The desire to live in a welfare state, the Harvard investigators concluded, was 'rooted in deep values of the Soviet citizen'.[44]

There was less agreement about the legitimacy of state action in what were regarded as the personal affairs of citizens: matters such as one's movements about the country, religion, political opinions and home life, it was thought, should not normally be of any concern to the government. Outside this sphere, however, most respondents were willing to conceive of a wide ambit for the legitimate exercise of state authority. Despite a readiness to declare themselves in support of civil liberties in the abstract, for instance, fewer than half those interviewed felt that the government had no right to intervene in an assembly when the purpose of that assembly was 'to attack the government', and only about a third of respondents believed that people should be allowed to say things that were 'against the government'. There was also a widespread belief that it should be the function of the government, not simply to attempt to regulate 'anti-social' beliefs and behaviour, but also to exercise an active and improving influence upon the lives of its citizens. The government, for instance, was expected to 'raise the level of the press so that the press will educate the people of the state'; it was expected to undertake the publication of literature designed to reduce the incidence of social ills such as crime and immorality; and it was expected to ensure that basic social values were preserved and that those who offended against them were punished. It was for its failure to direct public opinion towards objectives of which most respondents approved, rather than for its attempt to interfere in what were regarded as essentially private matters, that the Soviet government was most widely condemned in this connection.[45]

Interviews conducted with emigres in more recent years tend again to confirm these impressions. A number of emigres interviewed in Israel by the present author, for instance, were asked to choose between a government which guaranteed personal liberty and permitted criticism of its actions but did not guarantee full employment, and a government which provided work and a decent standard of living for its citizens but did not permit full freedom of speech and belief. Most respondents naturally wanted both if they could; but when forced to choose, they opted virtually without exception for the first option (civil liberties) rather than the second (a guaranteed standard of living). Respondents were also of the opinion that full freedom of criticism should be permitted, extending if necessary to attacks upon the government; and there was near to unanimous agreement, as in the earlier investigation, that the individual's private life must remain inviolate (religion, family affairs and so forth). A number of respondents, however, observed that these predominantly 'liberal' responses would not be typical of the Soviet population as a whole, or even of their own immediate family and friends. Most Soviet people, it was thought, would in fact prefer a greater degree of material well-being to a greater degree of civil liberty; and even well-educated respondents were likely to specify that, while freedom of criticism must of course be permitted, it should not be allowed to extend to denigration and abuse. 'Common sense must be observed', remarked a Minsk psychiatrist; and a Moscow chemical engineer, also in his thirties, insisted that 'proper limits must be observed'. Criticism must be 'courteous and informed, not malicious and insulting'; it should contain a 'positive and constructive programme', not simply abusive slogans such as 'Rabin [the then Israeli PM] is a fool'; and it should not lead to 'anarchy' or 'disorder'.

The same respondent was also of the opinion that the Israeli Communist Party should be banned; and while this view was not widely shared by other interviewees, most of whom were highly educated and to that extent less representative of the Soviet population as a whole, it is reportedly a fairly common sentiment within the emigre community as a whole. Other studies have found, for instance, that recent Soviet immigrants object to pictures of President Sadat of Egypt ('our enemy') appearing on the front page of Israeli newspapers, and that they complain about the pornography and 'too broad' freedom of the press which is permitted in most western countries. Soviet immigrants also question why the Israeli government does not do more to discipline the public behaviour of its population, especially of the younger generation, and why the government does not do more to restrict the activities of left-wing groups in Israel and to limit the sale of Soviet propaganda in Israeli bookshops.[46] Respondents interviewed by the present author in Israel frequently expressed the view that industrial disputes should not be allowed to proceed as far as strike action (this was 'anarchy' or 'sabotage', not the way in which intelligent adults should resolve their differences), and the manner in which the Soviet government resolved matters of this kind found considerable support. 'There is too much criticism here—there things are better', remarked a sixty-year-old pensioner; and a young engineering student went so far as to state: 'Criticism of the government must not be allowed'. Even allowing for the extent to which respondents may have had specifically Israeli circumstances in mind, the broadly authoritarian or at least paternal cast of mind of most respondents—their generally high level of education and overall hostility towards the Soviet system notwithstanding—emerges reasonably clearly. One recent immigrant, asked what was the greatest problem presently facing the USSR, gave a reply which illustrates this point nicely: the greatest problem of this kind, he explained, was the lack of democracy. Asked what could be done about it, he replied: 'The Soviet government should issue a directive to all state institutions and party organizations to introduce democratic procedures immediately'.[47]

Government and Citizens

Most emigres, predictably, are disposed in a hostile (and sometimes in an extremely hostile) manner towards the Soviet government and towards its individual members in particular. Most investigations, however, have found that the political institutions of the Soviet state do not necessarily arouse the same repugnance. In the inquiry conducted by Inkeles and Bauer at the end of the Second World War, for instance, there was strong hostility towards the 'absolutist' character of the political system and towards the 'terror and injustice' associated with the secret police. These two features, however, were generally regarded as abuses or perversions of the Soviet political system, not as vices which were inherent within it; and there was no suggestion that the citizen might best be protected from such abuses by a series of constitutional limitations upon the actions of government such as existed in most liberal democracies. Former Soviet citizens, on the contrary, were generally more concerned with moral justice and the public welfare than with formal procedures of this kind. A government might generally do anything, and be approved for so doing, provided its actions were regarded as in furtherance of the public interest; if a government was acting in a manner which was regarded as harsh, dictatorial and not in accordance with the public interest, on the other hand, then it would in the view of most respondents have lost its right to govern, whatever its constitutional authority to do so.

The Soviet citizen's ideal, it appeared, was a 'paternalistic state with extremely wide powers which it would vigorously exercise to control the nation's destiny, but which yet served the interests of the citizen benignly, which respected his personal dignity and left him with a certain amount of freedom of desire and a feeling of freedom from arbitrary interference and punishment'. For most respondents, if a government were 'good' in this sense—friendly, helpful and nurturant—then political parties and factions had little special place or meaning. It was the abuse of power, rather than the institutions through which that power was exercised, which aroused the greatest hostility. As one respondent put it: 'The system would not have been so bad. It depends on how the system is carried out. It depends on who "is in control".' Hostility against the regime was directed primarily against the top political leaders, over two-thirds of those interviewed believing that they should be put to death if the Soviet government were overthrown; it was directed to a much less extent against the rank and file membership of the party, and it was directed still less against the basic institutional framework of the system, particularly in the case of younger respondents. The main outlines of the system, the investigators concluded, seemed on the contrary to 'enjoy the support of popular consensus'.[48]

Interviews with those who have left the USSR in more recent years tend largely to confirm these impressions. There appears to be virtual unanimity among them, for instance, that the regime is firmly, perhaps even unshakeably, established. A group of emigres recently interviewed by the present author in Israel variously described it as 'unalterable for at least the next twenty or thirty years'; as 'eternal', or at least 'unlikely to change for the foreseeable future'; and as 'one of the most stable regimes in the world'. This was partly to be explained by force and coercion, or the fear that they might be applied (this was the view of two older respondents); and propaganda was also believed to play a role, in combination with a limited knowledge of political alternatives, at least outside the ranks of the intelligentsia. But most respondents felt that other factors were rather more important. Chief among these were the Russian political tradition, with its long history of autocracy and repression (Communism, one Moscow journalist maintained, was 'in his deep conviction, the expression of the national character of the Russian people'); and also of importance was the regime's provision of a modest but nonetheless tolerable and steadily improving standard of living for the mass of its population. Most people, a Leningrad chemical engineer observed, had in fact a vested interest in the preservation of the regime, paradoxical though this might at first sight appear. For industrial workers it provided job security and a guaranteed standard of living for no more than the routine performance of their duties and political passivity; for the political bureaucracy the benefits of maintaining the existing system were obvious enough; and even the intelligentsia enjoyed privileges of a sort, such as access to experimental cinema clubs to which the majority of the population would not be permitted to gain entry. Most people had thus some kind of interest in the preservation of the existing system, much though they might object to many of its individual features.

Another respondent, a Moscow historian in his forties who had enjoyed reasonably close contacts with Soviet workers through his activities in the dissident movement, pointed out that the majority of the people did not in fact suffer from the absence of political freedom in the USSR. The slogan 'The party and the people are united' was, he thought, '90 per cent correct'. This fact was often underestimated in the west, where it was commonly believed that a small clique held power against the wishes of the vast majority of the population. But nothing could be farther from the truth. Pay was sufficient for pressing needs, such as vodka, and many of the regime's policies were in fact quite popular, such as the intervention in Czechoslovakia in 1968 (a point which other respondents independently endorsed) and the Soviet government's pro-Arab stance in the Middle East. It was also suggested that the regime derived a good deal of support and authority from its apparently growing influence in international affairs, and from its firm and decisive domestic leadership compared with the weakness and vacillation of its western counterparts ('The Soviet Union is striding ahead'). No respondent suggested a widespread degree of enthusiastic commitment to the regime (about 10 per cent might be so disposed, according to one estimate, but in most cases this was simply careerism); neither, however, was any respondent prepared to argue that the regime encountered a significant degree of domestic opposition. Most people simply accepted it as 'no worse than others', and believed that 'with some reservations, it could be accepted'.

These more recent emigres, perhaps in part because of their disproportionately well-educated composition, were more convinced than their predecessors that it should be possible to form political parties without interference from the state (although the hope was frequently expressed that this would not lead to the formation of a multiplicity of competing groups, as in Israel, and two respondents, perhaps not coincidentally among the least educated, replied baldly: 'No, there should be only one party'). There was agreement with the earlier investigation, however, that the state should exercise supervision and control over a wide area of national life, from the provision of full employment, housing and welfare to the development of sport, the preservation of social unity and the determination of a single and binding set of national priorities. Many were concerned by the failure of the government in Israel to undertake functions of this kind; and even the excesses of the 1930s in the Soviet Union seemed justified, to some younger respondents, leading as they had done to the development of industry and the survival of the USSR as a state. Not all attributed the excesses of this period to Stalin ('He was advised by fools'); and in any case there 'had to be a master (*khozyain*)', a 'head of the household'. And prices had been low.[49]

Compared with a matched sample of American immigrants, another investigation found, Soviet immigrants in Israel were much more likely to favour a strong leadership and to defer to it, and to conceive of a wide scope for the proper exercise of state authority.

More than two-thirds of the Soviet group, for instance, were willing to agree that 'a few strong leaders can do more for the state than all the discussions and laws' (fewer than half the Americans took this view), and nearly as many agreed with the proposition that 'every person should have faith in some power whose decisions he obeys without question' (this contrasted sharply with the responses of American immigrants, more than three-quarters of whom disagreed). A majority of Soviet respondents also agreed that 'people can be divided into two distinct classes—the weak and the strong', whereas nearly three-quarters of the American respondents disagreed. Compared with the American immigrants, it was found, former Soviet citizens were generally less suspicious of authority and more willing to see the state as legitimately performing a guiding and educational role ('In Israel the government should be more active because the majority of the population are not yet ready for democracy', as one respondent put it). Former Soviet citizens were also more willing to allow 'the government or its bodies' to determine the boundaries within which freedom could legitimately be exercised; Americans, in contrast, placed less trust in government and were more likely to emphasise individual and group initiative.[50] The dissident writer Andrei Amalrik has commented in this connection:

Whether because of historical traditions or some other reason, the idea of self-government, of equality before the law and of personal freedom—and the responsibility that goes with these— are almost completely incomprehensible to the Russian people. Even in the idea of pragmatic freedom, a Russian tends to see not so much the possibility of securing a good life for himself as the danger that some clever fellow will make good at his expense. To the majority of the people the very word 'freedom' is synonymous with 'disorder' or the opportunity to indulge with impunity in some kind of anti-social or dangerous activity. As for respecting the rights of an individual as such, the idea simply arouses bewilderment.[51]

Like Nechvolodov in Solzhenitsyn's *August 1914*, most Russians appear to believe that for Russia the political order is 'not a set of shackles, but a clamp; that it [does] not fetter the country, but [preserves] it from disaster by binding it together'.[52]

Political Trust and Efficacy

It would be surprising if this faith in strong central leadership remained unaffected by the experiences of the Stalin era in the Soviet Union, when so many, at all levels of the society, lost their lives or liberty as a direct result of the actions of the party-state authorities. What the evidence suggests, however, is that it was not Stalin so much as his 'evil subordinates' who were generally held to blame. There is in fact no reason to doubt Stalin's personal responsibility for at least a large proportion of the excesses of these years.[53] Yet even in prison, Evgeniya Ginzburg found, there were many who 'managed strangely to combine a sane judgement of what was going on in the country with a truly mystical personal cult of Stalin'. One prisoner, for instance, condemned to solitary isolation, spent her time composing a poem to 'Stalin, giver of all good'; others, according to Yevgeny Yevtushenko, though tortured close to death, wrote 'Long live Stalin' with their blood on the walls of their prison cells.[54] Victor Fainberg had an uncle who returned from the prison camps in the 1950s with vivid memories of both the abuses to which he had been subjected and the absurdities in sentencing he had encountered (an illiterate peasant from the depths of the Ukraine, for instance, had been put in a camp for 'Zionism and being an English spy'). But 'he led his people like Moses', his uncle had commented about Stalin; 'When you cut wood, the chips must fly'.[55] Many other detainees, according to Solzhenitsyn, spent their time in prison writing countless appeals to Stalin for clemency, and remained convinced that as soon as the facts of the matter reached his attention they would be released. The fact that their appeals had not been answered was explained by the evil machinations of Stalin's subordinates, who must surely have intercepted them; and there was 'real pain' when the news of Stalin's death became known, many believing that their chances of release had now been ended.[56] Years later, Khrushchev recalled, there were still those who were prepared to argue that it 'wasn't God who was guilty but one of his angels', and who attributed the excesses of the period to the 'false reports' with which God had been provided.[57]

Even today, according to other accounts, there is still considerable latent support for Stalin and his firm, decisive style of leadership. The historical record, admittedly, remains shrouded in obscurity, and many young people appear to have only the most approximate idea of what precisely took place during the so-called 'period of the cult of personality'.[58] Even when the full circumstances are known, however, there appear to be many who are prepared to argue that the use of force on such a scale was unpleasant and excessive but nonetheless 'necessary for that time'. A taxi driver in Baku, for instance, told Hedric Smith: 'We love Stalin here. He was a strong boss. With Stalin, people knew where they stood'. A Moscow factory director lamented the loss of the labour discipline which had prevailed at that time; a librarian in Tashkent gave him credit for the entire Russian war effort, and claimed that the mistakes of the period had been made 'in his name by other people'. Ordinary people, Smith found, resented the petty dictation of their immediate superiors, and longed for a stern but just Stalin figure to redress their grievances. People missed the dignity and decorum of the earlier period; they valued the stable, tightly regulated social order with which it had been associated; and there had been great dismay, even panic, when he had died. 'We literally did not know what would happen to the country, how we would survive without Stalin', one intellectual recalled. An elderly writer explained:

They feel that he built the country and he won the war. Now they see disorganisation in agriculture, disorganisation in industry, disorganisation everywhere in the economy and they see no end to it. They are bothered by rising prices. They think that when there was a tough ruler, like Stalin, we did not have such troubles. They forget that things were bad then, too, and they forget the terrible price that we paid.[59]

Yet if a popular veneration of Stalin appears to remain, its converse remains also: a pervasive fear and mistrust, particularly among older people, whose continued existence it would be unwise to minimise. Its dimensions have been most fully explored by Solzhenitsyn. One of the consequences of this period, he has noted, was 'constant fear'. The pattern of arrests and repression had begun earlier than the 1930s, and it continued thereafter. 'Any adult inhabitant of this country, from a collective farmer up to a member of the Politburo, always knew that it would take only one careless word or gesture and he would fly off irrevocably into the abyss'. The fear was not only the fear of arrest; there were other kinds of threats as well, such as purges, inspections, investigations into one's family or social background, and deprivations of work or residence permits. This all-pervasive fear, as Solzhenitsyn has put it, led to a 'correct consciousness of one's own insignificance and the lack of any kind of rights'. The Russian language itself became saturated with expressions which had their meaning only within this special context. Secrecy and distrust replaced the friendship and cordiality of previous years; neighbour informed upon neighbour, husband upon wife, and child upon parent (a child who was murdered by his relatives because he informed upon his parents for attempting to assist the kulaks in the 1930s, Pavlik Morozov, is still a Soviet and Komsomol hero).[60] Many of those who profited from the silences of these years still occupy prominent positions in Soviet social and political life, and the uncovering of their crimes, begun in 1956, has not been allowed to proceed very far. It would not be surprising if the atmosphere of this period, with its characteristic evasions and hypocrisy, continued to influence the texture of Soviet politics for a good many years to come.

Another consequence of these years is likely to persist also: a feeling of powerlessness in relation to the political authorities, combined with a certain ambivalence in popular attitudes towards them. These, of course, are popular attitudes of long standing; but it would be surprising if the experience of Stalinism, in which power was exercised in a manner dictatorial even by the standards of previous Russian history, had not reinforced them further. Most Soviet citizens, for instance, appear to have little faith in their ability to influence government policy. As many as 91.9 per cent, in an investigation conducted among an emigre group in Israel, believed that the average Soviet citizen could exert no significant influence upon the government of any kind; and only 8 per cent, in another such study, regarded the Soviet government as acting in the interests of the mass public, compared with nearly 80 per cent who regarded it as acting in the interests of the party or other 'vested interests'.[61] As many as two-thirds of a group of Soviet emigres in the USA, in another more recent investigation, believed that even individual party members could have no effective influence at all upon its internal workings (among those with higher education there was nearly unanimous agreement—92 per cent—on this point).[62] In most cases, Hedrick Smith found, ordinary Russians would refer to the political authorities as *vlasti*, 'they', and there was rarely any identification with the regime as such or with any of its individual members. Most Russians kept their thoughts to themselves, or within the circle of their family and immediate friends; understandably, perhaps, they refrained from expressing their opinions openly—their political opinions at least—and made no attempt to bring their influence to bear upon the decisions of government.[63]

The result is a certain ambivalence in personality—'Two persons in one body', as a character in a novel by Dudintsev has put it, with 'two sides, the hidden one and the visible one'. It is the 'visible' man, in this metaphor, who repeats the phraseology of the authorities when required and takes part in ritual demonstrations of unity and commitment; the 'hidden' man, on the other hand, retains a set of older and more humanistic values and regards the actions of the 'visible' man with some scepticism. In Alexander Rashin's story 'The Levers', published in 1956, it was the 'visible' members of the collective farm community who took part in a meeting at which the requisite and previously-agreed resolution was passed in an atmosphere of pious rhetoric; but it was the same people who, as 'hidden' men, had been talking shortly before the meeting began in the frankest possible terms about the wretched situation in which the collective farm in reality found itself.[64] It would be wrong to regard the first *persona* as wholly spurious and the second as wholly authentic, or to regard the citizen's commitment to the regime as entirely formal and his real values as entirely at odds with those which the regime seeks to propagate; both *personae* in fact share elements of both spuriousness and authenticity. It would be wrong at the same time, however, to overlook the institutionalised hypocrisy which the Soviet system continues to demand of its citizens if they are to live a normal family and occupational existence within its boundaries, and the ambivalence and 'linguistic dualism' which these pressures impose upon them.[65] It would be presumptuous for an outsider to attempt to characterise these conflicting pressures further; their dimensions may perhaps best be explored in the pages of Soviet literary and philosophical writings, particularly of a *samizdat* or unofficial character.

It is as a blend of conformity and dissent, of genuine commitment to the Soviet system and pride in its achievements combined with considerable cynicism with regard to those presently responsible for its management, then, that the contemporary Soviet political culture may perhaps most aptly be characterised. We shall return to an examination of these themes, particularly as regards the important question of generational differences, in our final chapter. It remains, however, to consider more closely the impact of the regime's programme of specifically Marxist-Leninist socialisation upon the population as a whole, and to examine the social, ethnic and other sub-groups into which, for the purposes of a more detailed analysis, the larger national population must be divided. To these subjects our next two chapters are devoted.

6

The Impact of Marxism–Leninism

The extent of the Soviet government's commitment to the propagation of Marxism–Leninism has not seriously been questioned.[1] The USSR is a state, that is to say, within which the official teachings of Marxism–Leninism are understood to apply to all aspects of the activities of government and citizens, and in which no area of social life, from religion and family life to the use of leisure time and recreation, is regarded as beyond the scope of state action. The theorists of totalitarianism were among the first to draw attention to the 'politicisation of society' which thereby resulted. All totalitarian states, as the most influential of these theories put it, had six common traits or features, the first of which was an 'elaborate ideology, consisting of an official body of doctrine to which everyone in that society is supposed to adhere, at least passively'; an ideology, moreover, which was 'characteristically focused and projected towards a perfect final state of mankind' and based upon a 'radical rejection of the existing society [and the] conquest of the world for the new one'.[2] The Soviet authorities themselves proclaim the 'supreme goal' of the Soviet state to be the 'building of a classless communist society in which there will be public communist self-government', and the Communist Party of the Soviet Union more particularly claims to base itself 'in all its activities' upon the teachings of Marxism–Leninism.[3]

There has been less agreement about the extent to which the doctrine of Marxism–Leninism may be said in fact to influence the making of decisions by the Soviet government, or to imbue the consciousness of the average Soviet citizen. The regime itself certainly claims, as Brezhnev told the XXV Party Congress in 1976, that the long experience of Soviet rule has brought into being a new

'Soviet man' combining 'ideological conviction and enormous human energy, culture, knowledge and the ability to apply them', an 'ardent patriot' and a 'consistent internationalist'; a man who (in the words of a *Pravda* editorial) is 'in a word, always and in all things—a dedicated and active fighter for the party's great cause, for the triumph of communist ideas'.[4] Western scholars have generally been more sceptical, and many have pointed to the difficulty of attempting to assess such claims in the absence of independent evidence which bears directly upon them. Some, however, appear to have been convinced that a significant change in mass political values has indeed occurred. Alfred Meyer, for instance, has argued that 'Soviet citizenship training has succeeded and the basic tenets of the ideology have been internalised'; and Samuel Huntington, more recently, has gone so far as to declare that the Soviet Union is probably the 'most dramatically successful case [which exists] of planned political culture change'.[5]

In the remainder of this chapter it is proposed to examine this question somewhat more closely in the light of a body of little-known (and in some cases unpublished) research which has recently been appearing in the Soviet Union, concerned with the general question of the 'effectiveness of communist propaganda'.[6] The Soviet party authorities, it is perhaps not sufficiently realised, have at least as much reason to wish to find out the results of their massive and expensive propaganda campaign as do political scientists in the west, and since at least the beginning of the 1970s a much greater emphasis has been placed upon discovering the extent to which the party's message has indeed reached the 'hearts and minds' of its audience than upon the crudely quantitative indicators that were thought adequate in the past.[7] Research of this kind, much of it conducted by the Department for the Study of Party Propaganda and Political Information of the Academy of Social Sciences attached to the Central Committee of the CPSU, is the basis for most of what follows in this chapter.[8] It need hardly be repeated that much of the sociological material we shall consider is subject to a variety of methodological and other defects, and that no great weight should be attached to isolated or otherwise implausible findings which derive exclusively from such sources. When the same finding emerges from a number of different investigations, however, and is one which (such as the majority of those reported in this chapter) the party authorities might not ordinarily be expected to favour, it would seem not unreasonable to grant that finding at least a limited measure of validity.[9] We shall look in turn at four main areas of concern: 'mass-agitational work', or the political lectures and talks which are delivered to the mass of the population; the party-sponsored political education system; the lecturers and propagandists themselves; and then finally at such other forms of propaganda as the press, radio and television, and political posters.

Mass-agitational Work: Problems and Achievements

In purely quantitative terms, as we have seen, there can be no doubt of the regime's achievements in mass agitation as in other aspects of its political socialisation programme. The total number of lectures delivered, the size of the audience they have attracted, the knowledge and qualifications of those who have delivered them: all have recorded significant advances over the whole period of Soviet rule, and the proportion of the population presently exposed to such influences is higher than any that has previously been recorded (see pp. 75–83). A closer examination, however, makes it clear that the success of the mass-agitation programme is by no means as impressive as these figures might appear to indicate. The Soviet public, in the first place, appear to attend political lectures in large part simply because they have been obliged to do so. In Taganrog and Saransk, for instance, 35 per cent of those attending political lectures reported that the main reason for their attendance was 'party discipline', 'administrative pressure' or a 'feeling of duty or obligation'.[10] An investigation in the Chelyabinsk region found similarly that 27.8 per cent of those polled reported that they attended political lectures unwillingly; and comparable findings have been reported elsewhere.[11] Indifference and apathy are not, of course, encountered in every instance. In a poll of 3000 workers in the Urals area, for instance, nearly three-quarters (72.2 per cent) reported that they attended their *politinformatsii* 'with enthusiasm'; 64.4 per cent believed that such sessions 'widened their horizons'; 55.7 per cent said that they obtained replies to the questions that most concerned them; and 45 per cent reported that such sessions developed their independence and firmness of judgement.[12]

Political information sessions, however, appear to be consistently more popular than other forms of mass-agitational work, and the evidence does not suggest that agitational talks (*besedy*) or lectures (*lektsii*) are regarded with comparable enthusiasm. In an investigation at a tyre factory in Dnepropetrovsk, for instance, 86.2 per cent of those polled expressed an interest in *politinformatsii* as compared with only 61.8 per cent who expressed an interest in political lectures and 61.2 per cent who expressed an interest in agitational *besedy* (38.8 per cent said that they had no interest whatsoever in such sessions).[13] Another study, conducted at an industrial enterprise in Latvia, found that agitational *besedy* were placed together with political posters and slogans at the bottom of a popularity scale of various forms of ideological work.[14] Party spokesmen have acknowledged that many *besedy* and *politinformatsii* are 'superficial and lacking in content' and that they are 'held irregularly and attended unwillingly';[15] so far, however, no effective solution to this problem appears to have been found.

The subjects on which respondents most often wish to hear lectures again depart fairly markedly from what the party might ordinarily be expected to favour. There appears to be a great deal more interest in current events, for instance, than in questions of Marxist–Leninist theory. An investigation conducted in the town of Taganrog found that 61 per cent of those polled expressed a preference for more lectures of a current or topical character, compared with only 1 per cent who wished to have more lectures of a theoretical character. More than two-thirds (67 per cent) of the town's *Znanie* Society lecturers reported similarly that the questions they were asked were concerned most frequently with current events, compared with only 9 per cent who reported that they more frequently encountered questions of a theoretical character.[16] So far as individual subjects are concerned, again, there appears to be a marked preference for foreign affairs, sport and culture rather than for subjects such as Marxist philosophy and political economy. About 42 per cent of those who attended lectures provided by the *Znanie* Society in the Chelyabinsk region, for example, told investigators that they would like to hear more lectures on the international situation, compared with only 1.3 per cent who expressed an interest in further lectures on Marxist philosophy and 1.8 per cent who wanted more lectures on scientific Communism.[17] The distribution of preferences for individual subjects which was obtained in the Taganrog investigation is set out in Table 6.1. Similar findings have been reported elsewhere; and the general trend, for more lec-

TABLE 6.1   *Preferences in political lectures (percentages)*

	Population as a whole (N: 1020)			Those attending lectures			Those not attending lectures		
	Yes	No	DK	Yes	No	DK	Yes	No	DK
Marxist–Leninist philosophy	37	28	35	45	20	35	17	44	38
Political economy	40	27	31	50	20	30	22	44	34
Scientific Communism	37	26	37	45	19	36	19	41	40
Current international affairs	96	2	2	99	1	0	91	5	4
Current national affairs	95	2	2	96	1	3	92	4	4
Current local affairs	94	2	4	96	1	3	87	5	8

SOURCE   V. S. Korobeinikov (ed.), *Sotsiologicheskie Problemy Obshchestvennogo Mneniya i Sredstv Massovoi Informatsii* (Moscow, 1975) p. 103 (percentages rounded).

tures on current and international affairs rather than on Marxist philosophy and economics, is remarkably consistent.[18] It is perhaps the relative underprovision of such lectures at the expense of more orthodox themes which accounts for the relatively indifferent view most citizens appear to take of them: more than 30 per cent of those polled in the Chelyabinsk region, for instance, were not generally aware of the subject of the lecture to which they were going, and the vast majority (74.3 per cent) made no preparation for it whatsoever.[19]

The content of such lectures, not perhaps surprisingly, has also been giving rise to concern. There are repeated complaints, for instance, that lecturers simply repeat already familiar information, providing little that is fresh or original, and that they fail to relate their material to the particular circumstances of the audience they are addressing.[20] It is a frequent complaint that lecturers simply read out a prepared text, without attempting in any way to attract the attention of the audience to the subject they are discussing;[21] and it has even been known for a lecturer to repeat a simple grammatical error in the text of the lecture he was delivering, making it apparent that he had failed to do so much as glance through it beforehand.[22] Many agitators appear still to limit themselves to the reading aloud of newspaper extracts (a practice which may have had some purpose when the majority of the population was illiterate, it has been pointed out, but which can scarcely be justified in contemporary circumstances);[23] and there are repeated complaints of *politinformatory* who conduct their sessions at a low intellectual level and show little willingness to provide for at least a certain amount of group discussion of the themes they are addressing.[24] Questionnaires on this subject have consistently found a preference for more active forms of political instruction, such as 'evenings of questions and answers', 'thematic evenings', 'round table discussions' and so forth;[25] no more than 1.1 per cent, in an investigation of this subject, stated that they would listen with more attention to a lecturer who simply read out the text in front of him.[26] It is sessions of this kind, however, which appear generally to predominate.

Not all political lectures, admittedly, seem to suffer from these shortcomings. A Moscow teacher wrote to *Pravda*, for instance, to complain that at a political information session in her school a pupil had simply 'given a lively account of recent sporting sensations'. At other such sessions, she had heard, the proceedings were not infrequently given over to 'funny stories from the newspaper humour columns'.[27] In another case, reported recently in *Pravda*, a *politinformator*, sensing that the interest of his audience was beginning to evaporate, produced the following sensational fact which he had clearly reserved for such a contingency: 'King Ibn Saud of Saudi Arabia had a family of about 400', he told his startled audience. 'Besides his four legal wives, he had more than a hundred concubines, by whom he had 107 sons and 189 daughters.' When the party secretary later asked some members of the audience what they had gained from that day's political information session they all told him, laughing, that they had discovered a great deal about the family life of the King of Saudi Arabia. 'Apart from that', the party secretary complained to *Pravda*, 'nothing at all had remained in their memory'.[28] Not many political information sessions appear to be enlivened in this way, however, and complaints of the lecturer's 'lack of novelty', 'superficiality', 'avoidance of awkward questions' and 'monotonous delivery' are much more frequently encountered.[29]

The degree of satisfaction with political lectures and information sessions tends to vary considerably, depending upon which area, audience or type of lecture is considered. A recent large-scale investigation in the Chelyabinsk region, however, found that only 31.1 per cent of those polled were fully satisfied by the *politinformatsii* they attended. A further 47.7 per cent described them as satisfactory, and the remaining 21.2 per cent found them either unsatisfactory or refrained from answering the question.[30] As many as 80 per cent of respondents, in an investigation of *Znanie* Society lectures in Lithuania, complained similarly of their 'insufficiently convincing argumentation', and more than 13 per cent complained of the lecturer's boring or inexpressive delivery (40 per cent of those who organised the lectures, and 25 per cent of the lecturers themselves, shared these doubts as to their adequacy).[31] Comparable results have been obtained elsewhere.[32] From the point of view of the party authorities, moreover, it must be particularly disturbing to find that those with higher levels of education tend to be both more demanding of the political instruction they are offered and more critical of its present provision. A 'significant proportion' of the better educated members of the audience for mass political lectures, it has been found, complain of the lecturer's 'lack of competence', 'poor methodological preparation' and 'unconvincingness', and the level of dissatisfaction tends to increase with the level of education of the respondent concerned.[33] There is general agreement, moreover, that the number of propaganda measures which are undertaken is excessive and to the detriment of their overall quality.[34]

The impact of political talks and lectures is more difficult to assess. The levels of knowledge of those who attend such talks regularly, one important criterion of success, do indeed appear to be higher than the levels of knowledge of those who attend less regularly or not at all. The results obtained in a recent investigation into this matter at an industrial enterprise in the town of Gorky are set out in Table 6.2. The ability to provide satisfactory answers to major questions of current economic and political policy was consistently higher among those who attended *politinformatsii* regularly than among those who did not; and those who attended agitational *besedy* regularly were also better informed than those who did not do so, although the differences of knowledge in this case were less striking.[35] Overall levels of knowledge appear to be a good deal lower when the questions concern matters internal to the enterprise itself, such as plan targets and fulfilment; again, however, it is those who attend *politinformatsii* and *besedy* most regularly who appear to be consistently the best informed about such matters.[36]

Those who attend such sessions regularly are more likely to be better informed in the first place, however, and the evidence does not on the whole suggest that political lectures and information

TABLE 6.2 *Political knowledge and attendance at political information sessions (percentages)*

		Attend regularly	Do not attend
Knowledge of reasons for relaxation in inter- national tensions	Good	43.4	24.6
	Satisfactory	41.2	35.1
	Unsatisfactory	15.4	40.3
Knowledge of main events in development of relaxa- tion of international tensions	Good	49.6	29.8
	Satisfactory	38.1	31.6
	Unsatisfactory	12.3	38.6
Knowledge of means for improving effectiveness of national economy	Good	51.9	24.6
	Satisfactory	32.3	42.1
	Unsatisfactory	15.8	33.3

SOURCE V. G. Baikova, *Ideologicheskaya Rabota KPSS v Usloviakh Razvitogo Sotsializma* (Moscow, 1977) p. 150.

sessions play an important part for many people in increasing their political knowledge and levels of awareness. Only 3.9 per cent of those polled in Taganrog, for instance, indicated that they regularly received political information from the lectures and *politinformatsii* they attended; and no more than 2–6 per cent of those polled, in an investigation at a number of industrial enterprises in central Russia, reported agitational *besedy* as a principal source of information upon political and economic issues.[37] Only 3–5 per cent of those polled in an investigation at a number of collective farms in the Stavropol region, similarly, learned about the economic achievements and shortcomings of their local workgroup from agitators, although this is their primary function; a somewhat greater proportion were informed about such matters by *politinformatory* (5–7 per cent) and visual displays (6–9 per cent), but for most of those polled it was their workmates (30 per cent) and general meetings (50 per cent) which kept them abreast of such questions.[38] Fewer than a quarter of those polled, in a further investigation, were able to remember the subject of the last *politinformatsiya* they had attended and the name of the lecturer; and no more than the same proportion (23 per cent) felt that they would be able to make some practical use of the information they had received.[39] Inquiries elsewhere have found that more than a third of those polled were unable to name the agitator attached to their local workgroup, and that no more than a third of those polled came regularly into contact with him.[40]

The most detailed investigation of the impact of mass-agitational work so far to have been conducted was carried out at an aluminium plant in the Irkutsk region. More than 1900 workers at the plant were asked what effect they thought their involvement in such activity had had upon the 'development of their political and cultural horizons'. Their answers were distributed as follows: 22.5 per cent replied that they listened more frequently to political broadcasts on the radio and television; 21.8 per cent replied that they read more fiction; 17 per cent wished to know more and to be useful to society; 11.2 per cent wished to raise their educational and political level; 11.1 per cent took a more critical view of their colleagues' behaviour, and 9.1 per cent of television and the cinema; 8.6 per cent took a more active part in socio-political life; 5 per cent reported that they felt better equipped to take part in mass-political work; and 4.7 per cent read more socio-political literature. As many as 16.6 per cent, however, replied that their involvement in mass-political work had had no influence at all upon their subsequent behaviour, and about 30 per cent refrained from answering the question altogether.[41] These are scarcely the kind of results which party propagandists could find gratifying.

These, moreover, are the results achieved with those who attend political talks and lectures and fall within the ambit of mass-political work; but not all Soviet citizens do so to the same extent, and the party authorities appear presently to be concerned that a considerable proportion of the population may be wholly or partially outside its influence. In an investigation into attendance at political lectures in the Chelyabinsk region, for instance, it was found that the largest single group of workers (30.9 per cent of the total) had attended between three and five lectures in the previous year; a further 15.8 per cent had attended between six and ten lectures; and 9.6 per cent had attended more than ten lectures over the same period. Nearly a quarter of respondents (24.2 per cent), however, had attended only one or two lectures in the course of the previous year, and more than a fifth (20.4 per cent) had attended none at all.[42] An investigation conducted in a number of industrial enterprises in Tomsk found similarly that 34 per cent of those polled had attended no lectures (*lektsii*) over the three previous months; 40 per cent had attended no *politinformatsii*; and as many as 65 per cent had attended no agitational *besedy*.[43] Anti-religious lectures appear to suffer particularly acutely from this kind of differential turnout; most believers, it appears, avoid such sessions if at all possible, and those who do attend are generally already firmly committed to atheism.[44] Particular problems are also acknowledged to exist with night shifts, enterprises with a low proportion of party members, and with young workers resident in dormitories.[45]

The problem of non-involvement arises most acutely of all, however, in connection with those who live at home and are for one reason or another not members of the working population. In the Chelyabinsk region, for instance, it was found that young people under the age of 16 and those over the age of 50 were effectively outside the influence of mass-political work, and that women were much less likely to attend political lectures than their male counterparts.[46] It was to overcome problems of this kind that mass-political work on a residential basis has been extended, particularly since the late 1960s. The evidence, however, suggests that residential work may be no more successful than agitational work in other areas in achieving its objectives. A relatively small proportion of the local population appear to be embraced by such measures; they tend to be those who are in any case already actively engaged in political work elsewhere; work in this field appears to be given a particularly low priority among all forms of ideological work and is often carried out irregularly or not at all; and it is apparently not very popular with the mass of the population, the vast majority (91.3 per cent in one investigation) preferring political agitation and propaganda to be conducted at their place of employment rather than at their place of residence.[47]

The country population are also less likely to be reached by the oral propaganda network than their urban colleagues. Fewer than half as many, in one investigation, attended political lectures as did so in the main urban centre, and the average state or collective-farm worker was between four and five times less likely to attend a political lecture than an industrial worker from the same region.[48] In a number of less populated areas and districts, it appears, agitational collectives may not exist at all, or else they may spring briefly into existence when particular national campaigns are being mounted and then disappear again; and even in the major urban areas there may be a considerable disproportion in the provision of political lectures between one local neighbourhood and another.[49] The problem of differential saturation has received some attention in the party press, and a Central Committee official with responsibilities in this area has pointed to the danger that the party's propaganda may simply be 'informing the informed and agitating the agitated'.[50] So far, however, no satisfactory solution appears to have been found.

The problems attendant upon mass-agitational work generally were summed up in a Central Committee resolution, 'On raising the role of oral agitation in the fulfilment of the decisions of the XXV Congress of the CPSU', which was published in *Pravda* on 25 February 1977. Notwithstanding the party's successes in this field, the resolution made clear, there were still a number of serious short-comings. The higher levels of awareness and knowledge of the present-day Soviet citizen were not taken sufficiently into account; political information sessions and lectures were still far too often limited to a repetition of well-known facts, avoiding problem areas and providing no answers to the questions that concerned most members of the audience. Agitational work was conducted ir-regularly, leading specialists and managers had been allowed to exclude themselves from such work, and propaganda in residential areas, particularly on an individual basis, had been neglected. More attention should be paid, the resolution continued, to agitational work in remote areas beyond the reach of television, to recently formed and smaller workgroups, to enterprises employing mainly female labour, and to individual work in general, particularly with young people. Many such resolutions have been passed in previous years without any discernible improvement in the overall state of affairs, however, and it must remain to be seen whether this most recent resolution will be able to achieve what its predecessors have so manifestly been unable to accomplish.[51]

The Effects of Party-political Education

A very similar set of problems appears to attend the system of party-political education. Attendance at political education classes, in the first place, does not always appear to be distinguished by a firm commitment to the party's purposes, or indeed to be engaged in willingly at all. This is not always the case: an investigation in

Buryatia, for instance, found that 70.8 per cent of those polled attended their political education classes 'with enthusiasm', and another poll, conducted in the Komi ASSR, found that 61 per cent of respondents were similarly disposed.[52] Indifference and apathy, however, appear to be rather more frequently encountered. In the industrial town of Kamensk in the Rostov region, for instance, 39 per cent of those polled said that they attended political education classes 'because they were obliged to do so'; in Taganrog and Saransk about 20 per cent of those polled replied that they attended such classes because of 'party discipline', 'administrative pressure' or a 'feeling of obligation'; and at a number of industrial enterprises in Moscow, Chita and Polotsk as many as 50.8 per cent of those polled answered similarly that they attended their political education classes 'unwillingly' ('*bez zhelaniya*').[53] Even party members (31.2 per cent in one investigation) appear to be by no means enthusiastic in their attendance; and those with higher education were more than twice as likely to attend reluctantly than those whose education had been less advanced.[54] Lack of enthusiasm, however, is by no means a monopoly of the better educated. In a poll in a Leningrad factory, for instance, no fewer than 75 per cent of respondents declared that they attended political education classes only because they were obliged to do so by party or administrative pressure, and a further 5 per cent reported that they attended simply because they 'did not wish to offend the lecturer' (this interesting finding, not surprisingly, was omitted from the published version of this report).[55]

The classes themselves afford no greater grounds for satisfaction. Many students, in the first place, fail to consult the Marxist classics, or even the party literature that is prescribed for their course. More than two-thirds of those who attended political education classes in Rostov-on-Don, for instance, admitted that they rarely made use of the Marxist–Leninist classics in their studies, and a further 15 per cent confessed that they made no use of them at all.[56] As many as 78 per cent, in an investigation in the town of Kamensk, failed similarly to consult the Marxist classics in preparation for their classes, and more than 15 per cent made no use even of party documents for this purpose.[57] Similar results have been obtained in Khar'kov, Buryatia and elsewhere.[58] Indeed the second most common complaint about political education classes, in another such investigation, was that the lecturer required that the prescribed literature be read and its main points summarised. This accounted for 23.3 per cent of all objections; other complaints concerned the difficult and not always comprehensible material which was considered (26.2 per cent of all responses), and the fact that political studies appeared to be of little or no relevance to one's practical activities (18.7 per cent of all responses).[59] Those with less advanced education were more likely to experience difficulties in their study of the Marxist–Leninist classics; those with a higher education, however, were the most likely to be dissatisfied with their political education classes more generally.[60]

Many students appear in fact to have no great interest in their studies whatsoever. An investigation at an industrial enterprise in Dnepropetrovsk, for instance, found that 22.5 per cent of those polled expressed only a slight interest in their studies and that a further 15.1 per cent had no interest in their studies at all.[61] An investigation in the Tomsk region found similarly that no more than 38 per cent of the students involved had an interest in their studies that could be characterised as 'deep and stable'. The majority (60 per cent) had only an 'unstable and superficial' interest in their studies, and the remainder (2 per cent) were thought to have no interest in their studies whatsoever.[62] A survey conducted in the Tomsk and Mogilev regions found that levels of interest in party-political education depended a great deal upon which level of the party education system was being considered (Table 6.3). At no level, however, was there a degree of interest in political study that could be described as overwhelming; and at three of the four levels

TABLE 6.3   *Interest in party-political study (as assessed by the lecturers concerned, percentages)*

Level	Proportion of all students	Level of interest in studies		
		Deep and stable	Superficial and unstable	Non-existent
Primary	11	56	44	—
Intermediate	53	40	60	—
Higher	25	47	51	2
Komsomol	11	9	80	11

SOURCE   V. G. Baikova (ed.), *Politicheskoe Obrazovanie: Sistema, Metodika, Metodologiya* (Moscow, 1976) p. 224.

considered fewer than half of the students concerned had an interest in their studies which their lecturers could describe as 'deep and stable'. In the Komsomol political education system as many as 91 per cent of students were considered to have only a superficial interest in their studies or no interest at all, and even at the most advanced level of political education, composed for the most part of those proposing subsequently to take up some kind of career in party work, a majority of those enrolled were regarded as having a superficial interest in their studies or no interest whatsoever. Only at the primary level, embracing no more than 11 per cent of the total enrolment, were the majority of students considered to be fully committed to their studies.[63]

The content of political education classes, perhaps not surprisingly, has frequently given rise to complaint. Official theorists admit to two main shortcomings: either a tendency towards 'abstract theorisation cut off from life, from the concrete tasks of communist construction', at one extreme, or else 'unadorned empiricism, fact-mongering, and an underestimation of theory', at the other.[64] There are repeated complaints, for instance, of the 'low ideological and theoretical level' of many classes, of the lecturer's 'oversimplified approach' to many problems and of his failure to link the subject under discussion with the practical tasks facing the local workgroup in question.[65] Some propagandists conduct classes which are frequently cancelled, badly attended, and in which the lectures are simply a 'dry recapitulation of the various chapters of the textbook';[66] others, though ostensibly concerned with questions of Marxist–Leninist theory, in fact spend most of their time discussing current affairs.[67] The composition of study groups is frequently far from uniform in its educational and occupational makeup, and based upon the arbitrary choice of the party secretary in question;[68] and pedagogic methods appear often to leave a great deal to be desired. There are repeated complaints, for instance, of classes which are allowed to become a 'monologue of the propagandist' (about a third of the classes surveyed in the Tomsk and Mogilev regions were of this kind); of lecturers who 'organise' their classes unduly, allowing only a few previously-agreed members to contribute to discussion while the rest look on as passive spectators; and of propagandists who provide little or no fresh information in their lectures and force their students to prepare homework as if they were secondary schoolchildren.[69] A recent Central Committee resolution, 'On the tasks of party study in the light of the decisions of the XXV Congress of the CPSU', has called for greater use to be made of more active methods of study such as seminars and discussion groups, for the strict observance of the principle of the voluntary selection of level and subject of study, and for a greater effort to be made to constitute study groups from members whose educational and occupational backgrounds are broadly similar.[70] The deficiencies indicated have outlived previous resolutions to this effect, however, and it would not be surprising if they did so again.

The practical effect of the programme of party-political education is again somewhat difficult to assess. Those enrolled within the party education system, for instance, do appear to be better informed than their colleagues outside the political education system. The proportion of respondents with a good knowledge of the reasons for the relaxation of international tensions at a number of industrial enterprises in central Russia, in one recent investigation, averaged between 43.9 and 59.7 per cent for those who were attending party education classes, but between 25 and 38.5 per cent for a comparable group of non-students. There were similar differences in knowledge concerning the main differences between the capitalist and socialist ways of life and the main means for improving the effectiveness of the national economy, the proportion of those with a good knowledge ranging from 42.7 to 60.5 per cent in the case of students of the party education system and between 25.1 and 43.2 per cent in the case of non-students.[71] Analogous findings have been reported elsewhere.[72] Those who attended political education classes regularly were also more likely to be engaged in other forms of political propaganda (46.2 per cent of students of political education who were polled in an investigation in the Kalinin region regularly attended political information sessions, for instance, compared with 34.1 per cent of those who were not engaged in party study);[73] and they were more likely to read a newspaper regularly and to follow current events more closely.[74] Inquiries elsewhere have established that students of the party education system are also more likely to consider that they have a good knowledge of political developments and issues both at home and abroad.[75]

There are repeated complaints, however, that political education classes are too remote from daily life, and that students are unable to make practical use of the knowledge they have acquired. No more than 21 per cent of those polled in an investigation of Schools of Communist Labour in Chelyabinsk, for instance, said that they were able to put their knowledge into practical effect; and no more than 31 per cent, in an analogous investigation in Saransk, reported that they were able to make use of the knowledge they had acquired in their daily life and work.[76] Other studies have found that only a minority of students in fact take a more active part in their work and in socio-political life, their declared greater interest in such matters notwithstanding. More than two-thirds of those polled at a number of political schools in Moscow, for instance, reported that their studies had widened their political horizons, and more than half reported an increased interest in political questions; but fewer than a third reported that their political participation had become more active as a result, and no more than a quarter indicated that they spoke more regularly at the meetings they attended.[77] A similar inquiry in a small town in the Moscow region found that about half those polled reported that they had a better understanding of Marxist–Leninist theory as a result of their attendance at political education classes; but only 27 per cent indicated that they had become more active in socio-political life, and only 22 per cent reported that they had become more active at their place of work.[78] An inquiry in the Tomsk region found similarly that 47 per cent of those polled felt that their knowledge of national and international issues had been improved by their attendance at political education classes, and that 37 per cent considered that they had a better understanding of the production tasks of their collective; but only 19 per cent had been encouraged to take a more active part in socio-political life, no more than 9 per cent took a regular part in propaganda work, and as few as 7 per cent indicated that they had been stimulated to take a greater interest in political literature.[79]

Those who attended political education classes were more likely in the first place to be better informed and more interested in socio-political questions than the average, moreover, and it remains to be demonstrated that participation in political study plays a significant part for many students in developing their political knowledge and commitment in line with the party's requirements. Indeed even at the informational level the performance of the political education system appears to leave a great deal to be desired. The opinion of party propagandists as to the knowledge which their students had acquired in an investigation in the Tomsk and Mogilev regions, for instance, is set out in Table 6.4. Relatively satisfactory levels of

TABLE 6.4 *Level of knowledge of students of party-political education (assessment of lecturers, percentages)*

		Level of knowledge			
Level	Proportion of students	Good	Satis-factory	Unsatis-factory	Other
Primary	11	42	18	40	—
Intermediate	53	24	25	46	5
Higher	25	42	28	27	3
Komsomol	11	38	6	49	4

SOURCE V. G. Baikova (ed.), *Politicheskoe Obrazovanie: Sistema, Metodika, Metodologiya* (Moscow, 1976) p. 223 (percentages as in original).

knowledge were reported at the advanced level, 70 per cent of students being regarded by their lecturers as having acquired either a 'good' or a 'satisfactory' level of knowledge; but at the primary level as many as 40 per cent of students were regarded as having acquired an 'unsatisfactory' level of knowledge, and at the intermediate and Komsomol levels these proportions were even higher.[80] In another investigation conducted in the Moscow area more than half (53 per cent) of propagandists who were polled took the view that their students had absorbed the material covered and had not simply memorised it; but 43 per cent took the opposite view, and no more than 8.9 per cent thought that the knowledge their students had absorbed had been converted into firm personal convictions.[81] The higher the level of education and the more advanced the level of study, moreover, the less the students concerned believed that their knowledge of the subjects concerned had been significantly advanced.[82]

Tests of the levels of knowledge attained by students at various levels of the political education system tend largely to bear out these impressions. Investigations in Moscow and Tomsk, for instance, have found that at the end of a year of Marxist–Leninist study about a quarter of those polled were unable to define 'proletariat' or 'productive forces'; almost half were unable to define 'dictatorship of the proletariat'; and over 60 per cent were unable to define 'reformism'. Even lower scores were obtained by students at a School of the Fundamentals of Marxism–Leninism, whose subjects of study include the history of the CPSU and Marxist–Leninist philosophy.

Three-quarters of those polled were unable to distinguish between confiscation of the estates and nationalisation; only 16 per cent were able to distinguish between 'essence' ('*sushchnost*') and 'appearance' ('*yavlenie*'); and as few as 4 per cent were able to apply this distinction to the New Economic Policy period of the 1920s.[83] Even on a more straightforward topic, detente (or the 'relaxation of international tensions'), students were generally little better informed. Nearly 80 per cent of those polled in an investigation in Saransk, for instance, were unable to provide an acceptable answer as to why detente had become possible, and more than half were unaware that it would not lead to relaxation in the ideological as well as in other fields. This is a mistake about as basic as it is possible to make in this connection.[84]

Propagandists and Their Problems

A great deal in a system of this kind will clearly depend upon the attitudes, skills and qualifications of those responsible for conducting party propaganda, whether of a mass-agitational or party-political character. Inquiries have established that the educational level of such personnel, at least, has steadily been rising. Only 14 per cent of party propagandists in Estonia had a higher education in 1957–8, for instance, but 60 per cent had reached this level by 1965–6, and the present figure is reported to approach 80 per cent.[85] At a national level the proportion of party propagandists with a higher education has increased from 79.8 per cent in 1969 to 87.3 per cent in 1975, the latest year for which figures are presently available; and in some republics even higher levels have been recorded.[86] Most party propagandists have already spent some time at their job (an investigation in the Tomsk and Mogilev regions, for instance, found that 31 per cent of those surveyed at the primary level were conducting their classes for the first time, but that only 13 per cent at the intermediate level and 9 per cent at the advanced level were doing so); and a considerable proportion have been able to specialise in a particular field of instruction (in the same investigation between 23 and 28 per cent of propagandists reported that they had been able to specialise in a single subject of instruction, and a further 10–23 per cent reported that they had been able to limit themselves to only two or three such subjects).[87] Courses of retraining for lecturers and propagandists, and the assistance provided to them in terms of teaching materials, visual aids and so forth, have also been improved; and party committees have been given clear instructions to increase the amount and quantity of information they provide to their ideological activists and to devote more attention to this general area of work.[88] The overall position, however, remains far from satisfactory in a number of respects.

The qualifications of party lecturers and propagandists, in the first place, appear to vary a great deal both by the level of work in which they are engaged and by the subject in which they have specialised. About half of the *politinformatory* surveyed in most investigations, for instance, have a higher education (44.6 per cent of those in Estonia did so, according to a recent study, as did 47 per cent of those surveyed in the Stavropol region), and a relatively high proportion tend to be Communist Party members (about 70 per cent and 68 per cent respectively, in the same investigations) and of relatively senior occupational standing (more than half of those surveyed in the Stavropol region were technical and white-collar staff, for instance, and most of the remainder were executive personnel or academics).[89] The educational and occupational background of most *agitatory*, however, appears to be by no means so impressive. Fewer than 30 per cent of those surveyed in the Stavropol region, for instance, had a complete or incomplete higher education, and fewer than half (47 per cent) were Communist Party members.[90] Even lower proportions in both categories have been recorded elsewhere.[91] Other writers have complained that agitational work is not infrequently entrusted to 'unauthoritative, unqualified' people whose performance of their duties leaves a good deal to be desired. Many agitators, it appears, conduct their *besedy* irregularly, neglect individual for collective forms of activity, and fail to set an example in their own place of employment.[92] Even the better-qualified *politinformatory* do not necessarily conduct their work at a level which is beyond criticism: many of them, it appears, conduct their political information sessions irregularly or not at all, and elsewhere their supposed specialisation is either formal or else entirely non-existent.[93] Cases have even been reported in which all members of a workgroup had taken it in turn to give *politinformatsii* to each other, despite the supposed highly qualified nature of such work. Political information sessions of this kind, the journal *Agitator* commented with some asperity, were 'not usually distinguished by their profundity of content'.[94]

Party propagandists and lecturers (*dokladchiki*) are generally somewhat better qualified, and their work does not normally suffer from the kind of deficiencies that apply to the work of *agitatory* and *politinformatory*. Their levels of qualification and ability, however, do appear to vary considerably, depending upon the level and kind of lecturing or party education work being undertaken. A very high proportion of those lecturing on scientific and medical themes for the *Znanie* Society in Latvia, for instance, had a higher education (between 90 and 95 per cent of the total); but on socio-political themes the proportion with a higher education was less than 80 per cent, and on production and military themes, physical culture, agriculture and atheism it was still lower (50–60 per cent). No more than half of the lecturers surveyed, moreover, were lecturing on subjects connected with their own educational or occupational experience.[95] Party propagandists are less likely to suffer from such deficiencies in their educational background; but those who conduct classes at the primary level appear to be less well educated and to have less experience than those who work at more advanced levels.[96] To insist upon relatively high levels of qualification, moreover, has meant in practice that lecturers and propagandists have become composed to a disproportionate extent of academics and technical and white-collar staff, with relatively few young people, industrial workers or collective farmers among them.[97] The result is that in some areas, particularly in the country, there are too few adequately-qualified cadres to draw upon to provide for at least a minimal specialisation in propaganda and lecturing duties.[98]

The most serious problem facing lecturers and propagandists at all levels, however, appears to be the inordinate demands made upon their time by the number and variety of such duties they are called upon to perform. Nearly half the lecturers associated with the *Znanie* Society in the Krasnodar region, for instance, indicated that the main difficulty they encountered in their work was the fact that they had to combine their lecturing duties with three, four, five or more other such assignments.[99] Party propagandists appear even more likely to be overburdened by additional duties of this kind. In an investigation in Tomsk, for instance, only 20 per cent of those polled had no further calls upon their time; the majority (62 per cent) had one or two additional duties, and 18 per cent had three or more such duties to perform. Investigations in Moldavia and Chelyabinsk have found similarly that only about 18 per cent of propagandists had no further party-political duties to perform in addition to their party educational responsibilities.[100] It is this problem, the difficulty of satisfactorily discharging one's political educational duties because of the demands of one's basic employment or other party-political responsibilities, which is consistently cited as the main problem confronting party propagandists in their work.[101] One unfortunate activist wrote to *Pravda* in despair when he was given an eleventh such duty to perform; and cases of this kind, though unusual, do not appear to be exceptional.[102] It is not perhaps surprising that although many of those polled in a survey of propagandists in Belorussia indicated that they carried out their duties willingly, an equal proportion (40 per cent) reported that they did so only as a party obligation.[103]

Not all the additional duties of a propagandist are necessarily related to his main function of political education, moreover, and even the political educational duties which a propagandist has to perform do not always relate closely to his previous qualifications and experience. In the Tomsk and Mogilev regions, for instance, more than half the propagandists polled at the primary level indicated that they had been unable to specialise even to a limited extent in their duties, and at the intermediate and advanced levels an even smaller proportion (33 and 35 per cent respectively) had been able to do so. Many propagandists had in fact taught all the courses on offer at the primary and intermediate levels over the previous nine years.[104] Many propagandists, also, receive training for a subject area in which they are not subsequently engaged and do not in fact propose to engage. Only about a quarter of those who were specialising in philosophy at the Belorussian University of Marxism–Leninism, for instance, had been sent there by their local party committee with a view to their subsequently undertaking propaganda work in this field; and only about a fifth of those enrolled themselves intended to undertake duties of this kind upon their graduation.[105] A considerable proportion of the graduates of such institutions (between a quarter and a third, in various investigations) do not in fact undertake any propaganda work whatsoever upon their graduation;[106] and many others find themselves entrusted with political education duties which bear little relation to their previous area of specialisation. Graduates with a knowledge of scientific Communism or international relations, for instance, are 'frequently' employed in the system of economic education; and historians find themselves briskly 're-qualified' to teach political economy, and then a year or so later to teach philosophy. Such a 'universalisation' of propaganda duties, it has been noted, 'does little to assist propagandists to raise their theoretical level'.[107]

The consequences of this situation, in terms of the classes or lectures that ensue, are as might be expected. Almost three-quarters (74.8 per cent) of the propagandists surveyed in Voronezh, for instance, complained that they did not have enough time to prepare adequately for the classes for which they were responsible.[108] More than a quarter of the *Znanie* lecturers in the Chelyabinsk region, in a further poll, reported that they rarely had time to make use of the library, and 16 per cent had no library of their own to replace it (a small but still remarkable 0.1 per cent did not even bother to order a daily newspaper).[109] A 'good half' of the propagandists surveyed in the Krasnoyarsk region admitted that they only periodically found time to consult primary sources, such as Marxist–Leninist texts and party documents; more than 40 per cent of propagandists, in an investigation in Rostov-on-Don, reported similarly that they did not make use of the Marxist classics in their work, and almost as many (39.5 per cent) admitted to doing so rarely; and more than half (55.1 per cent) of the propagandists surveyed in the Karakalpak ASSR admitted frankly that they used nothing but the textbook in preparation for their classes.[110]

Even more important, from the party's point of view, are the ideological errors in political lectures and classes towards which the heavy burdens on lecturers and propagandists must in part have contributed. Many lectures on the role of the working class, it has been noted, have a 'schematic, declaratory character', and many lectures on international affairs provide no more than a chronological outline of events without attempting to give a Marxist–Leninist analysis of their underlying determinants.[111] Lectures on subjects like the Soviet state and the scientific-technical revolution are discussed without the necessary 'class approach'; the continued leadership of the working class in contemporary Soviet society is sometimes glossed over or minimised; and the development of detente with the USA is sometimes explained as if the imperialist character of American foreign policy had not remained unaltered.[112]

A variety of courses and seminars are available to assist lecturers and propagandists to improve their theoretical and methodological preparedness. There appears to be a good deal of dissatisfaction with such seminars, however, particularly at more advanced levels, and their contribution to the improvement of the political education system is by no means obvious. In an investigation in the Tomsk region, for instance, 85 per cent of the propagandists working at the primary level found the theoretical level of such seminars adequate but only 23 per cent thought their methodological level was sufficient; at the intermediate level 75 per cent of propagandists thought the theoretical level of the seminars was satisfactory but only 33 per cent were satisfied by their methodological level; while at the advanced level still fewer (55 per cent) thought the theoretical level of the seminars was adequate, and only 17 per cent found their methodological level satisfactory.[113] Another investigation, in the Chelyabinsk region, found that only 15.7 per cent of those polled were fully satisfied by the seminars conducted for their benefit; a majority (69 per cent) were only partially satisfied, and the remainder either found them unsatisfactory or refrained from expressing an opinion. Similar findings have been obtained elsewhere.[114] The seminars, it appears, involve those whose levels of education and experience differ widely; they are attended irregularly;[115] and those who do attend frequently find that 'exactly the same lectures are given year after year to exactly the same students'.[116]

Indeed the key problem appears to be that party committees, concerned above all with economic and organisational matters, have simply little time to devote to ideological work and to those responsible for its conduct. Complaints persist of a lack of knowledge of the work of lecturers and propagandists on the part of local party committees;[117] of measures being conducted simply *pro forma*, with the numbers involved exaggerated if necessary;[118] of elaborate proposals for campaigns of political propaganda which are then implemented partially or not at all;[119] and of party committees which fail to keep their ideological activists informed of the progress of their work and which fail to co-ordinate the various sectors of ideological work both with each other and with the party's overall objectives in this area.[120] The Central Committee in its resolution on oral agitation of June 1976 condemned party committees which 'do not regularly instruct their ideological *aktiv*, do not supply it with the necessary guidance, reference material and methodological recommendations, and do not place before them concrete and relevant tasks for the collective, town or district in question', and a number of attempts have been made to put such recommendations into practice by means such as the awarding of merit certificates to the best propagandists and their periodic re-accreditation.[121] Already there are reports of such procedures being regarded as 'short-lived campaigns', however, and in general it does not appear likely that the existing state of affairs will be significantly modified by such resolutions any more than it has been by those which have preceded them.[122]

'Visual Propaganda' and the Press

The situation with regard to two remaining types of propaganda, 'visual agitation' and the press, would appear to be little more satisfactory. 'Visual propaganda'—posters, placards and so forth—is certainly one of the modes of propaganda that is most likely to strike the first-time western visitor to the USSR. Its effect upon the population which is daily exposed to its influence, however, does not seem to be of a comparable order of magnitude. 'Abstract and banal' slogans were still being put up, the head of the Ukrainian party organisation has complained, such as 'Weeds are the enemies of the fields' and 'Harvesting is a serious matter'; they were placed beside safety or fire regulations; they were sometimes out of date by the time they were put up, particularly in more remote areas; and they were rarely changed.[123] An Astrakhan journalist, writing recently in *Pravda*, has pointed out that many of the slogans employed are in any case incomprehensible, at least to the population to whom they are presumably addressed. At a local jam factory, for instance, he had found a slogan declaring: 'Let us produce a *tub* of tomato paste above the plan!' The first worker he had asked, however, had been unable to tell him what a *tub* was, and only later had he established that it in fact referred to a standard unit of 1000 jars. At a local collective farm he had met the even more obscure slogan: 'Let us ideologically guarantee the collection of the harvest!' The slogan, he noted, if it meant anything at all, should presumably have been addressed to the local party committee and farm management rather than to members of the local workforce as a whole.[124] An investigation among industrial workers in Minsk found that between 26 and 30 per cent of those polled were unable to recall any example of propaganda of this kind; another established that only 15–17 per cent of those who walked past a poster paid it any attention; and a third found that only 7 per cent of those polled could recall the content of any of the textual placards they had seen.[125]

The mass media—press, radio and television—are rather more difficult to avoid, and the evidence leaves little doubt that all three are in fact widely available and widely consulted. Studies in the town of Taganrog, for instance, found that 97 per cent of those polled had a radio and that 74 per cent had a television set, and that more than 70 per cent read the newspapers at least three or four times a week.[126] A study in Leningrad found similarly that 93.3 per cent of homes surveyed had a television set and that 99.2 per cent of homes had access to at least a television set or a radio. More than 70 per cent of those polled watched television every day, more than 83 per cent listened to the radio on an average weekday, and 74.9 per cent read the newspapers every day (a further 19.1 per cent read them several times a week).[127] The newspaper appears normally to be preferred as a source of political information, followed by radio and then television; in the country, however, where national and even local newspapers are often late in arriving, it is radio which is most frequently regarded as the best source of such information.[128] Country residents are also less likely to possess a television set or to read books and newspapers, at least on socio-political themes. A variety of investigations have established, however, that even in relatively remote areas at least half the local population are likely to read a newspaper regularly and nearly a quarter to watch television, and younger people and the better educated—an increasing proportion of the total population—are likely to read the newspaper and watch television more regularly than the local population as a whole.[129] In general there appears to be no reason to doubt that the mass media do in fact carry the party's message into the vast majority of Soviet homes, and with the extension of the radio and television networks to the more outlying points of the USSR this proportion is bound to increase still further.

This is not to suggest, however, that the mass media are necessarily successful in propagating the world-view which the Soviet authorities would presumably wish them to propagate. There appears to be a good deal less interest, in the first place, in ideological and economic matters than in international affairs, culture, morality and sport. A study in the Sverdlovsk and Chelyabinsk regions, for instance, found that 19.6 per cent of workers who were polled regularly watched programmes on economic matters and that 29.5 per cent watched programmes on socio-political themes; 53.6 per cent, however, regularly watched sports programmes, and 85.2 per cent regularly watched feature films.[130] Comparable conclusions emerge from a study conducted in Leningrad, the most detailed investigation on the subject that appears so far to have been conducted. Feature films were again the most popular kind of viewing, followed by documentaries and variety programmes (91.5, 85 and 84 per cent respectively of regular viewers liked most of all to watch such programmes); economic and political themes, however, were again the least popular, and only 4 per cent of regular viewers opted for more programmes on economic matters, the least popular of all the twenty-seven types of programme considered. More than 70 per cent of respondents said that they regarded television as a 'means of entertainment, rest and relaxation'; more than 41 per cent said that too few entertainment programmes were shown, and 48 per cent believed that their quality should be improved. It was the better educated, moreover, who were generally the most critical of the existing range of programmes and the most insistent in their preference for more programmes of a non-political character.[131] The same conclusions emerge, substantially without variation, from such other studies of this matter as have been conducted.[132]

Newspaper readers tend generally to display a similar pattern of preferences to their television-watching counterparts, with party-political and economic subjects almost invariably less popular than international, cultural and moral themes. A detailed survey of the readership of *Pravda* and *Izvestiya*, for instance, found that the most frequently-consulted categories of material were international events (74 per cent in *Pravda* and 69 per cent in *Izvestiya*), moral themes (75 per cent in *Izvestiya* and 57 per cent in *Pravda*), official communications (81 per cent in *Pravda*), 'surprising stories' (71 per cent of *Izvestiya*'s readers), and satirical articles (64 per cent in *Izvestiya* and 57 per cent in *Pravda*). Only 30 per cent of *Izvestiya*'s readers were interested in its editorials, however; 23 per cent read its articles on economics; and only 18 and 17 per cent respectively read its articles on propaganda themes or on the work of the Soviets.[133] The same preferences emerge from a variety of other investigations, as Table 6.5 makes clear. No more than 27 per cent of the readers of *Trud*, the trade union paper, for instance, bothered to read its lead-

TABLE 6.5 *Preferences of newspaper readers (percentage expressing an interest in each category)*

	Pravda 1968–9	Trud 1967	Izvestiya 1967–8	Literatur-naya Gazeta 1968–9	Pravda Buryatii 1970	Za Kom-munizm 1971
International situation	64	52	67	42	88	48
Economy	21	28	24	23	31	29
Science and technology	25	42	48	42	65	n.d.
Satire, humour	57	74	60	72	67	75

SOURCE *Sotsiologicheskie Issledovaniya*, no. 3 (1975) p. 59.

ing article, and no more than 29.7 per cent of the readers of *Pravda Buryatii*, the main daily paper of the Buryat ASSR, did likewise.[134]

The Soviet reader, moreover, tends generally to take a somewhat sceptical view even of those parts of his daily paper which he does in fact consult. Interviews with emigres, for instance, have established that the Soviet media are generally regarded as unreliable in factual matters and interpretation, and there appears to be a greater degree of reliance upon word-of-mouth communication and even rumour than would be the case in most western countries.[135] The same impression emerges, albeit in a more oblique manner, from investigations that have been conducted within the USSR itself. *Izvestiya* readers, for instance, were asked if there had been cases in which they had disagreed with the newspaper on a matter of fact. About a quarter of respondents said that there had not been any such cases, 12 per cent said that they had sometimes occurred, and the remainder (63 per cent) refused to answer the question. Those who were more likely to disagree with the newspaper were drawn disproportionately from those with higher education (the least well educated were also sceptical), from those who read the newspaper the most regularly, and from those in better paid and more skilled occupations.[136]

It is of considerable importance to note, further, that the Soviet media now have matters by no means to themselves so far as the presentation and dissemination of information is concerned. The jamming of western radio broadcasts to the USSR, for instance, was ended in 1973, and British, American and other foreign services can now be received in most parts of the USSR without serious difficulty. Television viewers in the Baltic area have access to Finnish programmes as well as to Soviet-produced ones, and a number of nationalities in the peripheral areas of the USSR can in addition receive broadcasts in their national languages from the states adjacent to them beyond the Soviet border.[137] It has been estimated that the total audience for foreign broadcasts in the USSR is now approximately 60 million, a relatively high proportion of the total population, and clearly a still higher proportion of the urban adult population of European Russia must fall within the regular reception area.[138]

In such areas, indeed, foreign radio and television may well be among the most important sources of political news and information for many people, particularly for foreign news and for developments to which the Soviet media have not themselves yet had time to react. About 6 per cent of those who were polled in an investigation in Moscow, for instance, quoted foreign radio as one of their principal sources of political information; among those who were allowed to complete their questionnaires anonymously, however, almost three times as many (17 per cent) quoted this source as among their most important.[139] A study of television viewing habits in Tallin, the capital of Estonia, found similarly that most viewers turned first to foreign (in this case Finnish) television when they wanted political news and commentary, then to the Estonian television service, and only thirdly to the Russian-language national television service. Those who had a higher education were again the most likely to seek out foreign rather than domestic sources of information on such matters.[140]

It would be wrong to suggest that censorship and information control have become a thing of the past, or that they have altogether lost their efficacy. Controls upon access to and the dissemination of information clearly remain much more restrictive than in most liberal democracies, and a number of relatively crude misrepresentations of western politics and society have probably remained more or less unchallenged, at least so far as the broad mass of the population are concerned. The greater availability of western broadcasts and information services, however, combined with the greatly increased intercourse between the USSR and the west in terms of tourism, commerce, journalism and so forth, have made an alternative and competing version of social reality more widely available to Soviet citizens than perhaps at any time since the foundation of the state itself in 1917 (see pp. 82–3). It would not be surprising if such developments, buttressed as they are by international agreements such as that concluded at Helsinki and by the USSR's continued need of a variety of economic services from its major western neighbours, increased still further the already difficult problems faced by those responsible for the conduct of political propaganda in the USSR by means of the mass media as well as by the variety of other means we have considered in this chapter.

To what extent this whole programme of socialisation may be termed a 'study in failure' must obviously remain a matter of judgement.[141] There is certainly a danger in judging the performance of the Soviet propaganda agencies by altogether unrealistic criteria. Relatively large numbers of citizens in most liberal democracies, for instance, have no clear conception of what is meant by the word 'democracy', are poorly informed about the working of the political system and have little knowledge of political developments both at home and abroad, and yet we do not normally regard this as evidence of 'failure' on the part of the western governments concerned.[142] There is equally a long-standing tradition for Soviet official spokesmen, in ideological as in other matters, to devote at least a part of their speeches and writings to 'shortcomings' and 'unsolved problems', yet without providing any indication of the extent to which the 'problems' and 'shortcomings' they quote may be typical of the overall situation to which they are referring. We would be unwise to assume that all the 'shortcomings' are genuine, but that all the much-trumpeted 'achievements' are false; clearly both will be true, at least to some extent, and the relative proportions of both must in every case be a matter for the most careful individual judgement. An element of bureaucratic self-interest may also be involved: a large and well-staffed apparatus of propaganda and agitation is now in existence, and it would be surprising if it did not attempt to find reasons for its continued existence in terms of a variety of 'threats' and 'dangers' of greatly varying degrees of seriousness. Organisations elsewhere, at least, have been known to defend their position in such a fashion.[143]

It does, however, at least seem clear that the Soviet authorities have failed to bring about that total transformation of sociopolitical values to which (unlike western governments) they have for more than two generations been committed; and so far as one can judge from the increasing number of resolutions and decrees to this effect, there is presently a real measure of anxiety at the level of the political leadership about both the performance of the apparatus of political agitation and propaganda and the purposes it is meant to serve. It would also seem—although it is more difficult to justify such a conclusion on the evidence presented in this chapter—that the Soviet authorities have so far failed to bring about a commitment to Marxist–Leninist values among their population which would be sufficient in itself to legitimate their rule, whatever its constitutional standing, economic performance and so forth. We shall return to the implications of this point, particularly so far as the generational composition of Soviet political opinion is concerned, in our final chapter. First, however, we must examine more closely the ethnic and other political sub-cultures of which the larger national political culture is constituted.

7

Political Culture and Political Sub-cultures

A political culture, as we noted at the outset of this study (see pp. 14–15), may be divided for analytical purposes into a number of distinct or overlapping political sub-cultures. Useful though it may be to speak of a national political culture, the level at which we have so far operated, it may at times be a loose or even entirely notional unit of analysis; other beliefs and values, other foci of identification and loyalty, may compete with and sometimes replace those associated with the national territorial unit as a whole. It may be helpful to regard such political sub-cultures as either 'vertical' or 'horizontal' in nature. A 'vertical' political sub-culture may be defined as one which relates to the shared social or demographic attributes of its members; the distinction between the 'mass' political culture and the 'elite' political culture of the political decision-makers and their associates, for instance, is of this nature. A political culture, however, is capable of further sub-division upon this basis: particular occupations or roles may generate a variety of associated beliefs and forms of behaviour; different generational groups may share assumptions and behavioural patterns which mark them off from the rest of the population; and perhaps most important, social groups or classes may have similar and distinctive life experiences such as to cause their patterns of political belief and behaviour to diverge significantly from the national norm. It is with the last of these sub-divisions, the differentiation of political belief and behaviour associated with particular educational or occupational backgrounds, that we shall be primarily concerned in this chapter.

Important though such divisions may be, however, they may at times be modified or even displaced by attachments which are 'horizontal' or area-based in character, and these must also be given due consideration. There is certainly no lack of internal divisions of this kind within the USSR: of regional or local differences, for instance, or of historic rivalries between major cities such as Moscow and Leningrad.[1] By far the most important of such sub-divisions, however, are those associated with national or ethnic groups within the USSR, and it is these with which we shall be mainly concerned in this chapter. The majority Russian population is not an amalgam of immigrant groups, like the population of the USA, and it has enjoyed a long period of independent statehood within its traditional national frontiers, unlike, for instance, the populations of Italy and Germany. The identification of most Russians with the territorial unit within which they reside, accordingly, does not generally appear to be in question.[2] Other national groups within the USSR have had periods of independent rule and have languages and cultures of their own, however, and it is clear that in many cases such differences may constitute foci of identification which conflict with or altogether supersede those which relate to the national territorial unit as a whole. It is to the most important of this group of political sub-cultures, the nationalities, that we turn at the outset.

'Horizontal' Political Sub-cultures: the Nationalities

There can clearly be no place in a volume of this kind for an exhaustive general discussion of the Soviet nationalities question as a whole.[3] The main dimensions of the USSR's existence as a multinational state, however, should at least be apparent from Table 7.1. Altogether, according to the 1970 census, there were more than 100 different nationalities within the USSR, and the Russians, although the most numerous, accounted for only just over half of the total, a proportion which has been tending gradually to decline over the years. The USSR is in fact the only major power in which the dominant nationality accounts for barely a majority of the total population; and with the continued more rapid growth of the non-Russian and especially of the Muslim nationalities of the USSR, which already account for almost a fifth of the total Soviet population, the time is not too far distant when Russians may find themselves a minority within the state to which they have given their language and their leadership. The implications of this fact are sufficient to make population policy—family size, regional distribu-

TABLE 1.1 *Major Soviet nationalities, 1970 census*

Nationality	Population in 1970 (millions)	Percentage of USSR total	Linguistic group	Percentage habitually speaking native language		Traditional religion
				1959	1970	
Russians	129.0	53.4	East Slavic	99.8	99.8	Orthodox
Ukrainians	40.8	16.9	East Slavic	87.7	85.7	Orthodox
Uzbeks	9.2	3.8	Turkic	98.4	98.6	Moslem
Belorussians	9.1	3.7	East Slavic	84.2	80.6	Orthodox
Tatars	5.9	2.5	Turkic	92.1	89.2	Moslem
Kazakhs	5.3	2.2	Turkic	98.4	98.0	Moslem
Azerbaidzhanis	4.4	1.8	Turkic	97.6	98.2	Moslem
Armenians	3.6	1.5	Indo-European	89.9	91.4	Gregorian
Georgians	3.2	1.3	Japhetic	98.6	98.4	Orthodox
Moldavians	2.7	1.1	Romance	95.2	95.0	Orthodox
Lithuanians	2.7	1.1	Baltic	97.8	97.9	Roman Catholic
Jews	2.2	0.9	Germanic	21.5	17.7	Jewish
Tadzhiks	2.1	0.9	Iranian	98.1	98.5	Moslem
Germans	1.8	0.3	Germanic	75.0	66.8	Protestant
Chuvash	1.7	0.7	Various	90.8	86.9	Orthodox
Turkmenians	1.5	0.5	Turkic	98.9	98.9	Moslem
Kirgiz	1.4	0.6	Turkic	98.7	98.9	Moslem
Latvians	1.4	0.6	Baltic	95.1	95.2	Protestant
Mordvinans	1.3	0.5	Finno-Ugrian	78.1	77.8	Orthodox
Bashkir	1.2	0.5	Turkic	61.9	66.2	Moslem
Poles	1.2	0.5	East Slavic	45.2	32.5	Roman Catholic
Estonians	1.0	0.4	Baltic	95.2	95.5	Protestant

SOURCE *Itogi Vsesoyuznoi Perepisi Naseleniya 1970 goda*, tom 4 (Moscow, 1973) pp. 9–11.

tion and so forth—one of the most sensitive areas of Soviet political life generally.[4]

Nationality differences within the USSR have more than a purely ethnic, and in some cases an administrative, significance; many minority nationalities have a language, culture and level of socio-economic development which differentiates them sharply from the Russian-speaking majority, and the historical experience of many nationalities has also been very different from that of the Russians, who, since at least medieval times, have exercised the dominant influence upon the affairs of state. Russia proper, for instance, has been under continuous Soviet rule for more than sixty years, and its inherited political culture was of the centralised, relatively repressive character outlined above (Chapter 2). The Baltic nations, however, have had a very different political experience under German, Polish and Swedish as well as Russian control; their forms of government were generally of a more representative or 'western' character, serfdom was abolished relatively early, the bulk of the population adhered to the Protestant or Roman Catholic faiths rather than to Orthodoxy, and levels of social and economic development were generally far in advance of those of Russia proper up to the time of the incorporation of these republics into the USSR in 1940.[5] Moldavia was incorporated into the USSR in the same year; the bulk of its population is ethnically Rumanian and cultural affinities with neighbouring Rumania, of which most of the republic previously formed part, are still very strong.[6] Parts of the Ukraine have similarly come at various times under foreign control, and the whole of the republic, together with many other parts of the USSR, was under Nazi occupation and thus effectively beyond the control of the Soviet government for most of the Second World War. Although a Slavic nation and predominantly Orthodox, the Ukraine contains a substantial Roman Catholic (Uniate) minority which is opposed to the majority faith, and there are historic animosities between the two peoples which the passage of time appears to have done little to alleviate.[7]

The cultural disparities between minority nationalities and the rest of the USSR are perhaps most striking of all in the case of the traditionally Muslim republics of Central Asia. With regard to religion, for instance, it is clear that levels of observance (if not necessarily of belief) are considerably higher in these republics than is generally the case elsewhere. Up to 34 per cent of senior school pupils in Uzbekistan and up to 40 per cent in Tadzhikistan, it was found, thought it entirely proper to celebrate the Muslim feast of Kurban Bairam, and traditional customs such as the payment of bride-money (*kalym*), the postponement of co-habitation (*kaitarma*) and childhood betrothals continue to be practised.[8] Other traditional usages such as pilgrimages, fasting and the avoidance of 'unclean' meat have also persisted, and traditional Muslim law (the *Shariat*) continues to enjoy a good deal of influence.[9] There have been repeated complaints about the 'liberalism' of some party committees in dealing with these practices, and local party officials have indeed been known to take part themselves in such ceremonies on the grounds that they represent an expression of national tradition as much as of religious conviction (some have even described themselves as 'non-believing Muslims').[10] What official ideologists call a 'private-property mentality' has also survived relatively unscathed in these republics and in the Caucasian republics of Georgia and Armenia, whose people enjoyed long periods of independent statehood before their incorporation into the USSR and have since retained a lively sense of national distinctiveness.[11]

Soviet official spokesmen have generally argued that, considerable though such differences may presently be, they will diminish and ultimately disappear as social and economic standards throughout the USSR improve and become more uniform. There is certainly a good deal of evidence to suggest that developments of this kind are taking place (Table 7.2). The Soviet Union has become a more industrialised society; an increasing proportion of its population live in cities and are members of the industrial labour force; illiteracy has virtually been eliminated, and educational standards have risen greatly, particularly among the formerly more backward nations. A knowledge of the Russian language has become more widespread (more than three-quarters of the Soviet population were fluent in Russian, according to the 1970 census); and the circulation of printed matter, an increasing proportion of it in the Russian language, has increased greatly and become more evenly distributed between one union republic and another.[12] Membership of the Communist Party has also increased and become more uniform between one nationality and another.[13] The CPSU Central Committee, reviewing these developments, has gone so far as to declare that a 'new historical collectivity of people—the Soviet people' has now come into existence in the USSR, based upon the

TABLE 7.2   *Union Republics—some indices of development*

Union Republic	Industrial production (1913 : 100)		Urban population (percentage of total)			Literacy (percentage of population aged 9–49)			Newspapers (daily circulation per 100 population)	
	1940	1977	1913	1940	1977	1897	1939	1970	1940	1976
RSFSR	8.7	145	17	34	69	29.6	89.7	99.7	23	84
Ukraine	7.3	94	19	34	61	27.9	88.2	99.8	17	49
Uzbekistan	4.7	67	24	25	39	3.6	78.7	99.7	13	31
Belorussia	8.1	188	14	21	53	32.0	80.8	99.8	12	50
Kazakhstan	7.8	227	10	30	54	8.1	83.6	99.7	16	36
Azerbaidzhan	5.9	57	24	37	52	9.2	82.8	99.6	19	47
Armenia	8.7	307	10	28	64	9.2	83.9	99.8	18	52
Georgia	10	134	26	31	51	23.6	89.3	99.9	20	64
Moldavia	3.8	258	13	13	38	22.2	45.9	99.5	2	49
Lithuania	2.6	133	13	23	58	54.2	76.7	99.7	10	62
Tadzhikistan	8.8	131	9	19	36	2.3	82.8	99.6	18	33
Turkmenia	6.7	73	11	35	48	7.8	77.7	99.7	19	29
Kirgizia	9.9	316	12	22	39	3.1	79.8	99.7	12	35
Latvia	0.9	38	38	35	67	79.7	92.7	99.8	21	58
Estonia	1.3	54	19	34	69	96.2	98.6	99.8	18	81
USSR as a whole	7.7	145	18	33	62	28.4	87.4	99.7	20	66

SOURCES   *Narodnoe Khozyaistvo SSSR za 60 Let. Yubileinyi statisticheskii ezhegodnik* (Moscow, 1977) pp. 44 and 176; *Itogi Vsesoyuznoi Perepisi Naseleniya 1970 goda*, tom 3 (Moscow, 1972) pp. 570–1; *Pechat' SSSR v 1976g* (Moscow, 1977) pp. 178–80.

'common ownership of the means of production, unity of economic, socio-political and cultural life, Marxist–Leninist ideology, and the interests and communist ideals of the working class'. The present party Programme provides that this process should continue until ultimately the 'complete unity' of the Soviet people is achieved.[14]

There is certainly a good deal of evidence that might be produced in support of such assertions. The investigation conducted by Inkeles and Bauer among Soviet emigres in the 1950s, for instance, found that the nationality of most respondents had less influence upon their political beliefs and values than did other variables such as their social class and education. Nationality as such played little part in most respondents' educational life-chances or expectations; and educational attainment in turn was far more important than nationality as a determinant of occupational position, although Russians did enjoy some advantage in applying for minor bureaucratic positions because of their better knowledge of the language in which most state administration was conducted. There were relatively few differences between the Russians and Ukrainians who were surveyed in terms of their attitudes towards the welfare state and the proper limits for government action, and relatively few Ukrainians cited nationality policy as an aspect of the system which they would like to change compared with the very large numbers who, like their Russian counterparts, were in favour of the abolition of the collective farm system and the ending of police terror. Younger respondents, moreover, tended on the whole to take a more favourable view of the regime's nationality policy and to manifest less hostility towards Russians than did their elders, particularly if they were better educated. Overall class was a better predictor of political beliefs and values than nationality among all the national groups surveyed: a conclusion which might be seen as an endorsement of the present government's nationality policy, based as it is upon the raising and gradual equalisation of educational and occupational standards throughout the USSR.[15]

A variety of investigations within the USSR itself provide further evidence that Soviet nationalities policy may be achieving at least some of its objectives. Attitudes towards marriage with a member of a different nationality, for instance, appear to be more favourable among the urban than among the rural population, and they appear to be more favourable also among the increasing members of better-educated citizens than among those whose education is less advanced. The better educated appear in turn more likely to know Russian and to have a marriage partner and friends drawn from a nationality other than their own.[16] A detailed investigation into matters of this kind was conducted in the Tatar ASSR, whose social and demographic characteristics were found to be reasonably representative of the Soviet population as a whole. Russians and Tatars, it was found, were distributed in a broadly similar manner in the occupational hierarchy, received approximately the same remuneration, and were active in socio-political life in virtually the same proportions. Nationality as such was found to have little bearing upon patterns of friendship, reading of newspapers, watching of television, or attendance at theatres or concerts. There were slight differences between Russians and Tatars in levels of religious observance and average size of family; but these were more or less accounted for by differences in the age structures of the two groups. Education, moreover, was tending to reduce such differences as remained; the proportion of children receiving their education through Russian was steadily increasing (although it still fell short of the demand for educational provision of this kind), and Russian-speaking Tatars were found in turn to be more favourably disposed towards inter-nationality contact in their home and place of work and more likely to have friends of a different nationality than their Tatar-speaking counterparts. Those with a knowledge of Russian were also more likely to be better educated, and this was also likely to predispose towards an absence of inter-nationality hostility.[17]

Similar trends have been identified in investigations elsewhere. In the Baltic republics, for instance, between 27.3 and 45.3 per cent of the titular nationalities concerned reported in 1970 that they had a fluent knowledge of Russian, a proportion which has increased considerably since 1959, and the number of nationally mixed marriages has also been increasing, particularly in the larger cities.[18] A higher proportion of Belorussians are similarly residing in towns, conversing in Russian and marrying members of nationalities other than their own; the continued existence of the Belorussians as a distinct national entity, indeed, appears to be by no means certain.[19] The development of nationally mixed marriages and of a knowledge of the Russian language for each union republic are shown in Table 7.3; they make clear that, in these respects at least, the process of national integration has been advancing steadily among virtually all nationalities in the direction which the Soviet authorities would

TABLE 7.3   *Union Republics—some indices of assimilation*

Union Republic	Families of mixed nationality (per cent)		Knowledge of Russian (per cent)	Titular nationality as percentage of population		Russians as percentage of population	
	1959	*1970*	*1970*	*1959*	*1970*	*1959*	*1970*
RSFSR	8.3	10.7	96.2	83.3	82.2	83.3	82.2
Ukraine	15.0	19.7	56.7	76.8	74.9	16.9	19.4
Uzbekistan	8.2	10.9	30.3	61.1	64.7	13.5	12.5
Belorussia	11.0	16.6	66.6	81.1	81.1	8.2	10.4
Kazakhstan	14.4	20.6	77.1	29.8	32.4	43.2	42.8
Azerbaidzhan	7.1	7.8	29.2	67.5	73.8	13.6	10.0
Armenia	3.2	3.7	24.6	88.0	88.6	3.2	2.7
Georgia	9.0	10.0	32.6	64.3	66.8	10.1	8.5
Moldavia	13.5	17.9	50.6	65.4	64.6	10.2	11.6
Lithuania	5.9	9.6	43.9	79.3	80.1	8.5	8.6
Tadzhikistan	9.4	13.2	30.9	53.1	56.2	13.3	11.9
Turkmenia	8.5	12.1	33.3	60.9	65.6	17.3	16.5
Kirgizia	12.3	14.9	52.5	40.5	43.8	30.2	29.2
Latvia	15.8	21.0	66.9	62.0	56.8	26.6	29.8
Estonia	10.0	13.6	49.7	74.6	68.2	20.1	24.7
USSR as a whole	10.2	13.5	76.0	—	—	54.6	53.4

SOURCES   V. I. Kozlov, *Natsional'nosti SSSR* (Moscow, 1975) pp. 235 and 246; *Itogi Vsesoyuznoi Perepisi Naseleniya 1970 goda*, tom 4, *passim*.

appear to favour. A number of nationalities, indeed, have altogether disappeared (or become fully assimilated) over the period of Soviet rule: the census of 1926 recorded the existence of 194 ethnic groups but the census of 1959 recorded only 109 and the census of 1970 just over 100, an indication of the direction in which present policies would appear ultimately to be tending.[20]

The overall picture, however, is by no means as clear-cut as the evidence so far considered might appear to indicate. Levels of inter-marriage, in the first place, vary considerably from republic to republic and from nationality to nationality; and although the pro-portion of nationally mixed families at the national and republican levels may have been increasing, it by no means follows that the level of intermarriage between each of the major nationalities con-cerned has been increasing at a similar rate. The main increase in nationally mixed marriages appears in fact to have occurred among the western or Slavic nationalities of the USSR, and to some extent also between Slavs and Balts; intermarriage between the other major nationalities of the USSR, in particular between Slavs and Muslims, is much less common and provides rather less compelling evidence of the formation of a single 'Soviet nation'. It has indeed been reported that of the nationally mixed marriages contracted in Turk-menia over the past fifty years, not a single one has been between a Turkmen girl and a Russian man. Marriages between Muslim men and non-Muslim women, although not specifically prohibited by Islamic law, are also relatively uncommon.[21]

A greater knowledge of the Russian language, moreover, by no means necessarily implies a weaker attachment to the native langu-age of the nationality in question. Russian has indeed become more widely known; it serves as the language of administration and inter-nationality communication as well as a means of education and career advancement. Most Soviet citizens, however, appear to have remained loyal to their native language in their domestic and family life,[22] and there has been little sign of the disappearance of at least the major Soviet national languages, most of which are still spoken by 90 per cent or more of the population in question and some of which have in fact increased their influence during the Soviet period.[23] The Central Asian nationalities, again, appear to be the most resistant to Russification in this respect: no more than 1.1 per cent of any of the five nationalities involved claimed Russian as a native language in the 1970 census, a much lower proportion than for the non-Russian population as a whole, and levels of fluency in Russian were also much lower than among minority nationalities elsewhere in the USSR. Changes in the degree of attachment of the major Muslim nationalities to their native languages have in fact been 'negligible' over the whole Soviet period.[24]

The gradual assimilation of minority nationalities, moreover, has in practice operated less to the advantage of the Russian population as such than to the advantage of the larger nationalities as a whole, Russians among them, into which the smaller nationalities have been assimilated. The evidence deployed in Table 7.3, for instance, shows that the proportion of the population of most union republics belonging to the titular nationality has in fact been increasing, and that of the Russians decreasing, over the last inter-censal period. The major Soviet nationalities, that is to say, have been gaining strength and increasing their territorial preponderance, while the smaller nationalities have been losing it, over the period we have been considering. The consequence is that, so far from national differences losing their significance, they are now perhaps more sharply marked and more firmly based territorially than ever before.[25] There is also a good deal of evidence that the cultural self-consciousness of the minority nationalities has not been adversely affected by their increasing urbanisation, industrialisation and ability to use the Russian language. The circulation of native-language but not Russian-language newspapers has been increasing since 1960 among the Muslim nationalities of Central Asia, for instance; the local languages are being purged of the Russian loan words which were imported during the 1930s and 1940s; and the indigenous intelligentsia have shown little tendency to disown or minimise their national identity.[26] The vigour and assertiveness of cultural self-consciousness among nationalities elsewhere, particularly in the Caucasus, the Ukraine and the Baltic, is a matter of public record.[27]

Indeed the evidence suggests that present Soviet nationalities policy, so far from reducing national self-consciousness, may in fact be tending in some ways to increase it. The development of republican publishing industries, for instance, has brought into being a group of local writers and journalists who tend naturally to operate in terms of the culture with which both they and their readers are most familiar; the development of educational facilities has led to the emergence of a substantial native intelligentsia who see little reason for responsible positions in their locality to be filled by outsiders; and the local political elites, although originally intended to represent the interests of the central government within their area, appear increasingly to resent their limited control over key local appointments and investment decisions and to be increasingly willing to employ 'nationalist' arguments as a means of increasing their leverage upon the central political authorities in this connection. The very existence of a national-territorial framework in the USSR, indeed, so far from providing for the peaceful solution of the nationalities question which was originally envisaged, may in fact have led to precisely the opposite result by establishing a system in which sectional interests, denied any other form of expression, can in practice take only the form of 'nationalism'.[28] The extent to which such pressures are likely to grow in future decades can only be a matter for conjecture; it will depend upon a number of factors, including the response of the central government to such pressures, demographic trends, and developments in the outside world. It does at least seem clear, however, that the nationalities question in the USSR is by no means destined for the historical obsolescence to which official spokesmen would apparently wish to consign it, and it may be significant that recent pronouncements by the Soviet leadership in this connection have placed more emphasis upon the 'harmonious relations' which exist between the nationalities in the USSR than upon their ultimate disappearance.[29]

'Vertical' Political Sub-cultures: Social Groups and Classes

The division of a political culture into a number of political sub-cultures is premised upon the assumption that factors such as class, age and sex are likely to have an influence upon political beliefs and behaviour which will be sufficient in many cases to justify the delimitation of a separate sub-unit composed of the members of the total population who share the social attribute in question. Any large society, clearly, will manifest an almost infinite variety of political belief and behaviour, and it may sometimes appear arbitrary to select one variable rather than another as the basis for classifying a particular national population into a number of constituent subgroups. Even major social variables such as class and sex, moreover, may not always differentiate perfectly between one group of citizens and another in terms of their political beliefs and behaviour, and the variables concerned may often cross-cut rather than coincide with one another (the political orientations of women, for instance, will be likely to vary with the age-group to which they belong, and the political orientations of young people will in turn be likely to vary with their sex and social class). The term 'political sub-culture', accordingly, has been reserved in this volume for aggregates of individuals which are reasonably large in size, whose basic political orientations diverge to a significant degree from those of the larger national population, and whose members have sufficient in common in terms of their political beliefs and behaviour to justify their delimitation as a separate political sub-unit.[30] We have already dealt with perhaps the most important 'horizontal' lines of cleavage in the Soviet political culture which are of this nature, the political sub-cultures associated with particular national and territorial identities. It remains to consider what may be called the 'vertical' political sub-cultures based upon shared social attributes, the most important of which are those associated with class, sex and age-group.

The existence of differences in political belief and behaviour between males and females is of course a familiar finding from political research elsewhere. Virtually all investigations into this matter have found, for instance, that women tend to express less interest in politics, that they are less likely to vote or to belong to a political organisation, and that they converse less often about politics with their immediate family and friends.[31] Research conducted within the USSR tends largely to bear out these impressions. Women have become involved in Soviet political life to a much greater extent than in the past (see pp. 87–8); but they still tend to be much less politically involved than men, and to be involved to a progressively smaller extent the more senior and responsible the political position concerned (Table 7.4). Rather less information is available about the extent to which Soviet women are interested in politics and converse about it with their immediate family and friends; but there is no shortage of evidence that women in the Soviet Union, like their counterparts elsewhere, read newspapers and socio-political literature less often than men,[32] that they attend political education classes and lectures less frequently,[33] that they take a less active part in socio-political activities,[34] and that they are less interested in political issues in the newspapers and magazines they read than

TABLE 7.4   *Women in Soviet politics (percentages of total, by category)*

	Communist Party			Soviet state		
Population 1977	Membership 1977	Central Committee 1976	Politburo 1978	Local Soviets 1977	Supreme Soviet 1974	Council of Ministers 1978
53.5	24.7	4.0	0.0	49.0	31.3	1.0

SOURCES   *Narodnoe Khozyaistvo SSSR za 60 Let. Yubileinyi Statisticheskii Ezhegodnik* (Moscow, 1977) pp. 40 and 87; *Partiinaya Zhizn'*, no. 21 (1977) p. 32; *Materialy XXV S"ezda KPSS* (Moscow, 1976) pp. 242–6; *Verkhovnyi Sovet SSSR Devyatogo Sozyva. Statisticheskii Sbornik* (Moscow, 1974) p. 26; Wolfgang Berner *et al.*, *Sowjetunion 1977/78* (Cologne, 1978) various pages.

their male counterparts.[35] The same differences appear in investigations conducted in the country as in the town, in the 1920s as in the 1970s, and among the better educated as among the less educated.[36] It would not seem unreasonable, on the evidence so far considered, to conclude that women in the USSR constitute a distinctive political sub-culture characterised by lower levels of political interest and involvement than the national population as a whole.

Impressive though such evidence may be at a behavioural level, however, it by no means follows that there is a 'biological' difference between the sexes in their attitudes to politics, in the USSR or indeed elsewhere. Soviet women, in the first place, have simply less free time at their disposal in which to study, attend political lectures, or discharge the manifold responsibilities associated with membership of a political organisation or the tenure of an executive position. One recent investigation into this matter in the Chelyabinsk area, for instance, found that the women who were polled spent about three hours a day on household duties, compared with only one hour a day by their male counterparts. The men who were polled were in fact able to devote more time in an average day to rest and study than to their domestic duties, whereas the women who were polled spent up to three times as much time upon domestic responsibilities as they could devote to such other purposes.[37] The same conclusions emerge, substantially without variation, from most other studies of this matter.[38] Domestic responsibilities of this kind—the 'second shift', as it has been called—appear to have at least as much to do with Soviet women's less active participation in socio-political life as any prior hostility on their part to such involvement; the attitude of Soviet women towards socio-political activity, certainly, appears to be as favourable as that of men, and where they have no domestic responsibilities to discharge Soviet women tend in fact to take as active a part in political life as their male counterparts. There are indeed more female members of the Komsomol than there are male members;[39] and unmarried women have been found to be more active politically than their unmarried male colleagues.[40] There is also a certain amount of evidence to suggest that when Soviet women do take part in socio-political life they do so more willingly, and with more disinterested motives, than their male counterparts.[41]

Differences between the political behaviour of the sexes, moreover, although normally present to some degree within all social categories, are not unaffected by factors such as age, education and occupation; and when factors such as these are held constant, the male/female difference becomes much less where it does not disappear altogether.[42] It is differences of this kind, indeed, which appear to be most fundamental of all to the variations of political belief and behaviour with which political sub-cultures are associated. There is no shortage of evidence, for instance, that collective farmers are less likely to read socio-political literature, less likely to attend political meetings, and less likely to be members of the Communist Party than industrial workers; and it is the view at least of a number of well-qualified observers that their attitude towards the political system more generally is a combination of cynicism, indifference and resentment which perhaps accurately reflects their relative powerlessness in relation to the central political authorities.[43] The Soviet industrial worker, too, tends to lack control over those organisations which supposedly represent his immediate interests, and there have been periodic reports of industrial action and working-class unrest of an overtly political character.[44] There is unfortunately much less evidence than would be necessary for an adequate analysis of the political beliefs and values of the major social groups of which Soviet society is constituted, however, and the discussion which follows is therefore confined primarily to the variations in political behaviour associated with educational and occupational differences, a matter on which Soviet sources are rather more forthcoming.[45]

A greater degree of education and a non-manual occupation, in the first place, appear to be closely associated with more favourable attitudes towards socio-political activity (*obshchestvenno-politicheskaya rabota* or *deyatel'nost'*). Among highly qualified workers at a number of enterprises in Khar'kov, for instance, 87.8 per cent had a favourable attitude towards such activity, compared with 28.9 per cent of the less qualified and unskilled workers who were polled.[46] An investigation at a tractor factory in Kishinev found similarly that among highly qualified workers 5.6 per cent took an indifferent or hostile view of socio-political activity compared with 20.3 per cent of less skilled or unqualified workers, while 69.5 per cent of highly qualified workers but only 41.6 per cent of the less skilled and qualified took a favourable view of such activity. Technical and white-collar staff were still more favourably disposed towards socio-political activity than were industrial workers as a whole.[47] The relationship between education and attitudes towards socio-political activity is broadly similar. The results obtained by an investigation into this matter at Sverdlovsk and Kishinev, for instance, are set out in Table 7.5. In both cases the better educated took a consistently

TABLE 7.5   *Attitudes   towards   socio-political   activity   and   education*
(*percentages*)

| | Level of education | | | | | |
Attitude	4th class or less	5–6	7–8	9–11	Intermediate specialised	Higher education
Sverdlovsk investigation						
Favourable	77.4	79.3	88.0	86.1	87.6	96.0
Indifferent	18.7	19.2	11.8	12.8	12.4	4.0
Hostile	3.9	1.5	0.2	1.1	0.0	0.0
Kishinev investigation						
Favourable	50.0	70.9	75.9*	71.7†	92.2	92.4
Indifferent	29.1	16.7	8.7*	11.1†	4.8	3.0
Hostile	16.7	12.5	10.3*	14.8†	2.9	3.0

SOURCES   Sverdlovsk investigation—L. N. Kogan *et al.*, *Dukhovnyi Mir Sovetskogo Rabochego* (Moscow, 1972) p. 180; Kishinev investigation— V. N. Ermuratskii (ed.), *Sotsial'naya Aktivnost' Rabotnikov Promyshlennogo Predpriyatiya* (Kishinev, 1973) p. 105 (aggregated).
* 7 classes;   †8–9 classes.

more favourable view of socio-political activity than the less educated. In the Sverdlovsk case the average educational level of those favourably disposed towards such activity was 8 classes; of those who were indifferent it was 6.5 classes; and of those who were unfavourably disposed it was about 6 classes. The better educated and qualified, in both investigations, were also more likely to express a willingness to devote any additional free time at their disposal to socio-political activity and to have more disinterested motives for doing so.[48]

Education and social position, moreover, appear to be closely related to different levels of political knowledge and awareness. A detailed investigation into matters of this kind was made in the town of Taganrog. The workers who were polled were found to have much lower levels of knowledge about the country's economic situation than most other social groups: 20 per cent were 'totally uninformed' about recent economic reforms compared with only 3 per cent of technical staff (ITR), and no more than 6 per cent had a 'high' or 'very high' level of knowledge compared with 42 per cent of the technical staff who were polled. Those with lower levels of education were similarly less well informed than their better educated colleagues (63 per cent of those with no more than four years of education were 'completely uninformed' about the economic reforms compared with only 7 per cent of those with a higher education, and no more than 7 per cent had a 'high' or 'very high' level of knowledge compared with 30 per cent of those with a higher education). Technical staff and those with a higher education were also more likely to read newspapers and journals such as *Pravda* and *Ekonomicheskaya Zhizn'*; they were more likely to rely upon such periodicals as a source of information than upon the conversations of their family and friends; and they were more likely to attend political lectures and discussions than the other social groups represented within the sample (62 per cent of technical staff and 73 per cent of those with a higher education attended such sessions regularly, for instance, compared with 32 per cent of workers and only 4 per cent of those with no education beyond the 4th class).[49] Investigations elsewhere have found similarly that those with a higher education are more likely to be well informed about the economic performance of their enterprise and about international affairs, and that they are more likely to be interested in such matters, than those whose education is less advanced.[50]

The better educated and qualified, as these differences might suggest, are also more likely to possess socio-political literature and to read it. No more than 23 per cent of the workers who were polled in a nation-wide investigation into this matter had any socio-political literature in their domestic libraries, for instance, compared with 35 per cent of technical staff; and they were also less likely to possess the works of Lenin (about 25 and 33 per cent respectively did so).[51] Almost all qualified workers in an investigation in the Ukraine, similarly, had books in their homes and subscribed to two or three periodicals; only a third of the unskilled workers, however, had a domestic library, and almost a third ordered no periodicals whatsoever. Political books, in particular, were 'almost never' encountered in such homes.[52] The better educated and more highly skilled are also more likely to read such literature. An investigation in Tallin, for instance, found that 11 per cent of workers but 20 per cent of technical staff regularly read socio-political literature;[53] and a study in the Krasnodar region found similarly that between 24 and 29 per cent of executive personnel read such literature but that only between 3 and 9 per cent of unskilled workers did so.[54] The results of an investigation into this matter in the Krasnodar and Kalinin regions are set out in Table 7.6. The general tendency, for the better educated and more skilled to take a greater interest in socio-political affairs and to be more

TABLE 7.6   *Political information and occupation (percentages)*

	Unskilled and semi-skilled workers		Technical specialists	
	Krasnodar krai	*Kalinin oblast'*	*Krasnodar krai*	*Kalinin oblast'*
Proportion of total who				
Read newspapers	51	46	87	79
Listen to the radio	61	62	78	79
Watch television	26	26	61	54
Read literature	26	10	64	51
Read socio-political literature	3–9	n.d.	24–9	n.d.
Study in spare time	3	3	22	35

SOURCE   Yu. V. Arutyunyan, *Sotsial'naya Struktura Sel'skogo Naseleniya SSSR* (Moscow, 1971) pp. 176–9.

exposed to the mass media generally, is consistent with the conclusions of investigations that have been conducted elsewhere.[55]

Not only are the better educated and qualified more knowledgeable about politics and more favourably disposed towards socio-political activity than other workers, they tend also to take a more active part in socio-political life, both in their immediate work environment and in the wider society. Among young collective farmers in the Chelyabinsk and Kurgan regions, for instance, more than ten times as many respondents with a specialised higher education were found to be involved in socio-political activity as those with no education beyond the 4th class (67 per cent and 6.2 per cent respectively). The proportion of those involved increased consistently with every increase in the level of education.[56] The same relationship has been found in investigations conducted elsewhere in the USSR (Table 7.7). Party membership is similarly stratified: only 7 per cent of those aged over 25 with no education beyond the 8th class were party members in 1973 compared with 18 per cent of those with a completed secondary education, 31 per cent of those with a completed higher education, and 46 per cent of those with a higher degree.[57] An investigation conducted at a number of industrial enterprises in the Urals found similarly that 21.4 per cent of those with heavy manual or unskilled jobs had a high level of activism but that 60.4 per cent had a low one; while among those

TABLE 7.7 *Socio-political activity and education (participation by educational group, percentages)*

	To 4th class	5–6	7	8–9	Inter- mediate	Intermediate specialised	Higher education
Kishinev*	20.8	58.3	39.7	40.7	55.4	71.8	83.3
Urals†	23.8	37.1	—43.0—		51.4	60.8	72.3
Leningrad‡	—43.5—			58.5	67.5	79.7	82.3
Kazan'‡	—26.5—			34.2	49.7	72.6	85.8
Perm'§	—19.5—		—38.5—		42.4	79.3	n.d.

SOURCES * V. N. Ermuratsky (ed.), *Sotsial'naya Aktivnost' Rabotnikov Promyshlennogo Predpriyatiya* (Kishinev, 1973) p. 95; † M. T. Iovchuk and L. N. Kogan (eds), *Dukhovnyi Mir Sovetskogo Rabochego* (Moscow, 1972) p. 178; ‡ Yu. G. Chulanov, *Izmeneniya v Sostave i v Urovne Tvorcheskoi Aktivnosti Rabochego Klassa SSSR* (Leningrad, 1974) p. 67; § *Trud i Lichnost' pri Sotsializme*, vyp. 2 (Perm', 1973) p. 38.

engaged in highly qualified automated work the proportions were nearly reversed, 28.3 per cent manifesting a low level of socio-political activism but 44.8 per cent a high one.[58] A study at a number of enterprises in Leningrad showed similarly that 29.6 per cent of unqualified workers took part in socio-political activity compared with 81.9 per cent of those engaged in qualified mental and manual work.[59] The proportion of such activity which is of a more responsible or organisational character, moreover, appears to increase with each rise in the level of education or qualification.[60]

A broadly similar relationship may be discerned between occupation and socio-political activism. Technical and white-collar staff, in particular, have been found in almost every study of this kind to be considerably more involved in socio-political activity than the mass of industrial workers. The amount of time devoted to such activities, for instance, tends to vary directly by social group. The average peasant, in one recent investigation, spent about four hours a month engaged in socio-political activity; the average worker spent about six hours a month engaged in the same activity; but the average member of the technical and white-collar staff was found to spend about eight hours a month engaged in activity of this kind.[61] The same relationship was found by a group of investigators working in the Urals area. Almost twice as many workers as technical staff were found to spend not more than half an hour a week upon socio-political activities; while a third of the technical staff, but only a quarter of the workers, spent three or four hours a week thus engaged.[62] An investigation at an industrial enterprise in Leningrad found similarly that technical and white-collar staff spent considerably more time upon socio-political activity than industrial workers, particularly the less skilled. More than half (58.6 per cent) of the workers who were polled, and nearly three-quarters (73.8 per cent) of the unskilled workers, spent no time at all on such activities, compared with only a third (33 per cent) of technical staff. The technical and white-collar staff who were engaged in socio-political activity were also likely to spend more time upon it than the group of workers who were thus engaged (18.7 per cent of the white-collar and technical staff who were polled spent more than four hours a week upon socio-political activity, for instance, compared with 11.5 per cent of the workers and only 7.5 per cent of the semi-skilled workers who were polled).[63]

The proportion of those who are involved in socio-political activity tends also to vary widely by social and occupational group. One study, for instance, found that 66 per cent of all technical staff were engaged in socio-political activity but that only 36.3 per cent of all workers and 24.6 per cent of unskilled workers were thus engaged; another study, also conducted in Leningrad, found similarly that 64.4 per cent of all the technical and white-collar staff but only 36.6 per cent of the workers who were polled were involved in some form or other of socio-political activity; and a further study has shown that levels of activism among groups of unskilled workers may be as low as 7 per cent of the total.[64] It may be convenient to summarise such findings in tabular form (Table 7.8). In every

TABLE 7.8 *Socio-political activity and occupation*
(*percentage participation by category*)

	1	2	3	4	5	6
Workers	31	47.1	25.5	55	30.4	20.5
Technical and white-collar staff	65	79.9	57.5	70	57.3	67.2

SOURCES: (1) *Trud i Lichnost' pri Sotsializme*, vyp. 2 (Perm', 1973) p. 39; (2) V. N. Ermuratsky (ed.), *Sotsial'naya Aktivnost' Rabotnikov Promyshlennogo Predpriyatiya* (Kishinev, 1973) p. 95; (3) V. N. Pimenova, *Svobodnoe Vremya v Sotsialisticheskom Obshchestve* (Moscow, 1974) p. 282; (4) *Aktivnost' Lichnosti v Sotsialisticheskom Obshchestve* (Moscow, 1974) p. 255 (averaged); (5) L. N. Kogan (ed.), *Obshchestvenno-politicheskaya Aktivnost' Trudyashchikhsya*, vyp. 1 (Sverdlovsk, 1970) p. 222; (6) Yu. G. Chulanov, *Izmeneniya v Sostave i v Urovne Tvorcheskoi Aktivnosti Rabochego Klassa SSSR* (Leningrad, 1974) p. 66 (averaged).

case, it will be noted, the level of socio-political activism of white-collar and technical staff is higher than that of industrial workers, taken as a whole (the overall average is 34.9 per cent for industrial workers and 66.1 per cent for technical and white-collar staff). These data have been confined to investigations conducted during the 1970s in order to maximise comparability, but earlier studies have reached similar conclusions.[65] The differences between the two groups concerned, moreover, have not necessarily been declining over the years; on some evidence, indeed, they have increased.[66]

The evidence so far considered relates primarily to political behaviour and only secondarily to political beliefs and values. It should therefore be noted that the variations in political behaviour which have been outlined in this chapter may give only a very approximate impression of the distribution of political beliefs and values with which they are associated. The better educated, for instance, may be better informed about regime objectives simply because they are more likely to occupy a position in which such knowledge will be available to them; senior white-collar staff are more likely to be party members and thereby unavoidably involved in at least a minimum of political activity, whatever their attitude towards it; and the better educated and more senior are in turn more likely to know how they are 'expected' to regard such activity and more likely to reply accordingly. A political culture, however, is in our definition not simply the collective orientation towards politics; it also embraces the regular and expected forms of interaction within a society, its political 'way of life' as well as its political psychology, and at least at this level there can be little doubt of the existence of marked and interrelated differences within the Soviet political culture to which the term political sub-culture would appear quite properly to apply. Soviet society emerges, in fact, as a society which is stratified politically in a manner very similar to that of other developed (but capitalist) societies, in which the middle class is typically more active and better informed than the mass of industrial workers: a circumstance which may help to explain the relative reluctance of Soviet scholars to discuss such differences, sixty years after a revolution that was supposed to bring about their abolition.[67]

Soviet official spokesmen, however, emphasise that such differences, considerable though they may be, are no more than a transitory feature of a society which is developing from 'mature socialism' to full Communism; and there is no doubt that the account we have so far provided of Soviet political sub-cultures has indeed been essentially static, descriptive of existing patterns of political behaviour and belief rather than focusing upon the process of change within the political culture under the impact of socio-economic and other developments in the society within which it is located. The question of generational change is particularly important in this respect, for the future configuration of the political culture will clearly be profoundly influenced by the expectations, assumptions and behavioural patterns brought into the political culture by successive cohorts of younger citizens as successive cohorts of older citizens are leaving it. An extended discussion of the nature and direction of political change within the Soviet Union generally would lie beyond the scope of the present volume; but the process of change within the political culture, and in particular the impact upon it of changing political generations, must clearly be considered. To this our next and final chapter is devoted.

8

Political Culture and Political Change

The preceding chapters of this book have been concerned with the traditional political culture of the USSR and with its subsequent evolution over more than sixty years of Soviet government. The predominantly centralised, collectivist political culture which the Bolsheviks inherited in 1917, it was argued, has in many ways persisted up to the present day. The pre-revolutionary Russian economy was characterised by a relatively high level of state control and ownership which the Soviet government has since extended; the political system has become more effectively centralist with the improvement of transport and communications and the removal of those pockets of autonomy which were a real if subsidiary element of the pre-revolutionary system; and the predisposition of government to regulate matters of individual belief as well as behaviour has been strengthened further by the imposition of a mandatory official ideology. This is not to suggest that there have been no changes of significance in the Soviet political culture over the period we have been considering. Levels of political participation, for instance, have been rising, the exposure of the population to the means of mass communication has been increasing, and levels of religious observance have been falling, particularly among the younger generation. These, however, are primarily changes in political or socio-political behaviour; at the level of mass political values there has clearly been no wholesale conversion to the principles of Marxism–Leninism, and sub-cultural differences between social and ethnic groups have persisted in a form which appears to have been altered very little by the efforts of the Soviet authorities in that direction. An emphasis upon continuity rather than change in Soviet political culture, to this extent, would not appear to be misplaced.

A political culture, however, is not a 'given' which determines the performance of the political system and of individual citizens within it; it is itself the product of a distinctive pattern of historical evolution and of socio-economic change, and it will be affected by the changing socio-economic environment within which it is located at least as much as it will itself shape that environment. The traditional Russian political culture, as we argued at the beginning of this book, was the product of determinate historical circumstances of this kind. There was no powerful and autonomous landed aristocracy which might have limited the exercise of monarchical power; the industrial bourgeoisie was relatively weak and politically inert; and rural society was based upon a network of self-regulating communes which collectively administered the social as well as economic life of the population who comprised them. A social structure of this kind, itself varying markedly by region and changing rapidly from the later nineteenth century onwards, need not necessarily dictate any particular form of politics. There seems nonetheless to be more than a fortuitous connection between these aspects of its material environment and a number of the most distinctive features of the pre-revolutionary political culture, such as a relatively weak legal and constitutional order, a tendency to conceive of political authority in personalised terms, and a greater predisposition than might have been the case elsewhere to regulate all aspects of the life of the community by the collective decision of the community as a whole.[1] The pre-revolutionary political culture, that is to say, was deeply rooted in the social structure and economy of the society within which it was located.

It would be surprising, on this basis, if the Soviet political culture were not affected not only by the programme of political socialisation which the Soviet authorities have sponsored since 1917 but also by the rapid and striking changes in Soviet social and economic life that have been taking place over the same period. Of the magnitude of those changes there can certainly be no doubt (Table 8.1). The Soviet population has become a more urban and also a more educated one, with the numbers of school pupils, university graduates and technical specialists all increasing markedly both absolutely and as a proportion of the total population within the relevant age-groups. Industrial output has increased enormously, presently rivalling or exceeding that of the USA in a number of

TABLE 8.1   *Some indices of modernisation, 1913–77*

	1913	1940	1960	1977
National income (1913 : 1)	1	5.3	23	68
Urban population				
(percentage of total)	18	33	49	62
Industrial workers				
(percentage of population)	14.6	33.5	49.5*	61.6
Motor cars produced (thousands)	—	5.5	138.8	1280
Washing machines produced				
(thousands)	—	—	895	3600
Books (million copies p.a.)	99	462	1240	1737†
Periodicals (million copies p.a.)	117	245	779	3069†
Higher or secondary education per				
thousand popn aged 10 or over	n.d.	108§	361*	586
Graduates of higher education				
institutions (thousands)	12‡	126	343	752
Scientific workers (thousands)	11.6	98.3	354.2	1300

SOURCES   *Narodnoe Khozyaistvo SSSR za 60 Let. Yubileinyi statisticheskii ezhegodnik* (Moscow, 1977); *Narodnoe Obrazovanie, Nauka i Kul'tura v SSSR* (Moscow, 1977); *Pravda* (28 January 1978).
* 1959; † 1976; § 1939; ‡ 1914.

important respects; the proportion of the total population employed in industry has increased in parallel; and the output of consumer goods has also increased, although to a somewhat less dramatic extent. The circulation of books, newspapers and magazines, often considered a particularly discriminating indicator of 'modernity', has also increased considerably. The USSR, overall, has changed from a backward, predominantly agrarian society (though with a small, relatively advanced industrial sector and a talented literary intelligentsia) into a society whose levels of education, scientific research, health care, life expectancy, urbanisation and industrialisation are in most cases comparable with those of its major European and North American rivals.[2] What consequences have these changes had in terms of the country's political culture?

A number of such changes have already been considered. The average Soviet citizen, as we have seen, is a more frequent visitor to his local cinema and theatre; he visits the library and museum more often, and also the local club; and he is more likely to listen to the radio or watch television and to subscribe to the local and national press (see pp. 66–74). A number of more far-reaching theories have been put forward as to the likely impact of socio-economic change upon the political system, however, and it is with two of them in particular that we shall be concerned. The first is what may be called the 'political modernisation' theory: it posits a direct connection between the economy and the political system, and suggests that an increasing degree of development in the former will necessarily lead to changes of a liberalising or democratising character in the latter. The second theory is what may be called the theory of 'political generations'. This second theory, perhaps less accurately termed a theory than an approach or perspective upon the process of social and political change, accepts the link implied by the 'political modernisation' theory between the economy and the political system, but goes beyond it in emphasising the importance of the expectations and assumptions of successive generations of Soviet citizens which will intervene between and thus modify the impact of socio-economic change upon the polity. These two theories, both concerned with the important but problematic connection between socio-economic change and the evolution of the political culture, will be considered in turn. We begin with the theory of 'political modernisation'.

Political Change and 'Political Modernisation'

The theory of 'political modernisation' is in many ways a direct descendant of the evolutionary theories of the nineteenth century and earlier, which saw mankind progressing steadily through successive stages of social organisation until some final state of near-perfection was attained. Particular importance was attached in this sequence of development to the final or penultimate stage, the transition from the traditional society of the colonial and pre-industrial world to the dynamic industrial society which, in early nineteenth-century Europe, had succeeded it. Auguste Comte, in one of the earliest such formulations, spoke of this change as one from a theological or military stage of social development to one which was scientific and rational in character; Henry Maine defined the change in his *Ancient Law* of 1861 as one from 'status' to 'contract'; and Ferdinand Tönnies, in his *Gemeinschaft und Gesellschaft* of 1887, saw the transition as one from a 'community' mode of social organisation towards an industrial–capitalist society based upon 'association'. Evolutionary theories of this kind were very influential in their time: Marx and Engels, for instance, were strongly influenced by the American anthropologist Lewis Henry Morgan, whose *Ancient Society*, published in 1877, sought to establish that all societies passed (in the words of its sub-title) in a 'Line of Human Progress from Savagery through Barbarism to Civilisation' (which was to say the urban industrial America of his time).[3] Theories of this kind do not presently command much support within the social sciences; but their optimistic and unilinear assumptions do appear to lie behind a number of more recent theories of social change, among them the theory of 'political modernisation'.[4]

The theory of political modernisation may perhaps most conveniently be approached through the work of one of its principal modern exponents, Talcott Parsons.[5] Parsons, drawing explicitly upon Darwin, has suggested that social systems may be classified in terms of their development through a series of 'evolutionary universals', that is to say complexes of 'structures and associated processes the development of which so increases the long-run adaptive capacity of living systems in a given class that only systems that develop the complex can attain certain higher levels of general adaptive capacity'.[6] As a society emerges from the primitive level, Parsons writes, it will tend to evolve a system of social stratification based upon functional differentiation and achievement rather than upon kinship and ascription, and a specialised political function emerges which is independent of religious authority for its legitimation. An administrative bureaucracy and a system of money and markets come into existence, and a secular and impersonal legal system develops which is a prerequisite for the remaining universal in social evolution, the 'democratic association with elective leadership and fully enfranchised membership'. No institutional form basically different from this, Parsons writes, can legitimate power and authority in the general sense and also mediate its exercise by particular persons and groups in the formation of binding policy decisions. These evolutionary universals together constitute the 'main outline of the structural foundations of modern society'; they collectively confer upon those societies which possess them an adaptive advantage far superior to the structural potential of societies that lack them.[7]

The Communist-ruled societies of Eastern Europe have clearly advanced rather less far along this evolutionary continuum than the liberal-democratic societies of Western Europe and North America. Parsons, indeed, explicitly confirms that what he calls the 'communist totalitarian' states will prove structurally incapable of competing with liberal-democratic systems in their political and integrative capacity in the long run, and that they will be compelled to make adjustments in the direction of electoral democracy and a plural party system if they are not to regress into less advanced and politically less effective forms of social organisation. The legitimacy of Communist rule, Parsons argues, will be undermined if the party continues to be unwilling to trust the people it has educated, which means to entrust them with a share of political responsibility. 'This can only mean that eventually the single monolithic party must relinquish its monopoly of such responsibility.'[8] In the same way that strict Calvinism and Jacobinism were short-lived, Parsons has written elsewhere, 'it seems as certain as such things can be that Communism also will prove to be short-lived'. Even more than other systems of this kind, Parsons argues, Communist systems are bound to be undermined by the extent of their own success. The dictatorship of a single party will be unable in the long run to secure legitimation; emerging scientific and cultural elites will press for a greater measure of autonomy from the political decision-makers; and the increasing differentiation of the social structure will make a centrally dominated social order increasingly difficult to sustain. As a result of their own internal dynamics, Parsons writes, the Communist states must therefore evolve in the direction of the 'restoration—or where it has not yet existed, the institution—of political democracy'. This is the '*only* possible outcome—except for general destruction or breakdown'.[9]

The theory of political modernisation in relation to the Soviet Union and the other Communist-ruled states has been developed more fully by a number of other writers, many of whom have explicitly acknowledged their debt to Parsons.[10] Their point of departure is in many cases a conviction that the previously-dominant 'totalitarian' orthodoxy is no longer adequate as a description of contemporary Soviet and East European societies, and that it was probably at no time adequate as a basis upon which to assess the process of political development and change in these societies and in others like them. Like Parsons, modernisation theorists assume that Communist systems—variously categorised as 'mobilising' or 'modernising regimes'—will manifest the same linkages between socio-economic change and the polity as do political systems elsewhere. Robert Dahl has summed up these linkages as follows: a high socio-economic level and competitive politics are associated; not only competitive politics in general but polyarchy[11] in particular are significantly associated with relatively high levels of socio-economic development; and the higher the socio-economic level the more competitive the political system, and vice versa. 'Because of its inherent requirements', Dahl writes, 'an advanced economy and its supporting social structures automatically distribute political resources and political skills to a vast variety of individuals, groups and organisations.' Among these skills and resources are knowledge, income, esteem, the ability to organise and communicate, and access to organisations, experts and elites. These resources can be used to negotiate for individual or group advantages and to ensure that when conflicts arise, as they are bound to do, they will be resolved by negotiation and bargaining rather than by compulsion and coercion. The monopoly of political power enjoyed by the rulers of the Communist states, Dahl writes, is therefore being undermined by the programmes of social and economic development which they themselves have sponsored. The more the Communist leaders succeed in transforming the social and economic structures of the countries over which they rule, the more their political skills are threatened with obsolescence; but if they seek to retain their political hegemony by force alone they will be confronted by the enormous costs and inefficiencies of attempting to manage an advanced society by means more appropriate to a society at a less complex stage of development. The change from Stalin's hegemony to the post-Stalin system, Dahl argues, was a 'profound step towards liberalization'; further moves in this direction appear inescapable as a centrally dominated political system becomes increasingly difficult to reconcile with the pluralistic pressures of a modern economy and society.[12]

Most writers in the 'political modernisation' school point out that there need be no one-to-one correspondence between socio-economic and political change; external influences, cultural traits and so forth will intervene between and thus modify the impact of socio-economic change upon the polity.[13] The essential thesis, however, that the Communist states must eventually acquire the secular and bargaining political culture which corresponds to their economic and social modernity, is one that finds support across a surprisingly diverse spectrum of political opinion and scholarship. Roy Medvedev, for instance, speaks of some kind of democratisation in the USSR as an 'inevitable tendency'; Ghita Ionescu writes of 'pluralization and institutionalization' as an 'inevitable trend' which 'accompanies the process of economic, social and political development'; Michel Tatu writes that a move towards a parliamentary regime, or true liberalisation, 'cannot fail to occur' because it corresponds to the 'overall evolution of Soviet society'; and Karl Deutsch identifies an 'automatic trend towards pluralization and disintegration'.[14] Gabriel Almond, in perhaps the most far-reaching of such prognostications, speaks of the 'pluralistic pressures of a modern economy and society' and of a 'secular trend in the direction of decentralization and pluralism'. As their societies and economies develop, Almond writes, Communist systems will face the 'inevitable demands of a healthy, educated, affluent society' for both more material and what Almond calls 'spiritual consumer goods' (such as opportunities for participation and a share in the decision-making process). Already, Almond writes, 'Russian success in science, education, technology, economic productivity and national security has produced some decentralization of the political process. I fail to see how these decentralizing, pluralistic tendencies can be reversed, or how their spread can be prevented'.[15] To what extent can such a thesis—'political modernisation', in our terminology—be sustained?

It should first of all be noted that the modernisation thesis has not generally been borne out by the results of empirical examination. An investigation into the relationship between industrial development and individual 'modernity' in Ghana, India, Brazil and the USA, for instance, found that workers at more mechanised levels of industry did indeed score more highly on 'modern' values than did workers at less advanced levels, and that the range of variation in scores became less with each increase in the level of industrialism. There was little evidence of cross-national convergence of values with increasing levels of industrialisation, however; oil refinery workers, for instance, were no more similar in values to their counterparts in other countries than were the local farming populations, and more advanced workers had much more in common with less advanced workers in the same industry than did either group with their counterparts at a similar level of industrialism elsewhere. There was 'no evidence of a systematic erosion of workers' values as a function of industrialism', in other words; traditional values were being altered by industrialisation, but 'not in the direction of a greater degree of global consensus'.[16] Value differences, indeed, might be not diminishing but actually increasing with each increase in the level of industrialism.[17] A study conducted in Finland, Costa Rica, Japan, Mexico and the USA found similarly that a high level of industrialism need not necessarily lead to 'modern' and converging value systems. Japan, for instance, despite its high level of industrial development, more closely resembled Costa Rica in its value system than it did the United States of America or Finland; and national differences had generally a much greater impact upon most indicators of 'modernity' than did factors such as education or income. Nations, it was found, 'need not be universalistic to develop a modern industrial economy, and they do not necessarily become more universalistic in the process of becoming industrialized'.[18]

Empirical examinations of Communist political systems have similarly found little evidence that increasing levels of social and economic development need necessarily be associated with political liberalisation or democratisation. Daniel Nelson, for instance, has constructed an index of socio-economic development for nine of the East European Communist states based upon factors such as energy consumption per capita and levels of infant mortality, and examined its relationship to political change in those countries over a period of more than twenty years (1949-72). None of the variables considered—the educational level of the political leadership, the proportion of party members drawn from the intelligentsia, political instability or executive change—showed a strong positive correlation with either the level of socio-economic development or the rate of socio-economic change; in some cases, indeed, there was a moderately strong negative correlation. Overall 'no strong support was found for the hypothesis that relationships exist between political variables and socio-economic levels and/or rates of socio-economic change in communist states'.[19] Another study, devoted more particularly to the relationship between socio-economic change and patterns of participation in authoritative societal decision-making within the USSR over the post-Stalin period, found similarly that there was little evidence of a secular trend towards democratisation or pluralisation over the period considered. Sessions of the major decision-making bodies (the national legislature and party Central Committee) have on the contrary become less frequent, the number of those who have been able to articulate preferences within them has diminished, and their decisional output has also fallen, although to a somewhat smaller extent. There was no evidence of a movement towards more participatory and consultative norms, in these respects at least, over a period of major and far-reaching social and economic change; and no evidence that a centrally dominated political system need necessarily be incompatible with an advanced level of social and economic development.[20]

Indeed no very convincing grounds have yet been provided for supposing that competitive politics and social and economic 'modernity' need necessarily be associated in the first place. A number of contemporary states—the Soviet Union, Czechoslovakia and the GDR, for instance—have relatively high levels of national income per head but political systems that are centrally dominated and authoritarian in character; while a number of other states—India, and the United States in the early nineteenth century, for instance—have successfully combined a liberal-democratic political system with relatively low levels of urbanisation, industrialisation and per capita national income (in these and some other cases it might indeed be possible to argue the modernisation thesis in reverse—that competitive politics bring about social and economic development and not vice versa).[21] Even if changes of a broadly liberalising or democratising character have taken place in the USSR over the post-Stalin period, moreover, it by no means follows that such changes have been a consequence of the Soviet Union's socio-economic development over the same period or that they need lead ultimately to the formation of a 'modern' political culture similar to that by which the USSR's major western neighbours may presently be characterised. It is at least arguable that western liberal-democratic forms have as much to do with the unique or distinctive aspects of the historical experience of these societies as with their relatively advanced levels of social and economic development; and the adoption of similar patterns of politics elsewhere may be the result of emulation or implantation rather than the necessary consequence of increasing levels of social and economic 'modernity'.[22] The connection between liberal democracy and an advanced level of social and economic development, in other words, may be a largely fortuitous one; the two may be associated for reasons which are historically contingent and which offer no guarantee that a similar pattern of politics need necessarily reproduce itself in states which approach contemporary western levels of social and economic development.

The underlying dichotomy between 'tradition' and 'modernity', moreover, seems a hopelessly overstated one. No doubt there is a great deal modern societies have in common, and a great deal that serves to distinguish them, as a group, from societies of a pre-industrial or traditional character. But 'modern' societies also differ among themselves in many important respects, among them their degree of traditionalism or collectivism, and it is by no means obvious that such differences need necessarily be destined for historical obsolescence. We have properly been reminded of the 'modernity of tradition'.[23] Many traditional and customary usages, it is clear, need not necessarily obstruct the process of social and economic development; they may be compatible with a developed as well as with a pre-industrial economy.[24]

There would appear more generally to be little future in a theory of political modernisation which assumes a close connection between socio-economic change and the polity without taking into account that political change is ultimately effected by human beings, who may be influenced by religions, ideologies, historical experiences and other factors that bear little direct relation to the 'modernity' of the social and economic environment within which they find themselves. What may be of crucial importance in this connection is less social and economic change in itself than a population's perceptions and expectations in this regard—their perception of such changes both in their own country and in others of which they have cognisance, and their expectations with regard to the continuance of those trends in future years. Expectations and perceptions of this kind are likely to vary considerably by social group, nationality and so forth; but perhaps most important of all is the changing generational composition of the population, as each new cohort takes for granted the achievements of its predecessors and perceives the performance of government through eyes increasingly well informed as to the performance of other and competing social systems elsewhere. It is the changing generational composition of the Soviet population, then, through which social and economic change is refracted, and by which the influence of social and economic change upon the polity is ultimately regulated. It is to the question of political generations that we therefore turn in conclusion.

Political Change and 'Political Generations'

The generational approach to political change is predicated upon the assumption that successive generational groups will share common and distinctive experiences which will normally lead to some divergence between their political beliefs and values and those of the national population as a whole. Political scientists have identified three separate aspects of this question: generational effects, life-cycle effects, and period effects.[25] Generational effects, the first of these, arise when members of a particular age cohort undergo a set of experiences which affect all the members of that cohort relatively uniformly and which are sufficient to differentiate their political beliefs and values to some extent from those of earlier or later age cohorts. It is in this sense that one speaks, for instance, of a 'New Deal generation' or a 'Vietnam generation': a group of people of approximately the same age who have lived through important events at a relatively impressionable stage in their development and whose political views have to some extent been influenced thereby. Life-cycle or maturation effects arise simply from the process of ageing itself. The passage of years, it appears, does normally have an independent effect upon political beliefs and values, though it usually tends to confirm existing political beliefs and values rather than to change them in a conservative direction as has sometimes been hypothesised.[26] Period or *Zeitgeist* effects, finally, arise from events which have a marked and relatively uniform effect upon all generational groups together, such as a war or a period of rule of a wholly exceptional character. Each factor, operating individually, may have a marked impact upon the distribution of political beliefs and values within a society and thus to some extent upon its political development; more usually, however, they will exercise their influence in common and in varying combinations. We must bear in mind all three kinds of influence—generational, life-cycle and period— when we examine the impact of generational turnover upon political development in the USSR.

Of the existence of age-related differences in contemporary Soviet society there is certainly no lack of evidence. Press reports, for instance, speak regularly of youthful speculators and drop-outs, of 'hooligans' and delinquents, and of young people who 'display unhealthy attitudes' and 'forget their obligations to society'.[27] The report of one such group in the newspaper *Sovetskaya Latvia* ran as follows:

> Base instincts gradually brought these dissipated fellows together. The need for tape-recording so-called pop music gave rise to a great interest in the broadcasts of foreign radio stations hostile to us. What seemed at first glance harmless buffoonery and the desire thoughtlessly to imitate all kinds of 'hippies' and the Beatles led these young fellows into the filthy morass of moral dissipation and alienation from real life . . . They preferred to loaf, to be a burden on others. It took a long time to prove to them that in our time one cannot live as a deadbeat, that our society does not tolerate parasites or apostates from the established rules of our socialist community.[28]

Similar reports speak of young people who complain that 'interviews with celebrated collective farmers and vanguard workers are of no interest', who worship beat music and abstract art and the philosophy associated with them, and who dream of getting hold of a poster of Mick Jagger since, 'Alas, they are not sold at regular newsstands'. Such stories could be multiplied further.[29]

More serious scholarly inquiries have indicated similarly that significant proportions of young people devote relatively little time to socio-political activity and to the reading of political literature, that they are more interested in international affairs than in problems of Marxist–Leninist philosophy, and that such negative phenomena as card-playing and drunkenness have regrettably 'not yet been eliminated' among them (as any visitor to the Soviet Union could readily testify).[30] Many Soviet young people, it appears, even Komsomol members, have an inadequate grasp of political terminology and of the history of the CPSU, know very little about the responsibilities and work of state bodies, and have little appreciation of the importance of such qualities as socio-political activism and organisation.[31] Considerable proportions (26.2 per cent, in a recent national investigation) complain that socio-political activity interferes with their studies; and those who show the least enthusiasm are often those who are otherwise the most successful in their class and who obtain the highest marks for social scientific subjects.[32] The proportion of students and young people engaged in various forms of socio-political activity is broadly comparable to that of most other sections of the population: 44.4 per cent of students in a poll in Leningrad, for instance, took part in socio-political activity; 45.5 per cent at a number of institutions in the Urals and 44.6 per cent in the city of Gorky did so; 57.2 per cent of students, in an investigation in Belorussia and Tadzhikistan, were involved 'to some degree' in socio-political activity; and at two higher educational institutions in the Khar'kov area 51.2 and 54.7 per cent respectively were thus engaged.[33] A relatively high proportion of young people appear to take part only intermittently in activity of this kind, however, and those who do participate appear to do so with no great enthusiasm.[34] On some evidence, indeed, the proportion of young people involved in socio-political activity may have been falling somewhat in recent years, although in a longer-term perspective there can be no doubt that it has increased considerably.[35]

Evidence of this kind, however, provides little guidance as to the direction of change in Soviet political opinion at this or at any other level. Young people in most societies are generally more unruly than their elders, and reports of youthful cynicism provide no guarantee that attitudes of this kind will persist unchanged into the adult years or that successive generations of Soviet young people are becoming progressively more alienated from the political process. A good deal of evidence, indeed, suggests precisely the contrary. The survey of Soviet emigres conducted at the end of the Second World War by Inkeles and Bauer, for instance, gained a 'very definite impression of greater potential and actual support of the whole Soviet system by the rising younger generation', a support which 'developed "naturally" through time, becomes taken for granted by those who give it, and is not likely to be shaken by forces within the system itself'.[36] Younger Soviet citizens tended to take the system more and more for granted, to have specific rather than generalised complaints against it, to be less religious, and to be less inclined to seek to leave unless they had personally suffered arrest or imprisonment. Younger people were also more likely to favour the institutional structure of Soviet society, to believe that things would have been better if the leadership had been different, and to perceive the regime as a strong and authoritative one.[37] The regime might 'expect to increase the breadth and stability of its social support with the passage of time', the authors concluded, 'particularly as death claims the older generations who characteristically opposed the system on principle and could not easily be reconciled'.[38]

A very similar assumption is contained in two other theories, one western and one Soviet. The western theory argues that the legitimacy of a regime is a function, at least in part, of the length of time for which it has been in continuous existence. No regime, it has been hypothesised, may be said to be moving away from repudiation unless it has survived long enough to have been the predominant influence upon the political memories of more than half its adult population from childhood onwards; regimes that have been in existence for two or three generations, conversely, may gradually acquire legitimacy as an increasing proportion of their populations grow up knowing no other kind of system than that within which they have themselves been raised.[39] The Soviet Union by now abundantly satisfies these criteria: the regime has itself been in existence for more than sixty years and more than 84 per cent of the Soviet population have been born since its establishment, more than half of them since the Second World War. The Soviet political system should gradually have acquired legitimacy, on this interpretation, as those with conscious recollections of the pre-revolutionary order become a small and steadily diminishing proportion of the Soviet population as a whole.[40] Soviet official theory holds similarly that a fully developed socialist consciousness will come gradually into existence as those brought up under the old regime, and the capitalist mentality associated with them, become a steadily less considerable element within the total society. Survivals of this kind (*perezhitki*) have been defined as 'attitudes, norms, habits and traditions arising from pre-socialist socio-economic formations which have been preserved in the consciousness or behaviour of Soviet people and which are contrary to the principles of communist morality'; their gradual elimination is supposed to take place as socialist social relations and a socialist moral culture develop within the USSR in accordance with the formation of the material-technical basis of Communism.[41]

Deviant behaviour of this kind does indeed appear to become a steadily less conspicuous feature of the average Soviet citizen as he advances in years and in social and other responsibilities. The level of party membership, for instance, increases with age, from 3.5 per cent of males aged between 18 and 25 to 11.5 per cent of those aged between 26 and 30, 19.1 of those aged between 31 and 40, 22.4 per cent of those aged between 41 and 50, and 22.9 per cent of those aged between 51 and 60. The proportion of party membership has similarly been increasing over time within all but the youngest of these age-groups.[42] Younger people are also more likely to become involved in socio-political activity as they grow older, as Table 8.2

TABLE 8.2   *Age and socio-political participation* (*percentage by age-group*)

'Druzhba' furniture factory, Perm'* (*N* = 319)

16–24	25–29	30–39	over 40
34.6	42.5	41.2	31.8

Kishinev tractor factory† (*N* = 3300)

under 18	18–20	21–25	26–30	31–35	36–40	over 40
33.3	44.4	46.4	54.7	69.6	55.3	71.0

Twenty-one lathe-building factories, USSR‡ (*N* = 8000)

16–17	18–19	20–22	23–25	26–28	29–30	over 30
30.1	35.8	42.2	47.5	52.8	47.1	53.1

SOURCES   * *Trud i Lichnost' pri Sotsializme*, vyp. 2 (Perm', 1973) p. 40; † V. N. Ermuratskii (ed.), *Sotsial'naya Aktivnost' Rabotnikov Promyshlennogo Predpriyatiya* (Kishinev, 1973) p. 95; ‡ *Sotsiologicheskie Issledovaniya*, no. 1 (1978) p. 129.

demonstrates. The trend is not a uniform and consistent one; most studies have shown a slight decrease in levels of socio-political activism beyond the age of 50 or 60, and intervening variables such as occupation, education and party membership have a considerable influence upon the level and nature of socio-political activism whatever age-group is considered.[43] The bulk of the evidence, however, certainly suggests that youthful disaffection does not normally persist unchanged into the adult years; the trend, on the contrary, is towards a generally increasing level of conformity with regime-approved behaviour as the political life-cycle advances and as generation succeeds generation.[44]

These, however, are behavioural changes only; we have no evidence that political beliefs and values have been changing in a similar manner, and the increasing levels of participation recorded may indicate no more than that an increasing proportion of young people are attaining positions of responsibility in which party membership and a high level of socio-political activism are more or less obligatory, whatever their attitude towards them. It is also unlikely, to say the least, that the political beliefs and values of successive generations of Soviet citizens have been unaffected by the different circumstances in which they have been brought up within the USSR and by their different levels of knowledge of the outside world at formative periods in their political maturation. The rapid development of Soviet economic, social, cultural and diplomatic links with the outside world, particularly over the last ten or twenty years, is shown in Table 8.3. These foreign contacts are expected to expand still further in future years: the number of foreign tourists to the USSR and of Soviet tourists abroad between 1971 and 1975 were 15 and 11 million respectively, for instance, approximately equal to the

TABLE 8.3   *Soviet contacts with the outside world, 1950–76*

	1950	*1960*	*1970*	*1976*
Foreign trade as a percentage of GNP	2.6	3.3	7.9	6.3
International air transport network (thousand km)	19.1	36.1	224.6	255.6
Passengers carried on international flights (millions)	0.0	0.2	0.9	2.1
Foreign tourists (arrivals, millions)	0.5*	0.7	2.1	3.7†
of which from USA (thousands)	2.6*	17.4	66.4	98.8†
Foreign students in Soviet higher education (thousands)	5.2*	14.3§	27.9	30.6‡
Books translated (thousands)	0.8**	5.5	3.1	4.4††
of which from English (thousands)	0.0**	0.7	0.4	1.2††
Foreign states with which USSR has diplomatic relations	60	72	108	126

SOURCES   *United Nations Statistical Yearbook* (New York, various dates); *UNESCO Statistical Yearbook* (Paris, various dates); *Narodnoe Khozyaistvo SSSR za 60 Let. Yubileinyi statisticheskii ezhegodnik* (Moscow, 1977); A. A. Gromyko and B. N. Ponomarev (eds), *Istoriya Vneshnei Politiki SSSR 1917–1975*, vol. 2 (Moscow, 1976) pp. 620–9.
* 1956; † 1975; § interpolation; ‡ 1972; ** 1954 (incomplete data); †† 1973.

totals for the previous fifteen years, and over the next five years the number of tourists in both directions is expected to increase still further to 25 and 18 million respectively.[45] Unofficial contacts are necessarily less easy to document, but the evidence suggests that they too have been increasing rapidly in scope. Perhaps 2 per cent of the Soviet population were able to listen to a foreign radio broadcast in 1940 and about 8 per cent could do so by 1950, for instance, but about 50 per cent of the total population are estimated to be able to do so at present.[46] Information sources of this kind appear by now to be of some importance to a substantial and increasing proportion of the Soviet (and especially of the educated and urban) population, and official spokesmen must increasingly reckon with them in their policy and propaganda pronouncements.[47]

It would be surprising if such different levels of awareness of the outside world, together with the changing circumstances of the USSR itself within their own lifetimes, did not make for significant differences between one Soviet generational group and another in terms of their political assumptions, values and expectations. At the level of the political leadership this problem has already received some attention: a widening gulf is opening up, it appears, between an ageing group of Politburo members, most of whom had already attained positions of prominence under Stalin, and a mass of younger party members, nearly three-quarters of whom have had no direct experience of political life within the party during the Stalin period or before it.[48] Less attention, however, has been paid to the extent to which the successive crises of recent Soviet history may have marked off a series of 'political generations' within the Soviet population more generally. A Soviet author has suggested that five such groups may be identified: a 'generation of the October Revolution and the Civil War', of which there are presently few survivors; a 'generation of the builders of Communism', who reached their political maturity during the New Economic Policy and in the periods of collectivisation and industrialisation that followed it; a generation born during the 1910s and 1920s, whose formative political experiences were the Second World War and the years of post-war reconstruction; a generation born during the 1920s and 1930s, whose formative experiences were Khrushchev's virgin lands campaign of the 1950s and the 'criticism of the cult of personality' that followed the XX Party Congress in 1956; and finally a generation of those born during the 1950s and 1960s, a generation which the author describes as the 'active builders of a new society'. United though these generations are by their common values and objectives, Smirnov suggests, there will nonetheless be differences among them in terms of the attitudes they take towards the turbulent events of the past, which are for some a live memory and for others are no more than history.[49]

A Soviet demographer, Boris Urlanis, has examined one of these generational groups more closely, the members of the 'builders of Communism' generation who were born in the year 1906. In the year of their birth, Urlanis notes, only 7 per cent of Russian towns had a municipal electricity supply, only 3 per cent had a sewage system, only 5 per cent had a public transport system, and no more than 1 per cent had a telegraph service. Levels of literacy and education were low, and levels of disease and infant mortality were high (no more than 60 per cent of the children born in 1906, for instance, survived until the age of five).[50] Most children of this age-group were too young to have experienced the October revolution themselves, though a number, including Urlanis himself, saw Lenin and heard him make a speech. Nearly all the members of the cohort, however, were caught up in the rapid expansion of educational opportunities and of industry during the 1920s and 1930s (the champion miner, Alexei Stakhanov, was himself a member of the 1906 generation), and virtually all saw service of some kind during the Second World War, in the course of which about a third of the male members of the cohort lost their lives.[51] For most members of the 1906 generation this was probably their 'finest hour', a time when the links between the party and the people were perhaps at their closest and most genuine and when Slav or Russian nationalism was at an unusual pitch of intensity.[52] Both Brezhnev and Kirilenko, among the contemporary political leadership, were born in 1906; it would not be surprising if their attitudes and those of their contemporaries diverged to some extent from those of younger Soviet generations, for whom the major crises of earlier Soviet development are of no immediate personal significance and by whom the historic achievements of the past appear very largely to be taken for granted.[53]

We unfortunately dispose of no Soviet evidence which relates directly to this question, the variation of political beliefs and values between the generations. Such evidence as is available from other sources, however, does tend to confirm the impression that younger

Soviet citizens may often have perceptions, expectations and assumptions that differ markedly from those of generations raised within the more austere atmosphere of earlier decades. A comparison between the findings of Inkeles and Bauer and those obtained from interviews with a more recent generation of Soviet emigres, for instance, suggests a good deal of continuity both between samples and between generations in terms of their support for the basic socio-economic framework of the Soviet system. The Soviet system of agriculture was an exception, and both groups similarly took a hostile attitude towards the secret police system (although more recent emigres did not often spontaneously cite the KGB as a major source of disaffection, and when pressed more closely upon it they were more likely to remark that, objectionable though its activities no doubt were, there had been major and welcome changes in both the scope of its functions and in the manner in which they were exercised.) These two features apart, however, there was a considerable degree of support in both groups for many of the most distinctive attributes of the Soviet system. There was strong support in both cases for a wide degree of public ownership in industry; the Soviet health and educational systems found a similar degree of support in both groups; and there was widespread recognition of the achievements of the Soviet authorities in both economic and cultural development. More recent emigres were aware that there were many shortcomings in the services which the Soviet system provided: medical treatment was often poor and prescriptions hard to obtain, the standard of education in rural areas left a lot to be desired, and the choice of films, plays and books which was available, even in the major cities, was generally deplorable. It was these features of the system, however, which both groups of emigres were likely to regard as among its most praiseworthy features, and which there was least desire to change should the present administration lose power.[54]

The political institutions of the Soviet state, however, attracted no comparable degree of support; and although it would be hazardous to generalise from a small and biased sample to the Soviet population as a whole, it can at least be noted that comparisons within the more recent group of emigres reveal no tendency, such as that to which the Inkeles and Bauer study drew attention, for younger respondents to be generally less alienated and dissident than their elders. Respondents in their twenties, admittedly, were more likely to take a favourable view of the activities of Lenin than were those in older age-groups, and those who took a negative view were more likely to do so reluctantly or with qualifications—'Perhaps it wasn't his fault', 'His ideas were broadly positive, but their ultimate results were negative', and so forth (Table 8.4). Younger people were also more likely to take a favourable view of particular aspects of the system, such as the educational and health services, a 'fairly high level of culture', a relatively low crime rate, full employment, cheap housing and public transport, an absence of acquisitive consumerism, and so forth. As the Inkeles and Bauer study had hypothesised, this reflects the changed and improving circumstances in which most recent Soviet generations have grown up: younger respondents had had no direct experience of Stalinism (most of those over forty, in contrast, had themselves been arrested or had suffered the loss of family and friends); they had obviously been able to acquire none of the 'private-property mentality' associated with the pre-revolutionary social order; and their overall material circumstances in the USSR they generally regarded as either good or excellent, and improving.[55]

While they were willing to accept many of the social and economic institutions of the Soviet system, however, such as extensive public ownership and the comprehensive provision of welfare, younger respondents within the more recent group of emigres were generally committed to a thoroughgoing democratisation of Soviet political life and institutions. There was virtually universal support, for instance, for the principles of freedom of speech and of the press, freedom of belief (including religious observance), the right to choose one's place of residence, and a multi-party system. Virtually all the younger respondents believed that 'it should be possible for all who wish to do so to form their own political parties without interference from the authorities', and there was strong support for the right to criticise the actions of government to whatever extent was thought necessary. These younger respondents had been born and brought up under wholly Soviet conditions; they had parents who were often favourably disposed towards the regime (and in some cases held senior positions within it); and they had generally been in no serious material difficulty. Yet there could be no doubt, comparing these findings with those which the *Soviet Citizen* obtained in the early 1950s, of the extent to which younger respondents had become both more reform-minded and less inhibited in

TABLE 8.4 *Age and political beliefs* (N = 37)

	All		Under 30		31–40		Over 40	
	Number	(Per cent)	Number	(Per cent)	Number	(Per cent)	Number	(Per cent)
Attitude towards the system ('*Sovetskaya vlast*')								
favourable	1	(2.7)	1	(4.8)	0		0	
neutral	14	(37.8)	10	(47.6)	1	(25)	3	(25)
unfavourable	22	(59.5)	10	(47.6)	3	(75)	9	(75)
Attitude towards the activities of Lenin								
favourable	15	(42.9)	12	(63.1)	1	(25)	2	(16.7)
unfavourable	20	(57.1)	7	(36.9)	3	(75)	10	(83.3)
Attitude towards public ownership of heavy industry								
favourable	25	(86.2)	18	(94.7)	1	(50)	6	(75)
unfavourable	4	(13.8)	1	(5.3)	1	(50)	2	(25)

NOTE 'Don't knows' and other non-codable responses excluded.
SOURCE Stephen White, 'Continuity and change in Soviet political culture: an emigre study', *Comparative Political Studies*, XI (1978) p. 391.

expressing their views than their elders.[56]

It would be unwise to conclude upon this basis that reformist sentiment is necessarily widespread among Soviet youth, still less that an automatic 'liberalisation' of the regime will occur as this younger generation moves into positions of political responsibility and power. The sample employed is small and admittedly imperfect; and even if it were representative of the larger population (and it does, at least, appear to accord closely with the results of most other surveys of dissident opinion[57]) it would still be impossible to disregard the rewards and sanctions of which the regime additionally disposes as a means of encouraging those forms of behaviour of which it approves and discouraging those of which it does not. Findings such as these, however, do at least suggest that it should not simply be assumed that the passage of time will be sufficient in itself to enhance the legitimacy of the existing system in the USSR, or of its political arrangements more specifically. The better educated—on the evidence, at least, of such investigations—increasingly resent their inability to participate in social and political life any other than the regime's terms, together with the petty restrictions which are placed upon their work and self-expression; younger people appear to be no more willing to accept such restrictions than their elders, while they are more inclined to take the achievements of the past for granted and to be in a position to compare the performance of the Soviet government with that of its competitors elsewhere; and even Soviet industrial workers, however satisfied they may presently be with the modest but tolerable living standards with which the regime has so far provided them, may find their commitment disturbed by the price rises and increases in labour discipline to which the Soviet authorities have increasingly been having recourse in an attempt to arrest the steady fall in growth rates which the Soviet economy has been experiencing since the early 1960s.[58]

An economic growth rate of 5 per cent or so, the level which the Soviet economy attained for most of the early 1970s, is of course a creditable achievement compared with the laggardly performance of most western economies at this time; and even an economic growth rate of 3 or 4 per cent, the figure which most observers expect the Soviet economy to attain during the 1980s and beyond, may seem a reasonable performance in comparative terms, in an economy, moreover, in which inflation and unemployment officially do not exist and in practice have been confined to remarkably low levels.[59] The reduction in the rate of economic growth which even Soviet economists have forecast, however, combined with the reduction in social mobility with which it is associated, does mean that the expectations of rapid material and occupational advance which most Soviet citizens were able to entertain as recently as a decade ago must now be doomed to disappointment; and in turn it places a new emphasis upon the fact that the Soviet system, for all its many merits, has not yet provided an institutional mechanism for the resolution of the conflicts among competing interests which such a limited growth in real resources must necessarily imply. The objectives of virtually all social groups, institutions and regions could simultaneously be accommodated when, as during the later Stalin and Khrushchev years, the national product was itself rapidly expanding. In future, however, with an economy growing at a much more modest rate and an increasingly rigid and self-recruiting social structure, it may prove more difficult to contain the pressures which these circumstances entail within institutions of government to which the majority of the population appear to have developed only a limited and provisional attachment.

Overall, then, the evidence which we have reviewed suggests that the Soviet system may have achieved a relatively high level of legitimacy, or uncoerced support; and that many of its most distinctive attributes, such as public ownership of the means of production and the comprehensive provision of welfare, may have the support of a majority even of those who reject the system as a whole and have chosen to live elsewhere. The Soviet authorities appear to have had no comparable success, however, in generating support for the institutions by which policies are determined and formulated, or in bringing about a popular commitment to Marxist–Leninist values which would be sufficient in itself to legitimate their rule. This limited degree of commitment to the Soviet 'regime' as distinct from the Soviet 'system' was first identified by the *Soviet Citizen* team during the early 1950s, and subsequent investigations have tended on the whole to confirm it.[60] In turn it suggests the tentative conclusion that the Soviet political culture may not be unaffected by the unpalatable choices, economic and otherwise, which future decades appear likely to place before it. Liberal democracies, buttressed by the 'come rain or come shine' legitimacy which their political institutions confer upon them, may find it possible to survive a period of static or even falling living standards; a regime whose legitimacy is based more narrowly upon 'performance' criteria may find it rather less easy.

Further Reading

The documentation upon which this study is based is quoted fairly fully in the Notes and References section. This bibliographical note is therefore confined to a number of the more substantial English-language works on various aspects of Soviet political culture which the interested reader might be expected to find useful.

On the concept of political culture the classic study is still Lucian W. Pye and Sidney Verba (eds), *Political Culture and Political Development* (Princeton, 1965). More recent brief surveys include Dennis Kavanagh, *Political Culture* (London, 1972) and Walter A. Rosenbaum, *Political Culture* (New York and London, 1975). Pye has made two further contributions to the concept of political culture generally: 'Political Culture' in David Sills, (ed.), *International Encyclopedia of the Social Sciences*, vol. 12 (New York, 1968), and 'Culture and political science: problems in the evaluation of the concept of political culture', in Louis Schneider and Charles M. Bonjean (eds), *The Idea of Culture in the Social Sciences* (New York and London, 1973). Robert C. Tucker's interpretation of the concept of political culture is available in his 'Culture, political culture, and communist society', *Political Science Quarterly*, LXXXVIII (1973).

On Soviet political culture more specifically the pioneering contributions have been those of Frederick C. Barghoorn: see his chapter, 'Soviet Russia: Orthodoxy and Adaptiveness' in Pye and Verba (eds), *Political Culture and Political Development*, and his book *Politics in the USSR* (Boston, 1966; second ed., 1972). Other briefer studies are included in Adam Ulam, *The Russian Political System*, third ed. (New York, 1974); John S. Reshetar, *The Soviet Polity* (Toronto, 1971); and Darrell P. Hammer, *USSR: The Politics of Oligarchy* (Hinsdale, Ill., 1974). The present author contributed a chapter, 'The USSR: Patterns of Autocracy and Industrialism', to Archie Brown and Jack Gray (eds), *Political Culture and Political Change in Communist States* (London and New York, 1977), which also contains chapters on a number of other Communist nations and useful introductory and concluding discussions.

More sociologically-oriented considerations of aspects of Soviet political culture, based upon interviews with emigres, are contained in Alex Inkeles and Raymond A. Bauer, *The Soviet Citizen* (Cambridge, Mass. and London, 1959); Zvi Gitelman, 'Soviet political culture: insights from Jewish emigres', *Soviet Studies*, XXIX (1977), and the same author's 'Recent Soviet emigres and the Soviet political system: a pilot study in Detroit', *Slavic and Soviet Series*, II (1977); Jeffrey A. Ross, 'The composition and structure of the alienation of Jewish emigrants from the Soviet Union', *Studies in Comparative Communism*, VII (1974); and the present author's 'Continuity and change in Soviet political culture: an emigre study', *Comparative Political Studies*, XI (1978). Soviet sociological research on subjects of relevance to this study are reviewed in Mervyn Matthews, *Class and Society in Soviet Russia* (London and New York, 1972), and David Lane, *The Socialist Industrial State* (London and New York, 1976); see also Aryeh L. Unger, *The Totalitarian Party. Party and People in Nazi Germany and Soviet Russia* (London and New York, 1974), and Gayle Durham Hollander, *Soviet Political Indoctrination* (New York and London, 1972).

Literature and memoirs, finally, provide insights of a different kind as well as the atoms of individual experience of which sociological generalisations are ultimately composed. I have found the following to be particularly helpful for the purposes of this study: Evgeniya Ginzburg, *Into the Whirlwind* (London, 1967); Yevgeny Yevtushenko, *A Precocious Autobiography* (London and New York, 1963); Alexander Solzhenitsyn, *The Gulag Archipelago*, vol. 2 (London and New York, 1975); Konstantin Paustovsky, *Story of a Life*, 6 vols (London, 1964–74); and Nadezhda Mandelstam, *Hope against Hope. A Memoir* (New York, 1970, and London, 1971) and *Hope Abandoned. A Memoir* (New York, 1973, and London, 1974).

Notes and References

Chapter 1

1. For further general discussions of the concept of political culture, see Walter Rosenbaum, *Political Culture* (London, 1975); Dennis Kavanagh, *Political Culture* (London, 1972); Lucian Pye, 'Political Culture', in David Sills (ed.), *International Encyclopedia of the Social Sciences*, vol. 12 (New York, 1968); and Lucian Pye and Sidney Verba (eds), *Political Culture and Political Development* (Princeton, 1965). The definition here employed is close to that of Kavanagh, whose definition in turn relates closely to that of Almond (the 'particular pattern of orientations to political action' within which the political system is embedded); it differs from both, however, in comprehending a behavioural dimension (on this see more fully below, pp. 16–18).

2. F. M. Barnard, 'Culture and political development: Herder's suggestive insights', *American Political Science Review*, LXIII (1969) 392.

3. For Lenin's usage of the term see, for instance, his *Polnoe Sobranie Sochinenii*, vol. 41 (Moscow, 1958–65) p. 404; the Webbs' use of the term is noted in Archie Brown, *Soviet Politics and Political Science* (London, 1974) p. 100. Fyodor M. Burlatsky appears to be the first Soviet social scientist to make systematic use of the concept in his *Lenin, Gosudarstvo, Revolyutsiya* (Moscow, 1970) p. 327; he notes in a more recent work that the term is 'winning an increasing degree of recognition' in Soviet academic usage—*Sotsiologiya, Politika, Mezhdunarodnye Otnosheniya* (Moscow, 1974) p. 40.

4. Its originator is usually considered to have been Gabriel Almond in his article 'Comparative political systems', *Journal of Politics*, XVIII (1956) 391–409.

5. See, for instance, Gabriel Almond and James S. Coleman (eds), *The Politics of the Developing Areas* (Princeton, 1960) p. viii; and Lucian Pye in Pye and Verba (eds), *Political Culture and Political Development*, pp. 11 and 24.

6. The classic study in this genre is Theodor W. Adorno *et al.*, *The Authoritarian Personality* (New York, 1950); an earlier work was

Harold D. Lasswell, *Psychopathology and Politics* (Chicago, 1930). For recent general reviews of such studies, see Frederick W. Greenstein, *Personality and Politics* (Chicago, 1969), and Gordon J. DiRenzo (ed.), *Personality and Politics* (New York, 1974).

7. This point is considered in W. J. M. Mackenzie, 'The export of electoral systems', reprinted in his *Explorations in Government* (London, 1975) pp. 132–53.

8. Almond and Coleman (eds), *The Politics of the Developing Areas*, pp. vii–ix.

9. Gabriel Almond and Sidney Verba's *The Civic Culture* (Princeton, 1963) was perhaps the first extended attempt to apply the concept of political culture to political systems in the developed world; see also Seymour Martin Lipset's study of the United States as a developing nation, *The First New Nation* (London, 1964).

10. This argument is advanced in Herbert J. Spiro and Benjamin R. Barber, 'Counter-ideological uses of totalitarianism', *Politics and Society*, I (1970) 3–22, and in the present author's 'Political science as ideology: the study of Soviet politics', in Brian Chapman and Allen M. Potter (eds), *W.J.M.M. Political Questions: Essays in Honour of W.J.M. Mackenzie* (Manchester, 1975). General reviews of the totalitarian concept include Leonard Schapiro, *Totalitarianism* (London, 1972) and Carl J. Friedrich (ed.), *Totalitarianism in Perspective: Three Views* (New York, 1969); the classic study is still Carl J. Friedrich and Zbigniew K. Brzezinski, *Totalitarian Dictatorship and Autocracy*, revised ed. (Cambridge, Mass., 1965).

11. 'Varieties of de-Stalinization', in Chalmers Johnson (ed.), *Change in Communist Systems* (Stanford, 1970) pp. 135–6.

12. *Problems of Communism*, XXIII (November–December, 1974) 44.

13. Nathan Leites, *The Operational Code of the Politburo* (New York, 1951) pp. xi, xiii and *passim*.

14. Nathan Leites, *A Study of Bolshevism* (Glencoe, 1953); Nathan Leites and Eva Bernault, *Ritual of Liquidation* (Glencoe, 1954). A more general statement of Leites's position is available in his 'Psychocultural hypotheses about political acts', *World Politics*, I (1948) 102–19.

15. Daniel Bell, 'Ten theories in search of Soviet reality', *World Politics*, X (1958) 327–65, p. 331 and *passim*.

16. Leites, *The Operational Code*, pp. 4, 81, 30 and 71.

17. Leites, *A Study of Bolshevism*, pp. 137 and 403–4.

18. Geoffrey Gorer and John Rickman, *The People of Great Russia* (London, 1949); Gorer's essential theses were also published in the *American Slavic and East European Review*, VIII (1949) 155–66.

19. Gorer, *The People of Great Russia*, pp. 97–8 and 128.

20. Ibid., pp. 123–4, 139, 146, 152 and 174.

21. *Human Relations*, V (1952) 111–75. A condensed and revised version of Dicks's conclusions appeared as 'Some notes on the Russian national character' in Cyril E. Black (ed.), *The Transformation of Russian Society* (Cambridge, Mass., 1960) 631–52.

22. Henry Dicks, 'Observations on contemporary Russian behaviour' (1952) 136–39 and 162 (emphasis in the original).

23. Ibid., pp. 140–41, 169–70 and 174.
24. Other studies in this general idiom include Dinko Tomasic, *The Impact of Russian Culture on Soviet Communism* (Glencoe, 1953); Nicolas Vakar, *The Tap-root of Soviet Society* (New York, 1962); and Margaret Mead, *Soviet Attitudes towards Authority* (New York, 1951). A general review of these studies is available in Clyde Kluckhohn, 'Studies of Russian national character', in Alex Inkeles and Kurt Geiger (eds), *Soviet Society* (London, 1961) pp. 636–52.
25. A. Inkeles, E. Hanfmann and H. Beier, 'Model personality and adjustment to the Soviet socio-political system', *Human Relations*, XI (1958) 3–22; see also E. Hanfmann, 'Social perception in Russian displaced persons and an American comparison group', *Psychiatry*, XX (1957) 131–49.
26. Not all investigations, for instance, have found paranoid tendencies among former Nazi leaders; and completely divergent interpretations have been given of the character attributes of relatively small tribal groups such as the Pueblo—H. C. Duijker and N. H. Frijda, *National Character and National Stereotypes* (Amsterdam, 1960) pp. 63 and 51.
27. Sherif and Sherif, for instance, examining the proposition that Germans and Japanese are somehow 'inherently aggressive', have found that the nation engaged in the largest number of wars between 1850 and 1941 was in fact the United Kingdom. The interests of a far-flung Empire, they conclude, provide a better guide in such matters than speculative 'national character' hypotheses. Quoted in K. W. Terhune, 'From national character to national behaviour: a reformulation', *Journal of Conflict Resolution*, XIV (1970) 203–63, p. 241.
28. See also more generally A. R. Lindesmith and A. L. Strauss, 'A critique of culture and personality writings', *American Sociological Review*, XIII (1950) 587–600; Alex Inkeles and Donald J. Levinson, 'National character: the study of modal personality and socio-cultural systems', in G. Lindzey and E. Aronson (eds), *Handbook of Social Psychology*, vol. 4, second ed. (Reading, Mass., 1969) pp. 418–506; and Victor T. Barnouw, *Culture and Personality*, second ed. (Homewood, Ill., 1973).
29. Dicks, 'Observations', p. 137.
30. There is an admirable discussion of such 'problems of linkage' in Greenstein, *Personality and Politics*, Chapter 5; see also Neil J. and W. T. Smelser (eds), *Personality and Social Systems*, second ed. (New York, 1970) and Fred I. Greenstein and Michael Lerner (eds), *A Source book for the Study of Personality and Politics* (Chicago, 1971), which reprint a number of the more important contributions to this debate.
31. These problems have been pointed out, for instance, by Alex Inkeles, 'Sociological observations on culture and personality studies', in Clyde Kluckhohn and Henry A. Murray (eds), *Personality in Nature, Society and Culture*, second ed. (New York, 1969) p. 581. See also Donald D. Searing *et al.*, 'The primacy principle: attitude change and political socialization', *British Journal of Political Science*, VI (1976) 83–113, which reviews most of the secondary literature to date.
32. Gorer writes, for instance, that 'in all' he 'had access to between 300

and 400 interviews' (not all of them were conducted by himself personally); but at no point does he bother to indicate what proportion of this total were Russians, how many were women, what their age distribution was, and so forth (*People of Great Russia*, pp. 13–14). For a critical review of Gorer's findings, see Irving Goldman, 'Psychiatric interpretation of Russian history: a reply to Geoffrey Gorer', *American Slavic and East European Review*, IX (1950) 151–61, and Tadeusz Grygier, 'The psychological problems of Soviet Russia', *British Journal of Psychology*, XLII (1951) 180–4.

33. Dicks, 'Observations', pp. 139–40 (a similar point is made in Goldman, 'Psychiatric interpretation', p. 156).

34. On these distinctions see Pye and Verba (eds), *Political Culture and Political Development*, p. 15; Kenneth Jowitt, 'An organizational approach to the study of political culture in marxist-leninist systems', *American Political Science Review*, LXVIII (1974) 1171–91, p. 1173; and Archie Brown and Jack Gray (eds), *Political Culture and Political Change in Communist States* (London, 1977) pp. 7–9.

35. Rosenbaum, *Political Culture*, p. 4.

36. Archie Brown, *Soviet Politics and Political Science* (London, 1974) pp. 89–90.

37. Pye and Verba (eds), *Political Culture and Political Development*, pp. 513–16.

38. David Sills (ed.), *International Encyclopedia of the Social Sciences*, vol. 12, p. 218.

39. 'Culture and political science: problems in the evaluation of the concept of political culture', in Louis Schneider and Charles M. Bonjean (eds), *The Idea of Culture in the Social Sciences* (Cambridge, 1973) p. 68; Brown and Gray (eds), *Political Culture and Political Change*, p. 10.

40. Pye and Verba (eds), *Political Culture and Political Development*, p. 514.

41. David Sills (ed.), *International Encyclopedia of the Social Sciences*, vol. 12, p. 218; Leonard Binder *et al.*, *Crises and Sequences in Political Development* (Princeton, 1971) p. 103.

42. Pye and Verba (eds), *Political Culture and Political Development*, pp. 524–5.

43. Jowitt, 'An organizational approach', p. 1173.

44. Rosenbaum, *Political Culture*, p. 8; David W. Paul, 'Political culture and the socialist purpose', in Jane P. Shapiro and Peter J. Potichnyj (eds), *Change and Adaptation in Soviet and East European Politics* (New York and London, 1976) p. 4.

45. Robert C. Tucker, 'Culture, political culture, and communist society', *Political Science Quarterly*, LXXXVIII (1973) 173–90, especially pp. 176–9.

46. Almond and Verba, for instance, not infrequently construct indices of their respondents' subjective competence from their reported actions as well as from their opinions and perceptions (see, for example, *Civic Culture*, p. 231).

47. For some recent reviews of the literature on this subject, which can be pursued no further within the framework of the present study, see I. Deutscher, *What We Say, What We Do: Sentiments and Acts* (Brighton, 1973); A. E. Liska, 'Emergent issues in the attitude-behaviour consistency controversy', *American Sociological Review*, XXXIX (1974) 261–72; and Mary R. Jackman, 'The relationship between verbal attitude and overt behaviour: a public opinion application', *Social Forces* LIV (1976) 646–68.

48. This point was among those considered at a conference on political culture and comparative Communist studies, reported in the *Newsletter on Comparative Studies of Communism*, V (1972) 2–17, especially p. 6.

49. Almond and Verba, *Civic Culture*, p. 15.

50. Ibid., p. 34; see also pp. 278 and 368.

51. This point is effectively made in Brian Barry, *Sociologists, Economists and Democracy* (London, 1970) pp. 48–52; and in Carole Pateman, 'Political culture, political structure and political change', *British Journal of Political Science*, I (1971) 291–306.

52. Michael Mann, 'The social cohesion of liberal democracy', *American Sociological Review*, XXXV (1970) 423–39, p. 437 and *passim*.

53. Samuel H. Barnes and Giacomo Sani, 'Mediterranean political culture and Italian politics: an interpretation', *British Journal of Political Science*, IV (1974) 289–303.

54. Dennis H. Wrong, 'The over-socialized conception of man in modern sociology', *American Sociological Review*, XXVI (1961) 184–93.

55. Burkhard Strumpel (ed.), *Subjective Elements of Well-being* (Paris, 1974) pp. 144–5; a more detailed account is available in Arthur H. Miller, 'Political issues and trust in government: 1964–70', *American Political Science Review*, LXVIII (1974) 951–72.

56. The fact that this apparent withdrawal of generalised trust in government has not been accompanied by political instability or systemic change suggests that the emphasis placed upon the extent to which the political system was based upon the 'civic culture' of its citizens might in any case have been misconceived.

57. Zigurd L. Zile et al., *The Soviet Legal System and Arms Inspection* (New York and London, 1972) p. 8.

58. The relation is given an elegant though perhaps somewhat opaque formulation in the works of Louis Althusser, particularly *For Marx* (London, 1969) and *Lenin and Philosophy* (London, 1971).

Chapter 2

1. This chapter develops and extends part of my contribution to Archie Brown and Jack Gray (eds), *Political Culture and Political Change in the Communist States* (London and New York, 1977).

2. Hugh Seton-Watson, *The Russian Empire* (Oxford, 1967) p. 10.

3. M. N. Tikhomirov, *Drevnerusskie Goroda* (Moscow, 1956) pp. 217–28; A. P. Novosel'tsev *et al.*, *Drevnerusskoe Gosudarstvo i ego Mezhdunarodnoe Znachenie* (Moscow, 1965) p. 37.

4. Novosel'tsev, *Drevnerusskoe Gosudarstvo*, p. 33.

5. N. L. Podvigina, *Ocherki Sotsial'no-Economicheskoi i Politicheskoi Istorii Novgoroda Velikogo v XII–XIII vv.* (Moscow, 1976) p. 105; Tikhomirov, *Drevnerusskie Goroda*, p. 224.

6. M. N. Tikhomirov (ed.), *Novgorod* (Moscow, 1964) p. 27; M. A. D'yakonov, *Ocherki Obshchestvennogo i Gosudarstvennogo Stroya Drevnei Rusi*, fourth ed. (Moscow–Leningrad, 1926) p. 106.

7. Tikhomirov records an example of its usage in Pskov in the early seventeenth century (*Drevnerusskie Goroda*, p. 231).

8. G. S. Kalinin and A. F. Goncharov (eds), *Istoriya Gosudarstva i Prava SSSR* vol. 1 (Moscow, 1972), pp. 396–7.

9. The term 'Boyar Duma' is in fact a solecism; the institution was referred to at the time simply as the 'Duma'. For the standard account, see V. O. Klyuchevsky, *Boyarskaya Duma Drevnei Rusi*, fourth ed. (Moscow, 1909).

10. G. B. Gal'perin, *Forma Pravleniya Tsentral'nogo Gosudarstva XV–XVI vv.* (Leningrad 1964) p. 46.

11. N. P. Eroshkin, *Istoriya Gosudarstvennykh Uchrezhdenii Dorevolyutsionnoi Rossii*, second ed. (Moscow, 1968) pp. 64 and 79.

12. D'yakonov, *Ocherki*, pp. 356–60; S. O. Shmidt, *Stanovlenie Rossiiskogo Samoderzhavstva* (Moscow, 1973) p. 247.

13. 'It is only for such assemblies in the seventeenth century', A. R. Myers has written, 'that any serious comparison with the parliaments of the West can be attempted'; in *Parliaments and Estates in Europe to 1789* (London, 1975) p. 41. Authoritative general accounts include M. N. Tikhomirov, 'Soslovno-predstavitel'nye uchrezhdeniya (zemskie sobory) v Rossii XVI veka', reprinted in his *Rossiiskoe Gosudarstvo XV–XVIII vekov* (Moscow, 1973); Shmidt, *Stanovlenie*, Chapter 2; and L. V. Cherepnin, *Zemskie Sobory Russkogo Gosudarstva v XVI–XVII vv.* (Moscow, 1978).

14. Eroshkin, *Istoriya*, pp. 37, 53–54 and 104.

15. Shmidt, *Stanovlenie*, pp. 246–57; D'yakonov, *Ocherki*, p. 390.

16. Richard Pipes, *Russia under the Old Regime* (London, 1974) p. 108.

17. Eroshkin, *Istoriya*, pp. 266–7; Kalinin and Goncharov (eds), *Istoriya*, vol. 1, pp. 587–9.

18. Kalinin and Goncharov (eds), *Istoriya*, vol. 1, pp. 588–9.

19. P. N. Milyukov, *Russia Today and Tomorrow* (New York, 1922) p. 6.

20. Kalinin and Goncharov (eds), *Istoriya*, vol. 1, pp. 599–602; 'Basic Laws of the Russian State' (23 April 1906), in F. I. Kalynichev (comp.), *Gosudarstvennaya Duma v Rossii v Dokumentakh i Materialakh* (Moscow, 1957) p. 141.

21. Kalinin and Goncharov (eds), *Istoriya*, vol. 1, pp. 600–1, and 576–8.

22. This case is strongly argued in Marc Szeftel, 'The representatives and their powers in the Russian legislative chambers (1906–1917)', in *Studies presented to the International Commission for the History of Par-*

liamentary and Representative Institutions, xxvii (Louvain–Paris, 1965) 219–67.

23. Kalinin and Goncharov (eds), *Istoriya,* vol. 1, p. 583; V. V. Smirnova, 'Kritika dumskogo izbiratel'nogo prava', *Vestnik Moskovskogo Universiteta. Seriya Istoriya,* no. 6 (1971) 79–86; Alfred Levin, 'The Russian voter in the elections to the Third Duma', *Slavic Review,* xxi (1962) 660–77, pp. 667 and 675.

24. E. D. Chermensky, *Istoriya SSSR. Period Imperializma* (Moscow, 1974) pp. 172–3.

25. S. M. Sidel'nikov, *Obrazovanie i Deyatel'nost' Pervoi Gosudarstvennoi Dumy* (Moscow, 1962) p. 190; Milyukov, *Russia Today and Tomorrow,* p. 5. The new electoral law of 3 June 1907 is reprinted in Kalynichev (comp.), *Gosudarstvennaya Duma,* pp. 357–95.

26. Ruth A. Roosa, 'Workers' insurance legislation and the role of industrialists in the period of the Third Duma', *Russian Review,* xxv (1975) 410–52, p. 415.

27. Ruth A. Roosa, 'Russian industrialists look to the future: thoughts on economic development 1906–1917', in John S. Curtiss (ed.), *Essays in Russian and Soviet History* (Leiden, 1963) 198–218; P. A. Berlin, *Russkaya Burzhuaziya v Staroe i Novoe Vremya* (Moscow, 1922) pp. 243–4 and 269.

28. Michael Cherniavsky, *Tsar and People* (New York, 1969) p. 83.

29. Philip Longworth, 'The pretender phenomenon in eighteenth-century Russia', *Past and Present,* 66 (1975) pp. 61 and 70.

30. Paul Avrich, *Russian Rebels* (London, 1973) pp. 257 and 269–70. There is an admirable general discussion of the 'just Tsar' phenomenon in K. V. Chistov, *Russkie Sotsial'no-utopicheskie Legendy XVII–XIX vv.* (Moscow, 1967).

31. V. Dal', *Poslovitsy Russkogo Naroda* (Moscow, 1862) pp. 244–7.

32. V. K. Sokolova, *Russkie Istoricheskie Predaniya* (Moscow, 1970) pp. 55–80; V. I. Ignatov, *Russkie Istoricheskie Pesni. Khrestomatiya* (Moscow, 1970) pp. 16 and 38–9; V. K. Sokolova, *Russkie Istoricheskie Pesni XVI–XVIII vv.* (Moscow, 1960) p. 79.

33. N. M. Shanskii (ed.), *Etimologicheskii Slovar' Russkogo Yazyka,* tom 1, vyp. 4 (Moscow 1972) p. 150; M. Fasmer, *Etimologicheskii Slovar' Russkogo Yazyka,* vol. 1 (Moscow 1964) p. 448; D'yakonov, *Ocherki,* pp. 322–3.

34. Thornton Anderson, *Russian Political Thought* (Ithaca, 1967) p. 16; Fasmer, *Etimologicheskii Slovar',* vol. 1, p. 344.

35. Alfred Levin, *The Second Duma,* second ed. (Hamden, Conn., 1966) pp. 63 and 234.

36. A. I. Nil've, 'Prigovory i nakazy krest'yan vo II Gosudarstvennuyu Dumu', *Istoriya SSSR,* no. 5 (1975) 99–110; Oliver H. Radkey, *The Elections to the Russian Constituent Assembly of 1917* (Cambridge, Mass., 1950) pp. 57–63. See also more generally Eugene D. Vinogradoff, *The Russian Peasantry and the Elections to the Fourth Duma* (unpublished Ph.D dissertation, Columbia University, 1974).

37. Alfred Levin, *The Third Duma: Election and Profile* (Hamden, Conn.,

1973) pp. 89–90.
38. E. D. Chermensky, in *Voprosy Istorii*, no. 4 (1947) p. 35.
39. Milyukov, *Russia Today and Tomorrow*, p. 4.
40. Radkey, *The Elections*, p. 2. The term 'constitutional experiment' is taken from Geoffrey Hosking's account of the State Duma, *The Russian Constitutional Experiment* (Cambridge, 1973).
41. Paul N. Milyukov, *Russia and Its Crisis* (New York, 1962) p. 129.
42. Robert C. Tucker, *The Soviet Political Mind*, revised ed. (London, 1972) 121–42, especially pp. 122–5 (the quotation is on p. 124).
43. Eroshkin, *Istoriya*, pp. 206–9 and 278–9; *Sovetskaya Istoricheskaya Entsiklopediya*, vol. 14 (Moscow, 1961–76) cols. 393–4.
44. Eroshkin, *Istoriya*, pp. 230–1; Kalinin and Goncharov (eds), *Istoriya*, vol. 1, pp. 505–10; Roger Pethybridge, *The Social Prelude to Stalinism* (London, 1974) p. 266.
45. N. S. Psurtsev (ed.), *Razvitie Svyazi v SSSR 1917–1967* (Moscow, 1967) p. 19.
46. Jacob Walkin, 'The attitude of the Tsarist government towards the labour problem, 1905–1914', *American Slavic and East European Review*, XIII (1954) 163–84, pp. 174 and 183; Kalinin and Goncharov (eds), *Istoriya*, vol. 1, p. 607; *Sovetskaya Istoricheskaya Entsiklopediya*, vol. 11, cols. 654–62.
47. Berlin, *Russkaya Burzhuaziya*, p. 205.
48. Kalinin and Goncharov (eds), *Istoriya*, vol. 1, pp. 609–11; A. P. Kositsyn *et al.*, *Istoriya Sovetskogo Gosudarstva i Prava*, vol. 1 (Moscow, 1968) p. 53.
49. Eroshkin, *Istoriya*, p. 186.
50. John W. Atwell Jr, 'The Russian Jury', *Slavonic and East European Review*, LIII (1975) 44–61, p. 45 and *passim*.
51. Eroshkin, *Istoriya*, p. 241.
52. Kalinin and Goncharov (eds), *Istoriya*, vol. 1, p. 514; Eroshkin, *Istoriya*, p. 212; Marc Szeftel, 'Personal inviolability in the legislation of the Russian absolute monarchy', *American Slavonic and East European Review*, XVII (1958) 1–24.
53. Seton-Watson, *Russian Empire*, p. 480.
54. Maxim Kovalevsky, *Russian Political Institutions* (Chicago, 1902) p. 257.
55. Ibid., p. 263; David Lane, *Politics and Society in the USSR* (London, 1970) p. 459. See also more generally John S. Curtiss, *Church and State in Russia: the Last Years of the Empire, 1900–1917* (New York, 1940).

Chapter 3

1. M. S. Anderson, *Britain's Discovery of Russia 1553–1815* (London, 1958) provides a thoughtful and well documented account of such travelogues up to the early nineteenth century; see especially pp. 19–20.

2. There are classic statements of this problem in the work of Otto Hintze—see, for instance, his 'The preconditions of representative government in the context of world history', translated in Felix Gilbert (ed. and intro. by), *The Historical Essays of Otto Hintze* (New York, 1975)—and in the work of Max Weber—most accessibly perhaps in his *General Economic History* (London, 1923). See also an important but still little known essay by Friedrich Engels, 'Über den Verfall des Feudalismus und das Aufkommen der Bourgeoisie', in K. Marx and F. Engels, *Werke*, vol. 21 (Berlin, 1956–68) pp. 392–401. More recent contributions to the debate have been made by Reinhard Bendix, *Nation-building and Citizenship* (New York, 1964); Barrington Moore, *Social Origins of Dictatorship and Democracy* (London, 1967); Samuel Huntington, *Political Order in Changing Societies* (New Haven, 1968); Charles Tilly (ed.), *The Formation of Nation States in Western Europe* (Princeton, 1975); and Gianfranco Poggi, *The Development of the Modern State. A Sociological Introduction* (London, 1978).

3. The fullest account of this subject in English is Jerome Blum, *Lord and Peasant in Russia* (Princeton, 1961), and much of the following discussion is indebted to it.

4. Ibid., p. 42.

5. Ibid., pp. 80–81.

6. Ibid., pp. 84–5. The dating of the earliest known benefice has recently been challenged: see Richard Pipes, *Russia under the Old Regime* (London, 1974) p. 52.

7. Blum, *Lord and Peasant*, pp. 139 and 168–9.

8. Ibid., p. 143.

9. Ibid., p. 146.

10. Ibid., p. 151; 'Boyarstvo i Boyarskaya Duma', in *Bol'shaya Sovetskaya Entsiklopediya*, vol. 8 (Moscow, 1926–48).

11. An historiography of the debate is provided in Blum, *Lord and Peasant*, pp. 90–2; see also George Vernadsky, 'Feudalism in Russia', *Speculum*, XIV (1939) 300–23; Marc Szeftel, 'Aspects of feudalism in Russian history', in R. Colbourn (ed.), *Feudalism in History* (Princeton, 1956); Pipes, *Russia under the Old Regime*, pp. 48–54; and A. P. Novosel'tsev, V. T. Pashuto and L. V. Cherepnin, *Puti Razvitiya Feodalizma (Zakavkaz'e, Srednyaya Aziya, Rus', Pribaltika)* (Moscow, 1972).

12. The literature on this point is admirably summarised in Georges Balandier, *Political Anthropology* (London, 1970) Chapter 4.

13. Pipes, *Russia under the Old Regime*, p. 51

14. P. I. Lyashchenko, *Istoriya Narodnogo Khozyaistva SSSR*, vol. 1, fourth ed. (Moscow, 1956) pp. 192–3. It should be noted that there were considerable regional variations in this pattern of development, above all in the Grand Duchy of Lithuania, an independent state from the thirteenth century until 1569, most of whose territory was subsequently absorbed into Russia under the third partition of Poland in 1795; see further V. T. Pashuto, *Obrazovanie Litovskogo Gosudarstva* (Moscow, 1959) pp. 332–65; G. S. Kalinin and A. F. Goncharov

(eds), *Istoriya Gosudarstva i Prava SSSR*, vol. 1 (Moscow, 1972) pp. 237–50; and Novosel'tsev *et al.*, *Puti*, pp. 287 and 295ff.

15. 'Dvoryanstvo v Rossii', in *Bol'shaya Sovetskaya Entsiklopediya*, vol. 20; see also more generally A. P. Korelin, 'Russkoe dvoryanstvo i ego soslovnaya organizatsiya (1861–1904 gg.)', *Istoriya SSSR*, no. 5 (1971) 56–81, and the same author's 'Dvoryanstvo v poreformennoi Rossii', *Istoricheskie Zapiski*, LXXXVII (1971) 91–173.

16. The Table of Ranks is conveniently reprinted in George Vernadsky *et al.* (eds), *A Source-Book for Russian History from Early Times to 1917*, 3 vols, vol. 2 (New Haven and London, 1972) pp. 343–4.

17. These demands included the abolition of lifetime military service and the establishment of special schools and regiments for the nobility, and also an undertaking that important matters of state such as the declaration of war and peace and the raising of taxation should be subject to the approval of the Privy Council. The Empress initially agreed to these conditions but subsequently reversed her decision. For an account of this and a number of other abortive proposals for reform of the period, see Marc Raeff, *Plans for Political Reforms in Imperial Russia, 1730–1905* (Englewood Cliffs, 1966) pp. 41–52 and *passim*.

18. Marc Raeff, 'Imperial Russia: Peter I to Nicholas I', in Robert Auty and Dmitri Obolensky (eds), *Companion to Russian Studies*, vol. 1: *An Introduction to Russian History* (Cambridge, 1976) p. 167.

19. Terence Emmons, *The Russian Landed Gentry and the Peasant Emancipation of 1861* (Cambridge, 1968) pp. 9–10.

20. Daniel Field, *The End of Serfdom* (Cambridge, Mass., 1976) pp. 10–13.

21. Malcolm Falkus, *The Industrialisation of Russia, 1770–1914* (London, 1972) pp. 9–11.

22. Alec Nove, *An Economic History of the USSR* (London, 1969) pp. 12–17; Lyashchenko, *Istoriya Narodnogo Khozyaistva*, vol. 2, pp. 289–90.

23. I. F. Gindin, *Russkie Kommercheskie Banky* (Moscow, 1948) p. 372; S. L. Ronin, *Inostrannye Kapitaly i Russkie Banky* (Moscow, 1926) p. 104.

24. Lyashchenko, *Istoriya Narodnogo Khozyaistva*, vol. 2, pp. 378–80.

25. Ibid., vol. 2, p. 190; Olga Crisp, *Studies in the Russian Economy before 1914* (London, 1976) pp. 29–30.

26. In the metallurgical industry, for instance, state orders accounted for 40–50 per cent of total production in the years 1896–1900—A. L. Sidorov (ed.), *Ob Osobennostyakh Imperializma v Rossii* (Moscow, 1963) p. 120.

27. Gindin, *Russkie Kommercheskie Banky*, pp. 193 and 201; J. Garvy, 'Banking under the Tsars and the Soviets', *Journal of Economic History*, XXXII (1972) 869–93, pp. 873 and 881.

28. G. R. Naumova, 'Istochniki po istorii sbytovykh monopolii v Rossii', *Vestnik Moskovskogo Universiteta. Seriya Istoriya*, no. 3 (1974), 46–57; L. E. Shepelev, 'Tsarizm i aktsionernoe uchreditel'stvo v 1870–1910 godakh', in N. E. Nosov (ed.), *Problemy Krest'yanskogo*

Zemlevladeniva i Vnutrennei Politiki Rossi (Leningrad, 1972) pp. 274–6.

29. Margaret Miller, *The Economic Development of Russia, 1905–1914* (London, 1926) p. 191; A. Ermansky, 'Krupnaya burzhuaziya do 1905 goda', in L. Martov *et al.* (eds), *Obshchestvennoe Dvizhenie v Rossii v Nachale XX Veka*, vol. 1 (St. Petersburg, 1909–11) pp. 314–16.

30. Gindin, *Russkie Kommercheskie Banky*, pp. 64–5 and 97; P. A. Berlin, *Russkaya Burzhuaziya v Staroe i Novoe Vremya* (Moscow, 1922) pp. 142–4.

31. Lyashchenko, *Istoriya Narodnogo Khozyaistva*, vol. 2, p. 352; Berlin, *Russkaya Burzhuaziya*, p. 165.

32. Garvy, 'Banking under the Tsars and the Soviets', p. 884; Crisp, *Studies in the Russian Economy*, pp. 117 and 157.

33. Lyashchenko, *Istoriya Narodnogo Khozyaistva*, vol. 2, p. 185.

34. Theodore von Laue, *Sergei Witte and the Industrialisation of Russia* (New York, 1963) pp. 73–4.

35. Blum, *Lord and Peasant*, p. 477.

36. Miller, *The Economic Development of Russia*, p. 299.

37. This was the verdict of both Bolshevik and Menshevik commentators: see, for instance, M. N. Pokrovsky, 'Burzhuaziya v Rossii', *Bol'shaya Sovetskaya Entsiklopediya*, vol. 8; and A. Ermansky, in L. Martov *et al.*, *Obshchestvennoe Dvizhenie*, vol. 1, p. 313.

38. V. I. Lenin, *Polnoe Sobranie Sochinenii*, vol. 22 (Moscow, 1958–65) p. 62; P. V. Volobuev, *Proletariat i Burzhuaziya Rossii v 1917 godu* (Moscow, 1964) p. 52.

39. Berlin, *Russkaya Burzhuaziya*, p. 165; I. F. Gindin, 'Russkaya burzhuaziya v period kapitalizma, ee razvitie i osobennosti', *Istoriya SSSR*, no. 2 (1963) 57–80, p. 75.

40. V. Yu. Laverychev, *Krupnaya Burzhuaziya v Poreformennoi Rossii (1861–1900gg.)* (Moscow 1974) p. 190; L. E. Shepelev, *Aktsionernye Kompanii v Rossii* (Leningrad, 1973) pp. 223–93.

41. Louis Menashe, 'Industrialists in politics: Russia in 1905', *Government and Opposition*, III (1968), 352–68, p. 352; Carl A. Goldberg, *The Association of Industry and Trade 1906–1917: the Successes and Failures of Russia's Organized Businessmen* (unpublished Ph.D. dissertation, University of Michigan, 1974) pp. 17 and 25–7.

42. Goldberg, *The Association of Industry and Trade*, pp. 27–8 and 232.

43. James D. White, 'Moscow, Petersburg and the Russian industrialists', *Soviet Studies*, XXIV (1973) 415–16.

44. Volobuev, *Proletariat i Burzhuaziya*, pp. 76–82.

45. Ibid., p. 43.

46. Ibid., pp. 45–9; Gindin, 'Russkaya burzhuaziya', pp. 70–1. See also the interesting exchange on this subject between James D. White and Ruth Amende Roosa, *Soviet Studies*, XXIV (1973) 414–20 and 421–5.

47. Weber's views on developments in Russia are set out in two book-length articles, 'Zur Lage der bürglichen Demokratie in Russland' and 'Russlands Übergang zum Scheinkonstitutionalismus', both published in 1906; see further Richard Pipes, 'Max Weber and Russia', *World*

Politics, VII (1955) 371–401, and David Beetham, *Max Weber and the Theory of Modern Politics* (London, 1974) Chapter 7.

48. David Lane, *The Roots of Russian Communism* (London, 1975) pp. 175 and 186–7.

49. Lyashchenko, *Istoriya Narodnogo Khozyaistva*, vol. 2, p. 468; Menashe, 'Industrialists in politics', pp. 363–5. See also Alfred J. Rieber, 'The Moscow entrepreneurial group. The emergence of a new form in autocratic politics', *Jahrbücher für Geschichte Osteuropas*, XXV (1977) 1–20 and 174–99.

50. N. Peacock (ed.), *The Russian Yearbook for 1915* (London, 1915) p. 62.

51. A. G. Rashin, *Naselenie Rossii za 100 Let (1811–1913gg.)* (Moscow, 1956) pp. 322–38.

52. Ibid., pp. 140–1 and 144–5.

53. Maurice Dobb, *Soviet Economic Development since 1917* (London, 1948) p. 36; Theodore von Laue, 'Russian peasants in the factory, 1892–1904', *Journal of Economic History*, XXI (1961) 61–80.

54. There is an admirable short discussion in Blum, *Lord and Peasant*, Chapter 24, 'The Village Community', pp. 504–35; see also V. A. Aleksandrov, *Sel'skaya Obshchina v Rossii (XVII-nachalo XIX v.)* (Moscow, 1976), which contains an extensive historiographical introduction (pp. 3–46). *Obshchina* was a somewhat wider and looser term than *mir*; for a careful attempt to distinguish between them, see Steven A. Grant, '*Obshchina* and *Mir*', *Slavic Review*, XXV (1976) 636–51.

55. Sergei Pushkarev (comp.), *A Dictionary of Russian Historical Terms from the Eleventh Century to 1917* (New Haven and London, 1970) p. 95.

56. Rene Beerman, 'Pre-revolutionary Russian peasant laws', in William E. Butler (ed.), *Russian Law: Historical and Political Perspectives* (Leiden, 1977) pp. 179–92, p. 182.

57. Ibid., pp. 182–5.

58. Wayne S. Vucinich (ed.), *The Peasant in Nineteenth-Century Russia* (Stanford, Calif., 1968) pp. 146–7.

59. The reforms are well summarised in Nicholas V. Riasanovsky, *A History of Russia*, second ed. (London, 1969) p. 459.

60. John Keep, 'Imperial Russia: Alexander II to the Revolution', in Auty and Obolensky (eds), *Companion to Russian Studies*, vol. 1, p. 227.

61. The historiography of this question is briefly summarised in Blum, *Lord and Peasant*, pp. 508–10.

62. Ibid., pp. 523–4; Sula Benet (trans. and ed.), *The Village of Viriatino* (New York, 1970) pp. 44–6.

63. Benet, *The Village of Viriatino*, p. 35; Stephen and Ethel Dunn, *The Peasants of Central Russia* (New York, 1967) p. 10.

64. Geroid T. Robinson, *Rural Russia under the Old Regime* (London, 1932) p. 256.

65. William Shinn, 'The law of the Russian peasant household', *Slavic Review*, XX (1961) 601–21; Theodore Shanin, *The Awkward Class* (Oxford, 1972) pp. 28–32.

66. Shinn, 'The law of the Russian peasant household', p. 601.
67. A recent brief account is available in John Meyendorff, 'The Church', in Auty and Obolensky (eds), *Companion to Russian Studies*, vol. 1, pp. 315–30.
68. John Maynard, *The Russian Peasant and Other Studies*, vol. 2 (London, 1942) p. 375.
69. V. I. Lenin, *Polnoe Sobranie Sochinenii*, vol. 9 (Moscow, 1958–65) p. 357.
70. 'Zlomyshlennik', in A. P. Chekhov, *Polnoe Sobranie Sochinenii i Pisem*, vol. 4 (Moscow, 1974–) pp. 84–5; cf. Nicholas V. Riazanovsky, 'Afterword: the problem of the peasant', in Vucinich (ed.), *The Peasant in Nineteenth-Century Russia*, p. 270.
71. Maxim Gorky, 'On the Russian Peasantry', in R. E. F. Smith (ed.), *The Russian Peasant, 1920 and 1984* (London, 1977) pp. 12–19.
72. Terence Emmons, 'The Peasant and the Emancipation', in Vucinich (ed.), *The Peasantry in Nineteenth-Century Russia*, pp. 41–71; Daniel Field, *Rebels in the Name of the Tsar* (Boston, 1976) pp. 1–29.
73. Auty and Obolensky (eds), *Companion to Russian Studies*, vol. 1, p. 228.
74. *Narodnoe Khozyaistvo SSSR 1922–72* (Moscow, 1972) p. 35.
75. Carlo Cipolla, *Literacy and Development in the West* (London, 1969) p. 110.
76. Paul N. Milyukov, *Russia Today and Tomorrow* (New York, 1922) p. 10.

Chapter 4

1. *Kommunisticheskii Internatsional*, no. 1 (1 May 1919) cols. 38–44.
2. V. I. Lenin, *Polnoe Sobranie Sochinenii*, 55 vols (Moscow 1958–65) vol. 37, pp. 511 and 520; and vol. 39, p. 89.
3. *Vos'moi S"ezd RKP(b). Mart 1919 Goda, Protokoly* (Moscow, 1959) pp. 390–411.
4. N. Bukharin and E. Preobrazhensky, *The ABC of Communism* (London, 1969) p. 67.
5. As noted by E. H. Carr, 'The Bolshevik Utopia', in *The October Revolution: Before and After* (New York, 1969); and by Roger Pethybridge, 'Social visions 1917–21', in *The Social Prelude to Stalinism* (London, 1971).
6. *Vtoroi S"ezd Kominterna: stenograficheskii otchet* (Moscow, 1934) p. 11.
7. G. E. Zinoviev, *Sochineniya*, 16 vols (Leningrad, 1923–9) vol. 15, p. 281.
8. *Trinnadtsatyi S"ezd RKP(b): stenograficheskii otchet* (Moscow, 1924) p. 42.
9. Lenin, *Pol. Sob. Soch.*, vol. 45, p. 404; and vol. 42, p. 59.
10. See, for instance, Lenin's formulation of this point in his 'Infantile

Malady of "Leftism"', *Pol. Sob. Soch.*, vol. 41, pp. 3–4.

11. Marcel Liebman, *Leninism under Lenin* (London, 1975) p. 322.
12. Victor Serge, *Year One of the Russian Revolution* (London, 1972) p. 202.
13. *VIII S"ezd RKP(b). 18–23 Marta 1919g. Stenograficheskii otchet* (Moscow, 1919) p. 51; *Trinnadtsatyi S"ezd*, p. 681.
14. Ya. M. Shafir, *Gazeta i Derevnya* (Moscow, 1923) pp. 49–50 and 3–4.
15. Ya. Yakovlev, *Nasha Derevnya* (Moscow, 1925) p. 125.
16. M. Ya. Fenomenov, *Sovremennaya Derevnya* (Moscow–Leningrad, 1925) pp. 39 and 95–6; Yakovlev, *Nasha Derevnya*, p. 125.
17. S. A. Andronov *et al.* (eds), *KPSS vo glave Kul'turnoi Revolyutsii v SSSR* (Moscow, 1972) p. 40.
18. *Bol'shaya Sovetskaya Entsiklopediya*, vol. 1 (Moscow, 1926–48) pp. 416–24; T. A. Remizova (ed.), *Kul'turno-prosvetitel'naya Rabota v SSSR* (Moscow, 1974) pp. 61–2; L. V. Kislichenko, 'K istorii agitatsionno-massovoi raboty KPSS', in *Voprosy Teorii i Metodov Ideologicheskoi Raboty*, vyp. 2 (Moscow, 1973) pp. 266–7. See also Richard Taylor, 'A medium for the masses: agitation in the civil war', *Soviet Studies*, XXII (1970–1) 562–74.
19. Kislichenko, 'K istorii . . .', pp. 266 and 268.
20. *Narodnoe Obrazovanie, Nauka i Kul'tura v SSSR. Statisticheskii Sbornik* (Moscow, 1977) p. 9; T. H. Rigby, *Communist Party Membership in the USSR, 1917–1967* (Princeton, 1968) pp. 403–4; Lenin, *Pol. Sob. Soch.*, vol. 44, p. 174.
21. *Sovetskaya Istoricheskaya Entsiklopediya*, vol. 4 (Moscow, 1961–76) p. 463; Kislichenko, 'K istorii . . .', p. 271; M. S. Andreeva *et al.*, *Istoriya Kul'turno-prosvetitel'noi Raboty v SSSR*, Chast' II (Khar'kov, 1970) pp. 36–40 and 46–51. There is a good general account in Sheila Fitzpatrick, *The Commissariat of Enlightenment: Soviet Organization of Education and the Arts under Lunacharsky, October 1917–1921* (London, 1970).
22. Kislichenko, 'K istorii . . .', p. 271.
23. *Desyatyi S"ezd RKP(b). Mart 1921 goda. Stenograficheskii otchet* (Moscow, 1963) pp. 594–8.
24. Zev Katz, 'Party-political education in Soviet Russia, 1918–1935', *Soviet Studies*, VII (1955–6) 237–47, p. 237; E. H. Carr, *Socialism in One Country 1924–1926*, vol. 2 (London, 1959) p. 185 (the discussion that follows is much indebted to these accounts).
25. Carr, *Socialism in One Country*, vol. 2, p. 185.
26. Ibid., pp. 190–4. See further Samuel N. Harper, *Civic Training in Soviet Russia* (Chicago, 1929) Chapter 13, for a good contemporary account.
27. Harper, *Civic Training*, p. 281; E. H. Carr, *Foundations of a Planned Economy, 1926–1929*, vol. 2 (London, 1971) pp. 158–9.
28. Katz, 'Party-political education', pp. 239–44; Carr, *Socialism in One Country*, vol. 2, pp. 186–9.
29. *Bol'shaya Sovetskaya Entsiklopediya*, vol. 10, third ed. (Moscow 1969–) pp. 493–4.

30. Robert Conquest (ed.), *Religion in the USSR* (London, 1968) pp. 13–25; David E. Powell, *Antireligious Propaganda in the Soviet Union* (London, 1975) pp. 24–6. The standard scholarly study of this process is John S. Curtiss, *The Russian Church and the Soviet State 1917–50* (Boston, 1953).
31. Conquest, *Religion in the USSR*, pp. 17, 19 and 24; Powell, *Antireligious Propaganda*, pp. 28–9 and 36.
32. Conquest, *Religion in the USSR*, p. 22; Powell, *Antireligious Propaganda*, p. 30 and *passim*.
33. V. I. Pogudin, *Ideologicheskaya Deyatel'nost'—Moguchee Orudie Kommunisticheskoi Partii v Bor'be za Sotsializm* (Moscow, 1975) p. 25; Mark W. Hopkins, *Mass Media in the Soviet Union* (New York, 1970) Chapters 2 and 7.
34. Andronov, *KPSS vo Glave*, p. 117; G. I. Klyushin and S. N. Mostovoi, *KPSS—Vospitatel' Novogo Cheloveka* (Moscow, 1970) p. 50.
35. The decree on the press of 9 November 1917 is reprinted in *Dekrety Sovetskoi Vlasti*, vol. 1 (Moscow, 1957) pp. 24–5. The contemporary system of censorship is discussed in Martin Dewhirst and Robert Farrell (eds), *The Soviet Censorship* (Metuchen, N.J., 1973).
36. N. A. Petrovichev *et al.* (eds), *Partiinoe Stroitel'stvo. Uchebnoe Posobie*, fourth ed. (Moscow, 1976) pp. 301–3; *Pravda* (13 September 1977) pp. 2–3.
37. Petrovichev *et al.* (eds), *Partiinoe Stroitel'stvo*, pp. 301–2; V. D. Vetrov *et al.* (eds), *Raionnyi Komitet Partii* (Moscow, 1972), pp. 134–7; *Bol'shaya Sovetskaya Entsiklopediya*, vol. 19, pp. 240–1.
38. *Politicheskoe Samoobrazovanie*, no. 1 (1977) p. 107.
39. 'O zadachakh partiinoi ucheby v svete reshenii XXV S"ezda KPSS' (4 June 1976) in *Ob Ideologicheskoi Rabote KPSS. Sbornik Dokumentov* (Moscow, 1977) pp. 437–41, which reprints a number of other recent resolutions on this subject.
40. Petrovichev *et al.* (eds), *Partiinoe Stroitel'stvo*, pp. 307–9; Vetrov *et al.* (eds), *Raionnyi Komitet Partii*, pp. 158–65.
41. Vetrov *et al.* (eds), *Raionnyi Komitet Partii*, pp. 131–2.
42. Petrovichev *et al.* (eds), *Partiinoe Stroitel'stvo*, pp. 312–13; Vetrov *et al.* (eds), *Raionnyi Komitet Partii*, pp. 147–8, 'Prizvanie agitatora', *Pravda* (11 January 1978) p. 1.
43. Petrovichev *et al.* (eds), *Partiinoe Stroitel'stvo*, p. 313; Vetrov *et al.* (eds), *Raionnyi Komitet Partii*, pp. 148–50.
44. Petrovichev *et al.* (eds), *Partiinoe Stroitel'stvo*, pp. 312–16; Vetrov *et al.* (eds), *Raionnyi Komitet Partii*, pp. 144–6. The numbers engaged in mass-agitational work are as reported in *Partiinaya Zhizn'*, no. 10 (1976) p. 23.
45. See, for instance, N. S. Afonin (ed.), *Politicheskaya Agitatsiya v Trudovom Kollektive* (Saransk, 1976) p. 29; *Sotsiologicheskie Issledovaniya*, no. 4 (1976) p. 81.
46. See A. L. Unger, 'Politinformator or agitator: a decision blocked', *Problems of Communism*, XIX (September–October, 1970) 30–43.
47. Powell, *Antireligious Propaganda*, pp. 48–51; *Ezhegodnik Bol'shoi*

Sovetskoi Entsiklopedii 1977 (Moscow, 1977) p. 27.

48. *Narodnoe Obrazovanie, Nauka i Kul'tura v SSSR*, p. 348.
49. N. I. Mekhontsev *et al., Lektor i Slushatel'* (Moscow, 1975) pp. 16–18.
50. Vetrov *et al.* (eds), *Raionnyi Komitet Partii*, pp. 151–2; M. F. Nenashev, *Ratsional'naya Organizatsiya Ideologicheskoi Raboty* (Moscow, 1976) p. 121; *Agitator*, no. 13 (1976) pp. 42–5. See also Aryeh L. Unger, *The Totalitarian Party. Party and People in Nazi Germany and Soviet Russia* (London, 1974) pp. 128–39.
51. *Partiinaya Zhizn'*, no. 19 (1977) pp. 8–11.
52. *Partiinaya Zhizn'*, no. 20 (1977) pp. 5–16.
53. Unger, *The Totalitarian Party*, pp. 126–8; Ronald J. Hill, 'The CPSU in a Soviet election campaign', *Soviet Studies*, xxviii (1976) 590–8.
54. L. I. Brezhnev, *Leninskim Kursom*, vol. 5 (Moscow, 1976) p. 545.
55. O. E. Kutafin, *Postoyannye Komissii Mestnykh Sovetov po delam Molodezhi* (Moscow, 1974) pp. 4–14; E. Vasil'ev (ed.), *Formirovanie Novogo Cheloveka* (Moscow, 1974) pp. 61–77; *Ezhegodnik Bol'shoi Sovetskoi Entsiklopedii 1977*, pp. 22–5.
56. For a good general discussion of these points, see Nigel Grant, *Soviet Education*, third ed. (Harmondsworth, 1972); and Urie Bronfenbrenner, *Two World of Childhood: US and USSR* (London, 1971).
57. *Materialy XXIV S"ezda K.P.S.S.* (Moscow, 1971) p. 89.
58. *Narodnoe Khozyaistvo SSSR za 60 Let* (Moscow, 1977) p. 613. *The United Nations Statistical Yearbook 1976* (New York, 1977) gives the following figures for the circulation of 'daily and non-daily general interest newspapers per thousand population': France 220; USA 293; West Germany 289; USSR 388; United Kingdom 443; Japan 526 (pp. 884–8).
59. *Ezhegodnik Bol'shoi Sovetskoi Entsiklopedii 1977*, pp. 94–5.
60. *Narodnoe Khozyaistvo SSSR za 60 Let*, p. 613.
61. *Pravda* (21 February 1978) 3; *Ezhegodnik Bol'shoi Sovetskoi Entsiklopedii 1977*, pp. 95–6.

Chapter 5

1. *Materialy XXV S"ezda KPSS* (Moscow, 1976) p. 76.
2. V. I. Lenin, *Polnoe Sobranie Sochinenii*, vol. 33 (Moscow, 1958–65) p. 102; L. I. Brezhnev, *Leninskim Kursom*, vol. 2 (Moscow, 1970) p. 106.
3. *Materialy XXV S"ezda KPSS*, p. 77; Brezhnev, *Leninskim Kursom*, vol. 3 (Moscow, 1972) p. 287.
4. I. F. Protchenko, *Leksika i Slovoobrazonanie Russkogo Yazyka Sovetskoi Epokhi* (Moscow, 1975) pp. 108 and 30; see also Bernard Comrie and Gerald Stone, *The Russian Language since the Revolution* (Oxford, 1978) Chapter 5.
5. S. I. Ozhegov, *Leksikologiya. Leksikografiya. Kul'tura Rechi* (Moscow, 1974) pp. 32–33; Comrie and Stone, *The Russian Language*, pp. 197–9.
6. V. A. Nikonov (ed.), *Lichnye Imena v Proshlom, Nastoyashchem, Bud-*

ushchem (Moscow, 1970) pp. 34–5.

7. Ibid., pp. 87–8; *The Times* (22 January 1970) p. 10; and (30 January 1970) p. 11.
8. For a full discussion of this point, see Victor Zaslavsky and Robert J. Brym, 'The functions of elections in the USSR', *Soviet Studies*, xxx (1978) 362–71.
9. This is the so-called 'missing one per cent': see Jerome M. Gilison, 'Soviet elections as a measure of dissent: the missing one per cent', *American Political Science Review*, lxii (1968) 814–26.
10. See, for instance, Yu. V. Andropov as reported in *Pravda* (10 September 1977).
11. Andrew J. Milnor, *Elections and Political Stability* (Boston, 1969) pp. 99–100 and 120.
12. *Materialy XXV S"ezda*, p. 64.
13. Ibid., p. 63.
14. For a full discussion of this point, see Jerry F. Hough, 'Party "saturation" in the Soviet Union', in Paul Cocks *et al.* (eds), *The Dynamics of Soviet Politics* (Cambridge, Mass., and London, 1976).
15. The evidence on this point is considered in D. Richard Little, 'Mass political participation in the U.S. and the U.S.S.R.: a conceptual analysis', *Comparative Political Studies*, viii (1976) 437–60; and in Norman H. Nie and Sidney Verba, 'Political participation', in Fred I. Greenstein and Nelson W. Polsby (eds), *Handbook of Political Science*, vol. 4 (Reading, Mass., 1975).
16. D. Z. Mutagirov, 'Sotsial'noe planirovanie i razvitie obshchestvenno-politicheskoi aktivnosti trudyashchikhsya', *Chelovek i Obshchestvo*, iii (1968) 37.
17. This point is made in Mervyn Matthews, *Class and Society in Soviet Russia* (London, 1972) p. 254; there is a comprehensive review of the findings of such research in ibid., pp. 230–54, and in N. F. Tret'yakov, 'Problema sotsial'noi aktivnosti lichnosti v sotsiologii 60-kh godov', *Problemy Sotsiologicheskikh Issledovanii*, iii (1973) 21–32.
18. S. G. Strumilin, *Byudzhet Vremeni Russkogo Rabochego i Krest'yanina* (Moscow–Leningrad, 1924) pp. 24–6.
19. 3. G. Strumilin, *Rabochii Den' i Kommunizm* (Moscow, 1959) p. 15.
20. *Sotsial'nye Issledovaniya*, vi (1970) pp. 103–4.
21. L. Yu. Savitskii, *Obshchestvennaya Deyatel'nost' kak Faktor Vospitaniya Kommunisticheskogo Otnosheniya k Trudu* (avtoreferat kand. diss., Moscow, 1974) p. 9.
22. S. I. Tereshchenko (ed.), *Gor'kaya Balka* (Stavropol', 1972) p. 117; *Kommunist Moldavii*, no. 7 (1973) p. 55.
23. M. Sh. Tselishcheva, *Politicheskoe Vospitanie Trudyashchikhsya v period Stroitel'stva Kommunizma* (avtoreferat kand. diss., Leningrad, 1972) p. 17; M. Kh. Belen'kii, *Aktivnost' Narodnykh Mass* (Krasnoyarsk, 1973) p. 202; F. A. Baturin and V. M. Zasorin, *Vospitanie Aktivnosti Kommunistov* (Moscow, 1975) p. 39; T. Yaroshevskii and N. S. Mansurov (eds), *Aktivnost' Lichnosti v Sotsialisticheskom Obshchestve* (Moscow–Warsaw, 1974) p. 255.

24. Strumilin, *Byudhzet Vremeni*, p. 24.
25. G. E. Zborovskii and G. P. Orlov, *Dosug: Deistvitel'nost' i Illyuzii* (Sverdlovsk, 1970) p. 220.
26. *Usloviya Povysheniya Obshchestvennoi Raboty* (Volgograd, 1973) p. 140.
27. *Nauka Ubezhdat'* (Moscow, 1969) p. 439.
28. L. N. Kogan (ed.), *Molodezh': ee Interesy, Stremleniya, Idealy* (Moscow, 1969) pp. 196–7.
29. E. O. Kabo, *Ocherki Rabochego Byta* (Moscow, 1928) p. 200; A. M. Bol'shakov, *Sovetskaya Derevnya v Tsifrakh* (Leningrad, 1925) p. 109.
30. V. N. Sherdakov *et al.* (eds), *Ateizm, Religiya, Sovremennost'* (Leningrad, 1973) pp. 128–9.
31. See David E. Powell, *Antireligious Propaganda in the Soviet Union: a Study of Mass Persuasion* (London, 1975) pp. 134–6, and Barbara W. Jancar, 'Religious dissent in the Soviet Union', in Rudolf L. Tökés (ed.), *Dissent in the USSR* (London, 1975) pp. 191–230.
32. There is a good discussion of these and related questions in Christel Lane, *Christian Religion in the Soviet Union* (London, 1978).
33. For a comparative sociological discussion of these points, see Susan Budd, *Sociologists and Religion* (London, 1973); and James T. Borhek and Richard F. Curtis, *A Sociology of Belief* (London, 1975).
34. *Materialy Mezhvuzovskoi Nauchnoi Konferentsii po Probleme Vozrastaniya Aktivnosti Obshchestvennogo Soznaniya v period Stroitel'stva Kommunizma* (Kursk, 1968) pp. 361–2.
35. Ethel and Stephen P. Dunn, 'Religious behaviour and socio-cultural change in the Soviet Union', in Bohdan Bociurkiw and John W. Strong (eds), *Religion and Atheism in the USSR and Eastern Europe* (London, 1975) pp. 133–5.
36. Tereshchenko (ed.), *Gor'kaya Balka*, pp. 114–15; Alexandre Bennigsen, 'Islam in the Soviet Union: the religious factor and the nationality problem', in Bociurkiw and Strong (eds), *Religion and Atheism*, pp. 91–100.
37. Alex Inkeles and Raymond A. Bauer, *The Soviet Citizen. Daily Life in a Totalitarian Society* (Cambridge, Mass., and London, 1959).
38. This point is made in ibid., pp. 26–7; see also the admirable methodological discussion in Chapters 2 and 3, pp. 21–64, which has served as a point of departure for most subsequent emigre-based research of this kind.
39. For a general discussion of the sources that may be drawn upon in the study of Communist political culture, see Archie Brown and Jack Gray (eds), *Political Culture and Political Change in Communist States* (London, 1977) pp. 10–12.
40. As argued in Inkeles and Bauer, *The Soviet Citizen*, p. viii; see also Lewis A. Dexter, *Elite and Specialized Interviewing* (Evanston, Ill., 1970); and Raymond L. Gorden, *Interviewing: Strategy, Techniques and Tactics*, revised ed. (Homewood, Ill., 1975), who employs the term 'triangulation' to refer to a procedure of this kind for cross-checking the validity of one's findings (p. 40).

41. Inkeles and Bauer, *The Soviet Citizen*, pp. 242–6.
42. Stephen White, 'Continuity and change in Soviet political culture: an emigre study', *Comparative Political Studies*, xi (1978) 381–95, 386–7; this article contains a fuller presentation of these findings.
43. Inkeles and Bauer, *The Soviet Citizen*, p. 236.
44. Ibid., pp. 236–42.
45. Ibid., pp. 246–51.
46. Betsy Gidwitz, 'Problems of adjustment of Soviet Jewish emigrés', *Soviet Jewish Affairs*, no. 1 (1976) 27–42, pp. 35–6.
47. Zvi Gitelman, *Soviet Immigrants in Israel* (New York, 1972) p. 30.
48. Inkeles and Bauer, *The Soviet Citizen*, pp. 246–54 and 397.
49. White, 'Continuity and change in Soviet political culture', 384–7.
50. Zvi Gitelman, 'Soviet political culture: insights from Jewish emigrés', *Soviet Studies*, xxix (1977) 543–64, pp. 558–61.
51. Andrei Amalrik, *Will the Soviet Union survive until 1984?* (London, 1970) pp. 31–2.
52. Alexander Solzhenitsyn, *August 1914* (London, 1974) p. 528.
53. This point is admirably documented in Roy Medvedev, *Let History Judge* (London, 1972).
54. Evgeniya Ginzburg, *Into the Whirlwind* (London, 1968) pp. 169 and 223; Yevgeny Yevtushenko, *A Precocious Autobiography* (London, 1963) p. 13.
55. Victor Fainberg, 'Soviet dissidents', in Open University, Course D333: Soviet Government and Politics, *Supplementary Material: Broadcast Notes* (Milton Keynes, 1976) pp. 12–15.
56. Alexander Solzhenitsyn, *The Gulag Archipelago*, vol. 2 (London, 1975) pp. 328–37.
57. Edward Crankshaw (ed.), *Khrushchev Remembers* (London, 1971) pp. 317–18 (but cf. p. 285 where Khrushchev himself describes Beria as a 'wolf in sheep's clothing who had sneaked into Stalin's confidence and had been able to secure a high position by deceit and treachery')
58. Hedrick Smith, *The Russians* (London, 1976) pp. 194–6.
59. Smith, *The Russians*, pp. 195 and 246–7.
60. Solzhenitsyn, *Gulag Archipelago*, vol. 2, pp. 633–53.
61. Jeffrey A. Ross, 'The composition and structure of the alienation of Jewish emigrants from the Soviet Union', *Studies in Comparative Communism*, vii (1974) 107–18, p. 113; Gitelman, 'Soviet political culture', p. 555.
62. Zvi Gitelman, 'Recent Soviet emigrés and the Soviet political system: a pilot study in Detroit', *Slavic and Soviet Series*, ii (1977) 40–60, p. 57.
63. Smith, *The Russians*, pp. 255–6.
64. Quoted in Robert C. Tucker, *The Soviet Political Mind. Stalinism and Post-Stalin Change*, revised ed. (London, 1972) pp. 140–1.
65. The term 'linguistic dualism' is taken from Nadezhda Mandelshtam, *Hope against Hope: a Memoir* (London, 1971) p. 89.

Chapter 6

1. Some of the material contained in this chapter was first presented in the present author's 'Political socialization in the USSR: a study in failure?', *Studies in Comparative Communism*, x (1977) 328–42.
2. Carl Friedrich and Zbigniew K. Brzezinski, *Totalitarian Dictatorship and Autocracy*, second ed. (Cambridge, Mass., 1965) p. 22.
3. *Konstitutsiya (Osnovnoi Zakon) Soyuza Sovetskikh Sotsialisticheskikh Respublik* (Moscow, 1977) p. 5; *Ustav Kommunisticheskoi Partii Sovetskogo Soyuza* (Moscow, 1973) p. 5.
4. L. I. Brezhnev, *Leninskim Kursom*, vol. 5 (Moscow, 1976) pp. 548–9; *Pravda* (14 March 1976) p. 1.
5. Donald W. Treadgold (ed.), *The Development of the USSR* (Seattle, 1964) p. 24; Fred I. Greenstein and Nelson W. Polsby (eds), *Handbook of Political Science*, vol. 3 (Reading, Mass., 1975) p. 31.
6. To borrow the title of P. V. Pozdnyakov, *Effektivnost' Kommunisticheskoi Propagandy* (Moscow, 1975).
7. E. M. Kuznetsov, *Politicheskaya Agitatsiya: Nauchnye Osnovy i Praktika* (Moscow, 1974) p. 9 and pp. 3–11 *passim*.
8. The Academy, a party higher educational institution, was founded in 1946; it offers courses in a variety of party-relevant specialisms and sponsors a series of academic publications and periodicals.
9. For a general discussion of the character and reliability of Soviet sociological research, see Elizabeth A. Weinberg, *The Development of Sociology in the Soviet Union* (London, 1974) especially pp. 108–12.
10. N. S. Afonin, *Effektivnost' Lektsionnoi Propagandy* (Moscow, 1975) pp. 95–6.
11. *Voprosy Teorri i Metodov Ideologicheskoi Raboty*, vyp. 6 (Moscow, 1976) p. 107.
12. Ibid., p. 107.
13. Ibid., vyp. 4 (Moscow, 1975) p. 151.
14. *Kommunist Sovetskoi Latvii*, no. 6 (1972) p. 37, quoted in Aryeh L. Unger, *The Totalitarian Party. Party and People in Nazi Germany and Soviet Russia* (London, 1974) p. 146, n. 136.
15. *Pravda* (23 May 1977) 2.
16. V. S. Korobeinikov (ed.), *Sotsiologicheskie Problemy Obshchestvennogo Mneniya i Sredstv Massovoi Informatsii* (Moscow, 1975) pp. 102 and 104.
17. N. I. Mekhontsev *et al.*, *Lektor i Slushatel'* (Moscow, 1975) p. 65.
18. See, for instance, *Praktika Ideologicheskoi Raboty i ee Sovershenstvovaniya* (Vilnius, 1975) p. 101; Afonin, *Effektivnost' Lektsionnoi Propagandy*, pp. 87–8; *Voprosy Teorii i Metodov Ideol. Raboty*, vyp. 7 (Moscow, 1977) pp. 161–2.
19. Mekhontsev *et al.*, *Lektor i Slushatel'*, p. 97.
20. See, for instance, *Voprosy Teorii i Metodov Ideol. Raboty*, vyp. 3 (Moscow, 1974) p. 189; G. L. Smirnov *et al.* (eds), *Voprosy Teorii i Praktiki Partiinoi Propagandy* (Moscow, 1971) p. 243; N. N. Bokarev (ed.), *Sotsiologicheskie Issledovaniya v Partiinoi Rabote* (Moscow,

1973) pp. 29, 31 and 58: P. V. Pozdnyakov (ed.), *Politicheskaya Informatsiya. Nekotorye Voprosy Teorii i Praktiki* (Moscow, 1974) p. 87.
21. See, for instance, *Pravda* (11 November 1976) 3; (27 June 1977) 2; and (30 January 1978) 2.
22. *Pravda* (14 March 1975) 2.
23. Kuznetsov, *Politicheskaya Agitatsiya*, p. 275; see similarly *Pravda* (23 May 1977) 2, and (29 November 1977) 2.
24. See, for instance, Pozdnyakov, *Politicheskaya Informatsiya*, p. 87.
25. See, for instance, N. S. Afonin, *Lektor i Auditoriya* (Saransk, 1973) p. 48; *Voprosy Teorii i Metodov Ideol. Raboty*, vyp. 7, p. 162.
26. N. I. Mekhontsev *et al.*, *Lektsiya v Otsenke Slushatelei* (Moscow, 1973) p. 69.
27. *Pravda* (5 October 1976) 3.
28. Ibid. (3 March 1975) 2.
29. See, for instance, Pozdnyakov (ed.), *Politicheskaya Informatsiya*, pp. 24 and 87; *Voprosy Teorii i Metodov Ideol. Raboty*, vyp. 7, p. 163.
30. *Voprosy Teorii i Metodov Ideol. Raboty*, vyp. 6, p. 116.
31. *Sotsiologicheskie Issledovaniya*, no. 4 (1975) p. 115.
32. *Aktual'nye Voprosy Propagandistskoi i Massovo-politicheskoi Raboty na Sovremennom Etape* (Moscow, 1976) p. 138 and *passim*.
33. Afonin, *Lektor i Auditoriya*, p. 48; Pozdnyakov (ed.), *Politicheskaya Informatsiya*, p. 33; S. G. Novruzov, *Voprosy Sovershenstvovaniya Politicheskogo Informirovaniya Trudyashchikhsya* (avtoreferat kand. diss., Moscow, 1974) p. 14.
34. *Voprosy Teorii i Metodov Ideol. Raboty*, vyp. 3, p. 189.
35. V. G. Baikova, *Ideologicheskaya Rabota KPSS v Usloviakh Razvitogo Sotsializma* (Moscow, 1977) p. 150.
36. See, for instance, ibid., pp. 134–5 and 151–2.
37. Pozdnyakov (ed.), *Politicheskaya Informatsiya*, p. 109; Baikova, *Ideologicheskaya Rabota*, p. 138—but cf. *Partiinaya Zhizn'*, no. 8 (1977) 36–7.
38. *Voprosy Teorii i Metodov Ideol. Raboty*, vyp. 8 (Moscow, 1977) p. 97.
39. N. S. Afonin (comp.), *Politicheskaya Agitatsiya v Trudovom Kollektive* (Saransk, 1976) p. 28; Afonin, *Lektor i Auditoriya*, p. 73.
40. Afonin, *Lektor i Auditoriya*, p. 91; Baikova, *Ideologicheskaya Rabota*, p. 138.
41. G. I. Mel'nikov (ed.), *Kollektiv i Lichnost'* (Irkutsk, 1973) pp. 133–4.
42. M. V. Gramov (ed.), *Kompleksnyi Podkhod v Ideologicheskoi Rabote: Stil' i Metody* (Moscow, 1976) p. 96.
43. *Problemy Povysheniya Effektivnosti Kommunisticheskoi Propagandy*, vyp. 3 (Tomsk, 1975) p. 75.
44. David Powell, *Antireligious Propaganda in the Soviet Union: a Study in Mass Persuasion* (Cambridge, Mass., 1975) pp. 117–18 and 141–2.
45. M. V. Gramov and N. S. Chernykh (eds), *Ideino-vospitatel'naya Rabota v Proizvodstvennom Kollektive: Opyt, Problemy* (Moscow, 1976) p. 122.
46. Mekhontsev *et al.*, *Lektsiya v Otsenke Slushatelei*, pp. 27–8.
47. *Voprosy Teorii i Metodov Ideol. Raboty*, vyp. 1 (Moscow, 1972),

pp. 282–99; Pozdnyakov (ed.), *Politicheskaya Informatsiya*, p. 85.
48. Mekhontsev *et al.*, *Lektsiya v Otsenke Slushatelei*, p. 28.
49. *Pravda* (2 March 1977) 1, and (5 August 1977) 1; L. Ya. Zile (ed.), *Formy i Metody Ideologicheskoi Raboty Partii* (Riga, 1974) p. 169.
50. M. F. Nenashev in *Kommunist*, no. 4 (1977) 33.
51. A further resolution, 'On the state and measures for the improvement of lecture propaganda', was published in *Pravda* on 5 March 1978; it listed many of the deficiencies the earlier resolution had included.
52. G. I. Balkhanov, *Ustnaya Propaganda i ee Effektivnost'* (Ulan–Ude, 1974) p. 60; *Effektivnost' Partiinoi Ucheby. Iz Opyta Raboty Shkol Partiinoi i Komsomol'skoi Ucheby* (Syktyvkar, 1972) p. 7.
53. *Usloviya Povysheniya Obshchestvennoi Raboty* (Volgograd, 1973) p. 80; Afonin, *Effektivnost' Lektsionnoi Propagandy*, pp. 95–6; A. G. Efimov and P. V. Pozdnyakov, *Nauchnye Osnovy Partiinoi Propagandy* (Moscow, 1966) p. 101.
54. I. S. Soltan, *Politicheskaya Ucheba i Razvitie Obshchestvenno-politicheskoi Aktivnosti Rabotnikov Promyshlennogo Predpriyatiya* (avtoreferat kand. diss., Kishinev, 1973) pp. 18–19.
55. N. S. Afonin, *Sotsial'no-politicheskie Aspekty Povysheniya Effektivnosti Partiinoi Propagandy* (avtoreferat kand. diss., Moscow, 1973) p. 20 (the published version is the same author's *Lektor i Auditoriya*).
56. *Usloviya Povysheniya Obshchestvennoi Raboty*, p. 101.
57. *Usloviya Povysheniya Sotsial'noi Aktivnosti Rabochego Klassa v period Stroitel'stva Kommunizma. Sbornik Statei* (Rostov-on-Don, 1974) p. 88.
58. See White, 'Political Socialization in the USSR', p. 335.
59. Bokarev (ed.), *Sotsiologicheskie Issledovaniya v Partiinoi Rabote*, pp. 43–44.
60. N. N. Bokarev (ed.), *Sotsiologicheskie Issledovaniya v Ideologicheskoi Rabote*, vyp. 1 (Moscow 1974) p. 133; M. I. Fedorova, *Issledovaniya Putei Povysheniya Effektivnosti Raboty Sistemy Politicheskogo Prosveshcheniya v Zavodskikh Usloviakh* (avtoreferat kand. diss., Leningrad, 1968) pp. 12–13.
61. *Voprosy Teorii i Metodov Ideol. Raboty*, vyp. 4, p. 151.
62. Bokarev (ed.), *Sotsiologicheskie Issledovaniya v Ideol. Rabote*, vyp. 1, p. 108.
63. V. G. Baikova (ed.), *Politicheskoe Obrazovanie: Sistema, Metodika, Metodologiya* (Moscow, 1976) p. 224.
64. N. A. Petrovichev (ed.), *Partiinoe Stroitel'stvo. Uchebnoe Posobie*, fifth ed. (Moscow, 1978) p. 297.
65. See for instance Bokarev (ed.), *Sotsiologicheskie Issledovaniya v Partiinoi Rabote*, pp. 31 and 58; L. M. Molodtsov *et al.* (comps), *Deistvennost' Politicheskoi Ucheby* (Moscow, 1973) p. 41.
66. See, for instance, Zile (ed.), *Formy i Metody*, p. 120; *Partiinaya Zhizn'*, no. 20 (1975) p. 42; Baikova (ed.), *Politicheskoe Obrazovanie*, p. 82.
67. *Problemy Nauchnogo Kommunizma*, vyp. 2 (Moscow, 1968) p. 116.
68. Baikova (ed.), *Politicheskoe Obrazovanie*, p. 96; Zile (ed.), *Formy i Metody*, pp. 38–9, 51 and 119; *Pravda* (10 October 1976) 1.

69. Baikova (ed.), *Politicheskoe Obrazovanie*, p. 125; *Pravda* (13 November 1976) 1; *Politicheskoe Samoobrazovanie*, no. 5 (1977) 94.
70. *Pravda* (12 June 1976) 1.
71. Baikova, *Ideologicheskaya Rabota*, p. 148.
72. See, for instance, Baikova (ed.), *Politicheskoe Obrazovanie*, pp. 30–2.
73. Ibid., p. 32.
74. Soltan, *Politicheskaya Ucheba*, p. 15.
75. See, for instance, *Voprosy Effektivnosti Partiinoi Propagandy i Politicheskoi Informatsii*, vyp. 2 (Moscow, 1974) p. 129.
76. Gramov (ed.), *Kompleksnyi Podkhod*, pp. 92–3; Afonin, *Lektor i Auditoriya*, p. 73.
77. Yu. M. Khrustalev, *Formirovanie Politicheskogo Soznaniya Lichnosti v Usloviakh Razvitogo Sotsializma* (avtoreferat kand. diss., Moscow, 1974) p. 33.
78. *Voprosy Effektivnosti Partiinoi Propagandy i Pol. Informatsii*, vyp. 2, p. 129.
79. Bokarev (ed.), *Sotsiologicheskie Issledovaniya v Ideol. Rabote*, vyp. 1, p. 111.
80. Baikova (ed.), *Politicheskoe Obrazovanie*, p. 223.
81. Bokarev (ed.), *Sotsiologicheskie Issledovaniya v Ideol. Rabote*, vyp. 1, p. 142.
82. Baikova (ed.), *Politicheskoe Obrazovanie*, p. 204.
83. P. V. Pozdnyakov (ed.), *Effektivnost' Ideino-vospitatel'noi Raboty* (Moscow, 1975) pp. 106 and 110.
84. Afonin (comp.), *Politicheskaya Agitatsiya v Trudovom Kollektive*, p. 27.
85. *Politicheskoe Samoobrazovanie*, no. 9 (1976) 130.
86. *Partiinaya Zhizn'*, no. 21 (1977) p. 43 (and see also above, p. 77). The proportion of party propagandists in Belorussia with a higher education is presently 93 per cent, and in Moldavia it is 96 per cent—P. M. Masherov, *Ideinopoliticheskoi Rabote—Vysokaya Ideinost'* (Moscow, 1975) p. 68; P. K. Luchinskii, *Perspektivnoe Planirovanie Ideologicheskoi Raboty* (Moscow, 1975) p. 95.
87. Baikova (ed.), *Politicheskoe Obrazovanie*, p. 216.
88. See, for instance, the resolutions referred to in notes 120 and 121 below.
89. *Kommunist Estonii*, no. 9 (1977) 66; *Voprosy Teorii i Metodov Ideol. Raboty*, vyp. 8, p. 92.
90. *Voprosy Teorii i Metodov Ideol. Raboty*, vyp. 8, p. 92.
91. Only 17 per cent of agitators in the town of Taganrog, for instance, were reported to have a higher education in a study of the late 1960s—V. I. Brovikov and I. V. Popovich, *Sovremennye Problemy Politicheskoi Informatsii i Agitatsii* (Moscow, 1969) p. 106—and only 30 per cent of agitators in the Vologda region, more recently, were reported to be party members—*Partiinaya Zhizn'*, no. 8 (1977) 35.
92. *Agitator*, no. 11 (1977) 33–4; *Pravda* (12 April 1975) 2, and (24 July 1975) 2; Kuznetsov, *Politicheskaya Agitatsiya*, p. 8; *Agitator*, no. 18 (1977) 59; Yu. I. Leonov, *Ubeditel'no, Dokhodchivo, Nastu-*

216   Notes and References to pages 131–5

patel'no (Moscow, 1977) p. 76.
93. See, for instance, *Kommunist Estonii*, no. 9 (1977) 65; *Pravda* (12 April 1975) 2; *Agitator* (1977) no. 6, p. 5; no. 7, p. 10; and no. 18, p. 59.
94. *Agitator* no. 1 (1977) 62.
95. *Sotsiologicheskie Issledovaniya*, no. 4 (1975) 111–12 and 114; See similarly *Politicheskoe Samoobrazovanie*, no. 7 (1977) 120.
96. Baikova (ed.), *Politicheskoe Obrazovanie*, pp. 215–16.
97. See, for instance, *Sotsiologicheskie Issledovaniya*, no. 4 (1975) 110; Leonov, *Ubeditel'no*, pp. 78–9; *Voprosy Teorii i Metodov Ideol. Raboty*, vyp. 8, p. 92; Mekhontsev *et al.*, *Lektor i Slushatel'*, pp. 18–19.
98. Baikova (ed.), *Politicheskoe Obrazovanie*, p. 77; Smirnov *et al.* (eds), *Voprosy Teorii i Praktiki Partiinoi Propagandy*, p. 189.
99. *Sotsiologicheskie Issledovaniya*, no. 4 (1975) 112.
100. Baikova (ed.), *Politicheskoe Obrazovanie*, p. 78.
101. See, for instance, *Sotsiologicheskie Problemy Svobodnogo Vremeni Trudyashchikhsya* (Vilnius, 1974) p. 98; Mekhontsev *et al.*, *Lektor i Slushatel'*, p. 19.
102. *Pravda* (11 May 1975) 2; cf. Unger, *Totalitarian Party*, p. 112, n. 21.
103. *Politicheskoe Samoobrazovanie*, no. 1 (1975) 40.
104. Baikova (ed.), *Politicheskoe Obrazovanie*, pp. 216 and 75.
105. Ibid., p. 76; *Politicheskoe Samoobrazovanie*, no. 9 (1976) 133.
106. *Politicheskoe Samoobrazovanie*, no. 3 (1976) p. 131; and no. 8, p. 33.
107. *Politicheskoe Samoobrazovanie*, no. 3 (1976) 131; Leonov, *Ubeditel'no*, p. 73.
108. Baikova (ed.), *Politicheskoe Obrazovanie*, p. 78.
109. Mekhontsev *et al.*, *Lektor i Slushatel'*, p. 20.
110. Bokarev (ed.), *Sotsiologicheskie Issledovaniya v Partiinoi Rabote*, p. 105; *Problemy Nauchnogo Kommunizma*, vyp. 6 (Moscow, 1972) p. 232; D. Gilzatdinov, *Effektivnost' Partiinoi Propagandy* (Tashkent, 1971) p. 76.
111. Yu. M. Khrustalev, *Lektsionnaya Propaganda—Vazhnaya Forma Politicheskogo Vospitaniya* (Moscow, 1973) p. 21.
112. *Za Vysokuyu Effektovnost' Lektsionnoi Propagandy* (Moscow, 1975) pp. 16–20.
113. Baikova (ed.), *Politicheskoe Obrazovanie*, pp. 72–3.
114. *Voprosy Teorii i Metodov Ideol. Raboty*, vyp. 6, p. 118. See also Gramov (ed.), *Kompleksnyi Podkhod*, p. 161; *Sotsiologicheskie Issledovaniya*, no. 4 (1975) 114–15.
115. *Politicheskoe Samoobrazovanie*, no. 8 (1976) 33; *Sotsiologicheskie Issledovaniya*, no. 3 (1975) 126.
116. Smirnov *et al.* (eds), *Voprosy Teorii i Praktiki Partiinoi Propagandy*, p. 191.
117. See, for instance, *Pravda* (18 October 1976) 2, (13 November 1976) 1, (22 November 1976) 2, and (9 December 1977) 2; *Agitator*, no. 11 (1977) 36 and 45; *Politicheskoe Samoobrazovanie*, no. 8 (1976) 35.
118. See, for instance, *Pravda* (30 July 1977) 2; (7 September 1977) 1; and (29 November 1977) 2.
119. See, for instance, *Pravda* (7 September 1977) 1.

120. See, for instance, the recent resolution on the work of the Orsk party committee in this connection, *Pravda* (24 August 1977) 1.
121. *Pravda* (12 June 1976) 1; *Politicheskoe Samoobrazovanie*, no. 7 (1977) 118–23.
122. *Politicheskoe Samoobrazovanie*, no. 7 (1977) 120.
123. V. V. Shcherbitskii, *Vospitat' Soznatel'nykh, Aktivnykh Stroitelei Kommunizma* (Moscow, 1974) p. 28; I. P. Rudoi and A. V. Shumakov, *Naglyadnaya Agitatsiya—Sredstvo Vospitaniya* (Moscow, 1974), pp 9-10; *Agitator*, no. 7 (1977) 45.
124. *Pravda* (26 May 1977) 2.
125. *XXIV S''ezd i Problemy Povysheniya Proizvodstvennoi i Obshchestvenno-Politicheskoi Aktivnosti Trudovykh Kollektivov* (Minsk, 1972) p. 69; A. M. Shumakov, *Naglyadnaya Agitatsiya* (Moscow, 1973) p. 191; *Pravda* (25 December 1977) 3.
126. B. A. Grushin (ed.), *Gorodskoe Naselenie i Ekonomicheskaya Reforma* (mimeo., Moscow, 1973) p. 55; V. L. Popov, *Politicheskaya Informatsiya v Gazete kak Faktor Ideologicheskogo Vozdeistviya* (avtoreferat kand. diss., Moscow, 1972) p. 3.
127. *Sotsiologicheskie Issledovaniya*, no. 1 (1975) 113–17.
128. Pozdnyakov (ed.), *Politicheskaya Informatsiya*, p. 88; V. I. Benesh and M. V. Balamasova, *Sotsiologiya i Propaganda* (Leningrad, 1971) p. 82.
129. *Sovetskaya Etnografiya*, no. 1 (1971) pp. 8–9.
130. E. P. Mikhailova, *Televedenie v Sisteme Dukhovnoi Kul'tury Sotsialisticheskogo Obshchestva* (avtoreferat kand. diss., Sverdlovsk, 1972) p. 16.
131. B. M. Firsov, *Televedenie Glazami Sotsiologa* (Moscow, 1971) pp. 117–26.
132. See, for instance, B. Rubin and Yu. Kolesnikov, *Student Glazami Sotsiologa* (Rostov-on-Don, 1968) p. 149; M. T. Iovchuk and L. N. Kogan (eds), *Dukhovnyi Mir Sovetskogo Rabochego* (Moscow, 1972) pp. 376–7.
133. Quoted in Gayle D. Hollander, *Soviet Political Indoctrination* (New York, 1972) pp. 62–9.
134. E. O. Dobolova, *Vozrastanie Roli Gazety v Kommunisticheskom Vospitanii Trudyashchikhsya* (avtoreferat kand. diss., Irkutsk, 1972) pp. 12–13.
135. See, for instance, Hollander, *Soviet Political Indoctrination*, pp. 168 and 181–3.
136. Ibid., pp. 67–74.
137. Maury Lisann, *Broadcasting to the Soviet Union* (New York, 1976) passim.
138. *Guardian Weekly* (12 September 1976) 8.
139. Quoted in Rudolf L. Tökés (ed.), *Dissent in the USSR* (London, 1975) pp. 130–1.
140. Jane Shapiro and Peter J. Potichnyj (eds), *Change and Adaptation in Soviet and East European Politics* (New York, 1976) p. 138.
141. White, 'Political socialization in the USSR: a study in failure?', pp. 339–42.

142. The classic study on this point is Philip Converse, 'The nature of belief systems in mass publics', in David Apter (ed.), *Ideology and Discontent* (New York, 1964); see also Michael Rush and Phillip Althoff, *An Introduction to Political Sociology* (London, 1971) pp. 160–84.
143. This point is argued in Walter D. Connor, 'Generations and politics in the USSR', *Problems of Communism*, xxiv (September–October, 1975) p. 23.

Chapter 7

1. See, for instance, the rivalries of this kind reported in Stephen F. Cohen, *Bukharin and the Bolshevik Revolution* (London, 1974) pp. 234–5; and in Alec Nove, *The Soviet Economic System* (London, 1977) pp. 71–3.
2. An admirable general discussion of the problems of national identity in this connection is available in Lucian W. Pye and Sidney Verba, *Political Culture and Political Development* (Princeton, N.J., 1965) pp. 529–35. On the national self-consciousness of Russians more generally, see Dmitri S. Likhachev, *Natsional'noe Samosoznanie Drevnei Rusi* (Moscow, 1945); Hans Rogger, *National Consciousness in Eighteenth-century Russia* (Cambridge, Mass., 1960); and Nicholas V. Riasanovsky, *Nicholas I and Official Nationality in Russia, 1825–1855* (Berkeley, 1959).
3. The most useful general treatment of this subject is Zev Katz (ed.), *Handbook of Major Soviet Nationalities* (London, 1975).
4. See particularly John F. Besemeres, 'Population politics in the USSR', *Soviet Union*, ii (1975) 50–80 and 117–44.
5. Katz (ed.), *Handbook of Major Soviet Nationalities*, pp. 73–140 *passim*.
6. Ibid., pp. 415–33.
7. Ibid., pp. 21–48; for some recent statements of Ukrainian nationalist or dissident opinion, see Ivan Dzyuba, *Internationalism or Russification?*, second ed. (London, 1970), and Michael Browne (ed.), *Ferment in the Ukraine* (London, 1971).
8. *Lenin i Molodezh'* vyp. 10 (Moscow, 1974) p. 95; *Literaturnaya Gazeta* (28 May 1975) 13; Alexandre Bennigsen and Chantal Lemercier-Quelquejay, *Islam in the Soviet Union* (London, 1967) pp. 21 and 237.
9. Alexandre Bennigsen, 'Islam in the Soviet Union: the religious factor and the nationality problem', in Bohdan R. Bociurkiw and John W. Strong (eds), *Religion and Atheism in the USSR and Eastern Europe* (London, 1975) pp. 94–8.
10. Ibid., pp. 99–100; *Partiinaya Zhizn'*, no. 5 (1977) 26.
11. Katz (ed.), *Handbook of Major Soviet Nationalities*, pp. 143–88; Archie Brown and Michael Kaser (eds.), *The Soviet Union since the Fall of Khrushchev*, second ed. (London, 1978) pp. 256–9.
12. V. I. Kozlov, *Natsional'nosti SSSR* (Moscow, 1975) p. 221; *Narodnoe Obrazovanie, Nauka i Kul'tura v SSSR. Statisticheskii Sbornik*

(Moscow, 1977) pp. 405–6.
13. T. H. Rigby, 'Soviet Communist Party membership under Brezhnev', *Soviet Studies*, XXVIII (1976) 325–7; *Partiinaya Zhizn*', no. 21 (1977) 30–1.
14. *Spravochnik Partiinogo Rabotnika*, vyp. 12 (Moscow, 1972) p. 43; *Programma Kommunisticheskoi Partii Sovetskogo Soyuza* (Moscow, 1971) p. 113.
15. Alex Inkeles and Raymond A. Bauer, *The Soviet Citizen. Daily Life in a Totalitarian Society* (Cambridge, Mass., 1961) pp. 338–73.
16. V. N. Pimenova, *Svobodnoe Vremya v Sotsialisticheskom Obshchestve* (Moscow, 1974) p. 298; *Sovetskaya Etnografiya*, no. 4 (1973) 7–12.
17. Yu. V. Arutyunyan (ed.), *Sotsial'noe i Natsional'noe. Opyt Etnosotsiologicheskikh Issledovanii po materialam Tatarskoi ASSR* (Moscow, 1973) pp. 26–8, 52–3 and 266–89.
18. *Itogi Vsesoyuznoi Perepisi Naseleniya 1970 goda*, vol. 4 (Moscow, 1973) pp. 273, 281 and 317; A. I. Kholmogorov, *Internatsional'nye Cherty Sovetskikh Natsii* (Moscow, 1970) pp. 86–95.
19. Steven L. Guthier, 'The Belorussians: national identification and assimilation, 1897–1970', Part 2, *Soviet Studies*, XXIX (1977) 280–3.
20. Kholmogorov, *Internatsional'nye Cherty*, p. 37; *Itogi*, vol. 4, p. 3.
21. J. A. Newth, 'Demographic developments', in Brown and Kaser (eds.), *The Soviet Union since the Fall of Khrushchev*, pp. 85–9; Alexandre Bennigsen, 'Islam in the Soviet Union', in Bociurkiw and Strong (eds), *Religion and Atheism in the Soviet Union and Eastern Europe*, p. 97.
22. See, for instance, Katz (ed.), *Handbook of Major Soviet Nationalities*, pp. 114 and 305 (Latvia and Uzbekistan respectively).
23. Kholmogorov, *Internatsional'nye Cherty*, mentions Bashkir, Uzbek, Azerbaidzhani and a number of other languages in this connection (p. 154).
24. Brian Silver, 'Bilingualism and maintenance of the mother tongue in Soviet Central Asia', *Slavic Review*, XXXV (1976) 406–24, pp. 409–10.
25. Richard Pipes in Katz (ed.), *Handbook of Major Soviet Nationalities*, pp. 3 and 5.
26. Michael Rywkin, 'Religion, modern nationalism and political power in Soviet Central Asia', *Canadian Slavonic Papers*, XVII (1975) 271–85, p. 275; Edward Allworth (ed.), *The Nationality Question in Soviet Central Asia* (New York, 1973) pp. 3–18 and *passim*.
27. See the sources quoted in notes 5, 7 and 11 above.
28. Teresa Rakowska-Harmstone, 'The dialectics of nationalism in the USSR', *Problems of Communism*, XXIII (May–June, 1974) 1–22, especially 10–22.
29. Brezhnev in his speech on the adoption of the new Soviet Constitution in October 1977, for instance, warned against proposals to abolish the union republics and other national–territorial units of this kind, and urged that 'we would be taking a dangerous path if we were artificially to step up this objective process of national integration'—*Kommunist*, no. 15 (1977) 10–11.
30. See Walter A. Rosenbaum, *Political Culture* (London, 1975) p. 151.

31. The evidence on this point is reviewed in Robert E. Dowse and John A. Hughes, *Political Sociology* (London, 1972) pp. 192–4.
32. Yu. V. Arutyunyan, *Sotsial'naya Struktura Sel'skogo Naseleniya SSSR* (Moscow, 1971) pp. 180–1.
33. B. Grushin, *Svobodnoe Vremya. Aktual'nye Problemy* (Moscow, 1967) p. 78.
34. V. N. Ermuratskii (ed.), *Sotsial'naya Aktivnost' Rabotnikov Promyshlennogo Predpriyatiya* (Kishinev, 1973) p. 95; *Trud i Lichnost' pri Sotsializme*, vyp. 2 (Perm', 1973) p. 46.
35. L. N. Kogan *et al.*, *Rol' Pechati v Kommunisticheskom Vospitanii Trudyashchikhsya* (Sverdlovsk, 1966) pp. 8 and 16.
36. V. D. Patrushev in M. N. Rutkevitch (ed.), *Problemy Sotsialisticheskogo Obraza Zhizni* (Moscow, 1977) pp. 175–86. The most recent general survey is Dorothy Atkinson, Alexander Dallin and Gail Warshofsky Lapidus (eds), *Women in Russia* (London, 1978).
37. *Problemy Sotsial'noi Aktivnosti*, vyp. 1 (Chelyabinsk, 1974), p. 62.
38. See, for instance, *Sotsial'nye Issledovaniya*, vyp. 6 (Moscow, 1970) p. 193; Pimenova, *Svobodnoe Vremya*, pp. 275–77; L. A. Gordon and E. V. Klopov, *Chelovek posle Raboty* (Moscow, 1972) Prilozhenie, pp. 14–17.
39. *Spravochnik Partiinogo Rabotnika*, vyp. 17 (Moscow, 1977) p. 472.
40. V. G. Mordkovich, *Obshchestvenno-politicheskaya Aktivnost' Trudyashchikhsya* (avtoreferat dokt. diss., Moscow, 1974) p. 25.
41. See, for instance, *Trud i Lichnost' pri Sotsializme*, vyp. 2, p. 46; Ermuratskii, *Sotsial'naya Aktivnost'*, p. 110.
42. Arutyunyan, *Sotsial'naya Struktura*, p. 183.
43. Andrei D. Sakharov, *My Country and the World* (New York, 1975) pp. 20–3; Hedrick Smith, *The Russians* (London, 1976) pp. 246–60.
44. M. Holubenko, 'The Soviet working class', *Critique*, 4 (spring 1975), 5–25; cf. David Lane, *The Socialist Industrial State* (London, 1976) pp. 97–101.
45. The value of Soviet *samizdat* as a guide to political values and beliefs should not be underestimated, but its insights are somewhat impressionistic in character and they apply mainly to the intelligentsia, a relatively small proportion of the total population. See further F. J. M. Feldbrugge, *Samizdat and Political Dissent in the Soviet Union* (Leiden, 1975) especially pp. 1–25.
46. T. Yaroshevskii and N. S. Mansurov (eds), *Aktivnost' Lichnosti v Sotsialisticheskom Obshchestve* (Moscow, 1976) pp. 163–4.
47. Ermuratskii, *Sotsial'naya Aktivnost'*, pp. 105–6.
48. L. N. Kogan *et al.*, *Dukhovnyi Mir Sovetskogo Rabochego* (Moscow, 1972), pp. 180–1; Ermuratskii, *Sotsial'naya Aktivnost'*, pp. 106 and 110.
49. B. A. Grushin (comp.), *Gorodskoe Naselenie i Ekonomicheskaya Reforma* (rotaprint, Moscow, 1973) pp. 68, 54, 33 and 57–8.
50. Ermuratskii, *Sotsial'naya Aktivnost'*, p. 24; V. G. Baikova, *Ideologicheskaya Rabota KPSS v usloviakh Razvitogo Sotsializma* (Moscow, 1977) p. 145; *Obshchestvenno-politicheskaya Zhizn' Sovetskoi Sibirskoi Der-*

evni (Novosibirsk, 1974) p. 153.
51. G. L. Smirnov *et al.* (eds), *Voprosy Teorii i Praktiki Partiinoi Propagandy* (Moscow, 1971) pp. 332–3.
52. N. M. Sapozhnikov, *Struktura Politicheskogo Soznaniya* (Minsk, 1969) p. 136.
53. P. V. Pozdnyakov, *Effektivnost' Kommunisticheskoi Propagandy* (Moscow, 1975) p. 86.
54. Arutyunyan, *Sotsial'naya Struktura*, p. 179.
55. See, for instance, Gordon and Klopov, *Chelovek posle Raboty*, Prilozhenie, tables 30–7; V. E. Poletaev (ed.), *Sotsial'nyi Oblik Kolkhoznoi Molodezhi* (Moscow, 1976) p. 110; A. M. Gelyuta and V. I. Staroverov, *Sotsial'nyi Oblik Rabochego-Intelligenta* (Moscow, 1977) p. 157.
56. V. G. Mordkovich (ed.), *Obshchestvennaya Aktivnost' Molodezhi* (Moscow, 1970) p. 88.
57. Jerry F. Hough, 'Political participation in the Soviet Union', *Soviet Studies*, xxviii (1976) 3–20, p. 13, n. 28.
58. Yaroshevskii and Mansurov, *Aktivnost' Lichnosti*, p. 166.
59. *Sotsiologicheskie Issledovaniya*, no. 4 (1977) p. 42.
60. Yaroshevskii and Mansurov, *Aktivnost' Lichnosti*, p. 166.
61. L. M. Arkhangel'skii (ed.), *Dukhovnoe Razvitie Lichnosti* (Sverdlovsk, 1967) p. 174.
62. G. E. Zborovskii and G. P. Orlov, *Dosug: Deistvitel'nost' i Illyuzii* (Sverdlovsk, 1970) p. 220.
63. *Chelovek i Obshchestvo*, vyp. 3 (Leningrad, 1968) p. 39.
64. Ibid., vyp. 3, p. 40; *Voprosy Obshchestvennoi Aktivnosti Mass i Razvitie Politicheskoi Organizatsii Sovetskogo Obshchestva* (Khar'kov, 1968) p. 110; Yu. G. Chulanov, *Izmeneniya v Sostave i v Urovne Tvorcheskoi Aktivnosti Rabochego Klassa SSSR* (Leningrad, 1974), p. 68.
65. See, for example, *Sotsial'nye Problemy Truda i Proizvodstva* (Moscow–Warsaw, 1969) p. 297; and Arkhangel'skii (ed.), *Dukhovnoe Razvitie Lichnosti*, p. 181.
66. See, for instance, Chulanov, *Izmeneniya*, p. 69; *Sotsiologicheskie Issledovaniya*, no. 4 (1977) 42.
67. The evidence on this point is conveniently reviewed in Dowse and Hughes, *Political Sociology*, pp. 289–321.

Chapter 8

1. See, for instance, Richard Pipes, *Russia under the Old Regime* (London, 1974) p. 191; and above, Chapter 3.
2. The most convenient source of data on such matters is Charles L. Taylor and Michael C. Hudson, *World Handbook of Political and Social Indicators*, second ed. (New Haven and London, 1972); see also *Narodnoe Khozyaistvo SSSR za 60 Let. Yubileinyi statisticheskii ezhegodnik* (Moscow, 1977) pp. 93–137.

3. For a general review of evolutionary theory, see Lucy Mair, *An Introduction to Social Anthropology* (Oxford, 1965); and Marvin Harris, *The Rise of Anthropological Theory* (London, 1969).

4. James Coleman, 'Modernization: Political Aspects', in David L. Sills (ed.), *International Encyclopedia of the Social Sciences*, vol. 10 (New York, 1968) pp. 395–402, provides a convenient overview.

5. In what follows we shall be able to consider only part of the work of a complex and prolific social theorist; see, for a general introduction, William C. Mitchell, *Sociological Analysis and Politics. The Theories of Talcott Parsons* (Englewood Cliffs, N. J., 1967).

6. Talcott Parsons, 'Evolutionary universals in society', *American Sociological Review*, xxix (1964) 339–57, pp. 340–1.

7. Ibid., pp. 341–56.

8. Ibid., p. 356.

9. Talcott Parsons, 'Communism and the West: the sociology of the conflict', in Amitai and Eva Etzioni (eds), *Social Change: Sources, Patterns and Consequences* (New York, 1964), pp. 396–8.

10. Samuel Huntington has included David Easton, David Apter and Gabriel Almond among those who have developed the Parsonian tradition: see Fred I. Greenstein and Nelson W. Polsby (eds), *Handbook of Political Science*, vol. 3 (Reading, Mass., 1975) p. 3.

11. A regime that maximises public contestation and participation: see Robert A. Dahl, *Polyarchy* (New Haven and London, 1971) p. 7.

12. Ibid., pp. 64–5, 76–9 and 218.

13. Dahl, for instance, makes this reservation in ibid., p. 71.

14. Roy Medvedev, *Kniga o Sotsialisticheskoi Demokratii* (Amsterdam and Paris, 1972) p. 118; Ghita Ionescu, *The Politics of the European Communist States* (London, 1972) pp. 271–3; Michel Tatu, *Power in the Kremlin* (London, 1969) p. 538; Karl W. Deutsch, 'Cracks in the monolith: possibilities and patterns of disintegration in totalitarian systems', in Harry Eckstein and David E. Apter (eds), *Comparative Politics: A Reader* (New York, 1963) p. 506.

15. Gabriel A. Almond, *Political Development* (Boston, 1970) pp. 318–20. For some other general considerations of this question, see Charles A. Gati (ed.), *The Politics of Modernization in Eastern Europe* (New York, 1974); Carmelo Mesa-Lago and Carl Beck (eds), *Comparative Socialist Systems* (Pittsburgh, 1975); Mark G. Field (ed.), *The Social Consequences of Modernization in Communist Societies* (Baltimore and London, 1976); and Jan F. Triska and Paul M. Cocks (eds), *Political Development in Eastern Europe* (New York, 1977).

16. Frederick C. Fliegel, 'A comparative analysis of the impact of industrialism on traditional values', *Rural Sociology*, xli (1976) 431–51, pp. 446–7.

17. Andrew J. Sofranko and Frederick C. Fliegel, 'Industrialism and modernity: economic and noneconomic orientations', *Rural Sociology*, xlii (1977) 496–516, pp. 511–12.

18. Miles Simpson, 'Universalism versus modernity: Parsons' societal typology reconsidered', *International Journal of Comparative Socio-*

logy, XVI (1975) 174–206, p. 202.

19. Daniel N. Nelson, 'Socioeconomic and political change in Communist Europe', *International Studies Quarterly*, XXI (1977) 359–88, p. 384; see similarly the same author's 'Political convergence: an empirical assessment', *World Politics*, XXX (1978) 411–32.

20. Stephen White, 'Communist systems and the "iron law of pluralism"', *British Journal of Political Science*, VIII (1978) 101–17.

21. Dahl, *Polyarchy*, pp. 68–70.

22. This point is made in Reinhard Bendix, 'Tradition and modernity reconsidered', *Comparative Studies in Society and History*, IX (1966–7) 292–346; and in T. Anthony Jones, 'Modernization theory and socialist development', in Field (ed.), *The Social Consequences of Modernization*, p. 25.

23. To borrow the title of the book by Lloyd K. and S. H. Rudolph (Chicago, 1967).

24. See further Joseph R. Gusfield, 'Tradition and modernity: misplaced polarities in the study of social change', *American Journal of Sociology*, LXXII (1966–7) 351–62; Bendix, 'Tradition and modernity reconsidered'; Georges Balandier, *Political Anthropology* (London, 1970) Chapter 7; and Alejandro Portes, 'The factorial structure of modernity: empirical replications and a critique', *American Journal of Sociology*, LXXIX (1973–4) 15–44.

25. M. Kent Jennings and Richard G. Niemi, 'Continuity and change in political orientations: a longitudinal study of two generations', *American Political Science Review*, LXIX (1969) 1316–36, pp. 1317–19. The question of 'political generations' more generally is considered by Marvin Rintala, 'Political generations', in Sills (ed.), *International Encyclopedia of the Social Sciences*, vol. 6, pp. 92–6; Martha W. Riley, 'Aging and cohort succession: interpretations and misinterpretations', *Public Opinion Quarterly*, XXXVII (1973) 35–49; Neil C. Cutler, 'Towards a generational conception of political socialization', in David C. and Sandra K. Schwartz (eds), *New Directions in Political Socialization* (New York, 1975); Neil C. Cutler, 'Generational approaches to political socialization', *Youth and Society*, VIII (1976–7) 175–207; and Neil C. Cutler, 'Political socialization research as generational analysis: the cohort approach versus the lineage approach', in Stanley H. Renshon (ed.), *Handbook of Political Socialization* (London, 1977).

26. For the 'senescence theory' see David Butler and Donald Stokes, *Political Change in Britain*, second ed. (London, 1974) p. 62 and pp. 48–66 *passim*.

27. *Komsomol'skaya Pravda* (10 August 1977) 4; ibid. (19 January 1978) 4; A. Shishkov, *Tsentral'naya Zadacha Ideologicheskoi Raboty Partii* (Moscow, 1973) p. 52.

28. Quoted in Paul Hollander, *Soviet and American Society: A Comparison* (New York, 1973) p. 359.

29. *Pionerskaya Pravda* (12 August 1977) 2; see further Ruth W. Mouly, 'Values and aspirations of Soviet youth', in Paul Cocks *et al.* (eds), *The Dynamics of Soviet Politics* (Cambridge, Mass., and London, 1976)

pp. 221–38, and Hedrick Smith, *The Russians* (London, 1976) Chapter 7.
30. *Chelovek i Obshchestvo*, vyp. 13 (Leningrad, 1973) p. 71, and *Voprosy Sotsial'noi i Professional'noi Orientatsii Molodezhi* (Sverdlovsk, 1972) p. 52; B. N. Dukovich *et al.*, *Molodezh'. Obrazovanie, Vospitanie, Professional'naya Deyatel'nost'* (Leningrad, 1973) p. 154; Ya. R. Volin (ed.), *Trud i Lichnost' pri Sotsializme*, vyp. 1 (Perm', 1972) p. 145.
31. L. M. Molodtsov *et al.* (comps), *Deistvennost' Politicheskoi Ucheby* (Moscow, 1973) p. 55, and P. M. Masherov, *Ideino-politicheskoi Rabote—Vysokaya Ideinost'* (Moscow, 1975) p. 64; *Lenin i Molodezh'. Problemy Pravovogo Vospitaniya Molodezhi* (Moscow, 1974) p. 75; *Chelovek i Obshchestvo*, vyp. 13, pp. 16–17.
32. S. N. Ikonnikova, *Molodezh': sotsiologicheskii i sotsial'no-psikhologicheskii analiz* (Leningrad, 1974) p. 117; Masherov, *Ideino-politicheskoi Rabote*, p. 93, and Ts. A. Stepanyan and V. D. Timofeev (eds), *Puti Formirovaniya Sotsial'noi Aktivnosti Lichnosti pri Sotsializme* (Moscow, 1972) p. 130.
33. V. Lisovskii, *Eskiz k Portretu* (Moscow, 1969) p. 139; V. I. Turanskii, *Sotsial'naya Aktivnost' Molodezhi v Trudovom Kollektive* (avtoreferat kand. diss., Gorky, 1972) p. 9; Stepanyan and Timofeev (eds), *Puti Formirovaniya Sotsial'noi Aktivnosti*, p. 128; A. N. Iliadi *et al.* (eds), *Materialy Mezhvuzovskoi Nauchnoi Konferentsii po probleme Vozrastaniya Aktivnosti Obshchestvennogo Soznaniya v period Stroitel'stva Kommunizma* (Kursk, 1968) pp. 478–9.
34. Ya. R. Volin *et al.* (eds), *Trud i Lichnost' pri Sotsializme*, vyp. 2 (Perm', 1973) pp. 36–7; V. T. Lisovskii and A. V. Dmitriev, *Lichnost' Studenta* (Leningrad, 1974) pp. 101–20.
35. Lisovskii, *Eskiz k Portretu*, p. 139.
36. Raymond A. Bauer, Alex Inkeles and Clyde Kluckhohn, *How the Soviet System Works* (Cambridge, Mass., 1956; paperback ed., 1960) p. 230.
37. Alex Inkeles and Raymond A. Bauer, *The Soviet Citizen* (Cambridge, Mass., and London, 1959) pp. 254 and 274–85.
38. Bauer, Inkeles and Kluckhohn, *How the Soviet System Works*, p. 230 and pp. 222–31 *passim*. See also Raymond A. Bauer, 'Some trends in sources of alienation from the Soviet system', *Public Opinion Quarterly*, xix (1955–6) 279–91, especially pp. 285–9.
39. Richard Rose, *Governing Without Consensus* (London, 1971) p. 35.
40. These population figures are drawn from *Vestnik M.G.U. Seriya Zhurnalistika*, no. 3 (1977) 8.
41. 'Perezhitki proshlogo v soznanii i postupakh lyudei', in V. T. Syzrantsev (ed.), *Kratkii Slovar'-spravochnik Agitatora i Politinformatora* (Moscow, 1977) p. 225.
42. Jerry F. Hough, 'Party "saturation" in the Soviet Union', in Cocks *et al.*, *The Dynamics of Soviet Politics*, 117–33, pp. 121 and 128 (Methodology 'A').
43. See, for instance, ibid., p. 121; V. D. Ermuratskii (ed.), *Sotsial'naya Aktivnost' Rabotnikov Promyshlennogo Predpriyatiya* (Kishinev, 1973)

p. 95; Iliadi *et al.* (eds), *Materialy*, pp. 441–2; I. M. Slepenkov and B. V. Knyazev, *Molodezh' Sela Segodnya* (Moscow, 1972) pp. 112–17; V. G. Mordkovich (comp.), *Obshchestvennaya Aktivnost' Molodezhi* (Moscow, 1970) pp. 85–9.

44. See, for instance, Turanskii, *Sotsial'naya Aktivnost' Molodezhi*, p. 19; I. T. Levykin (comp.), *Sel'skaya Molodezh'* (Moscow, 1970) p. 65; Stepanyan and Timofeev (eds), *Puti Formirovaniya Sotsial'noi Aktivnosti*, p. 52; T. P. Bogdanova, *Trud i Sotsial'naya Aktivnost' Molodezhi* (Minsk, 1972) p. 153.

45. *Pravda* (10 August 1977) 3. Between 1965 and 1977 cultural exchange between the USSR and foreign countries increased two and a half times in volume—*Pravda* (28 July 1977) 3.

46. Ithiel de Sola Pool, 'Communication in totalitarian societies', in Ithiel de Sola Pool *et al.* (eds), *Handbook of Communication* (Chicago, 1973) p. 479.

47. Ibid., pp. 474–91; and Gayle Durham Hollander, 'Political communication and dissent in the Soviet Union', in Rudolf L. Tökés (ed.), *Dissent in the USSR* (London, 1975) 233–75.

48. John D. Nagle, 'A new look at the Soviet elite: a generational model of the Soviet system', *Journal of Political and Military Sociology*, III (1975) 1–13; Peter Frank, 'The changing composition of the Communist Party', in Archie Brown and Michael Kaser (eds), *The Soviet Union since the Fall of Khrushchev*, second ed. (London, 1978) 96–120.

49. G. L. Smirnov, *Sovetskii Chelovek. Formirovanie Sotsialisticheskogo Tipa Lichnosti*, second ed. (Moscow, 1973) pp. 322–5.

50. B. Ts. Urlanis, *Istoriya Odnogo Pokoleniya* (Moscow, 1968) pp. 44 and 114.

51. Ibid., pp. 120, 206, 181 and 142.

52. Vera Dunham, *In Stalin's Time. Middle-class Values in Soviet Fiction* (Cambridge, 1976) pp. 70–1; John A. Armstrong, *Ideology, Politics and Government in the Soviet Union*, third ed. (London, 1974) pp. 99–100.

53. Bogdanova, *Trud i Sotsial'naya Aktivnost'*, p. 43.

54. Stephen White, 'Continuity and change in Soviet political culture: an emigré study', *Comparative Political Studies*, XI (1978) 389–90.

55. Ibid., pp. 390–1.

56. Ibid., p. 392.

57. See, for instance, Tökés (ed.), *Dissent in the USSR*, pp. 99–100, and F. J. M. Feldbrugge, *Samizdat and Political Dissent in the Soviet Union* (Amsterdam, 1975), pp. 28–37.

58. Price increases in a number of goods and services, as well as some relatively insignificant reductions, were announced in January 1977 and March 1978; further increases are expected to take place as increases occur in the costs of production—*Pravda* (5 January 1977 and 2 March 1978). The prices of basic foodstuffs have, however, remained unaltered, despite the heavy budgetary subsidies they require. On increases in labour discipline more generally see *Literaturnaya Gazeta* (4 May 1977) 11, and *Izvestiya* (23 June 1977) 4.

59. Philip Hanson, 'The Soviet economy in 1977' (paper prepared for the Annual Conference of the National Association of Soviet and East European Studies, Cambridge, April 1978) pp. 1–7.
60. Inkeles and Bauer, *The Soviet Citizen*, pp. 252–4.

Index

Novgorod 23, 24, 61
Novosibirsk 90

occupational structure (in pre-
revolutionary Russia) 48, 55
occupations: and socio-political
activity 158, 162–4; and
political knowledge 159; and
socio-political literature 160–1
October revolution 66, 75, 183,
184; celebration of 81
Octobrist party 52
Oprichnina 43
Orthodox Church 39; doctrine of
59; *see also* religion

Paris Commune 66
Parsons, T. 170–1
parties, political 32, 106, 186
party education system *see*
political education system
Paul, D. W. 17
peasant commune: *see mir*
peasant revolts 34
peasant society (in pre-
revolutionary Russia) 55 ff.
peasantry (in pre-revolutionary
Russia): political attitudes of
60–1; legal status of 61
Peter I 'the Great' 10, 31–2, 39,
44
Peter III 31
Pioneers 82
Pionerskaya Pravda 83
Plato 2
Plekhanov, G. V. 69
Poland 34
Politburo 7, 109, 183
political behaviour *see* socio-
political activity
political beliefs and values 96 ff.,
142; and political behaviour
16–18, 84–5, 163–4; and
performance of political system
18–19
political change, theories of
169–90
political communications,
development of 74

political culture: definition of 1;
origins of concept of 1–6; use
of in relation to USSR 2, 6–14;
sub-divisions of 14–15; and
political change 15–16, 166–90;
and political behaviour 16–18,
84–5, 95; problems of analysis of
16–21; causal status of 19–21;
'traditional Russian' 40, 64;
contemporary 84 ff.
political education classes: motives
for attendance 123–4;
preferences in 124–5;
satisfaction with 125; interest
in 125–6; content of 126–7;
CC resolution on 127; and
political knowledge 127–30;
and political behaviour 127–8;
and women 155
political education system:
development of 70–2; present
structure of 75–7; effectiveness
of 123 ff.; *see also* political
education classes
political elite 10, 12; in national
areas 154
Political Enlightenment, Houses of
78
political generations 183–4;
theories of 177 ff.
political information sessions
(*politinformatsii*) *see* political
lectures
political informers
(*politinformatory*) 79, 80, 118,
120; qualifications of 131–2;
problems of 132–6
political institutions: attitudes
towards 103–7, 110–11, 149,
185 ff.; *see also* state,
government
political knowledge 68–9, 105,
119–20, 127–30, 141; in pre-
revolutionary Russia 32–3;
educational and occupational
differences in 159; and outside
world 182–3; generational
differences in 185–8